Faith Shattered and Restored
Judaism in the Postmodern Age

MAGGID

Rabbi Shagar
Shimon Gershon Rosenberg

FAITH SHATTERED
AND RESTORED
JUDAISM IN THE POSTMODERN AGE

TRANSLATED BY
Elie Leshem

EDITED BY
Dr. Zohar Maor

PREFACE BY
Aryeh Rubin

AFTERWORD BY
Rabbi Shalom Carmy

Maggid Books

Faith Shattered and Restored
Judaism in the Postmodern Age

First Edition, 2017

Maggid Books
An imprint of Koren Publishers Jerusalem Ltd.

POB 8531, New Milford, CT 06776-8531, USA
POB 4044, Jerusalem 9104001, Israel
www.maggidbooks.com

Cover design: Tani Bayer

The publication of this book was made possible through the generous support of the Targum Shlishi Foundation and Torah Education in Israel.

ISBN 978-1-59264-464-3, *hardcover*

A CIP catalogue record for this title is
available from the British Library

Printed and bound in the United States

Contents

Preface *vii*

Introduction *xi*

Uncertainty as the Trial of the Akeda *1*

My Faith: Faith in a Postmodern World *21*

Religious Life in the Modern Age *41*

Freedom and Holiness *67*

Living with Nothingness *85*

Justice and Ethics in a Postmodern World *105*

Mysticism, Postmodernism, and the New Age *119*

Love, Romance, and Covenant *131*

Self-Actualization and Society *153*

Seventy Bullocks and One Sukka: The Land of Israel, Nationalism, and Diaspora *173*

Afterword: An Individualist Religious Thinker, Without Grand Narrative *193*

Works by Rabbi Shagar *209*

Index *213*

Preface

The Sacred Literature of Rabbi Shagar

L ike many of my generation who grew up in the Modern Orthodox world of the 1950s and 1960s, I have often needed to work hard to
reconcile the conflicts of modernity with Jewish life and to integrate
the modernist mindset with some of our difficult-to-reconcile ideologies. This quest led me to the work of many great thinkers: I studied the
philosophies of Rabbi Kook while a student in Yeshivat Merkaz HaRav
in the early 1970s, and as a layman in my later adult years, I explored
the works of the thinkers Emmanuel Levinas and Yehezkel Kaufmann.
Yet the psychological and spiritual strains between the modern world
and some of the Jewish belief system remained ever-present. The integration of heart and mind, soul and intellect, within the context of our
tradition has often escaped me.

As I entered my seventh decade, this search led me to the work of
Rabbi Shagar, and his work introduced to me a new language for a new
generation. In his philosophy, the strict doctrine of the yeshiva world
is challenged; his is a Judaism that focuses not on obedience, but on

how the text and the law relate to the individual. Using the tools and language of the postmodernist, Rabbi Shagar helps the reader relate to the world around him, engaging the student in a stimulating dialogue that allows for a much richer spiritual experience.

Until now, Rabbi Shagar's works were known mostly within Israel; very few were available in English. So when asked to help subsidize the translation of some of his more approachable works, I immediately agreed. The anglophone world should appreciate this volume; after all, as an audience at once more individualistic and less integrally involved in the nationalist collective than their Israeli brethren, English-speaking Jews should resonate deeply with Rabbi Shagar's sensitivity to the individual's search for an independent approach. Rabbi Shagar's views are in complete opposition to the doctrinaire philosophy force-fed to many within the American yeshiva system: an approach that relies on top-down authority and leaves little room for the exploration of individual spiritual needs. I believe that many readers will be assuaged both psychically and spiritually by the enveloping and open-minded philosophy of Rabbi Shagar.

In a documentary on Rabbi Shagar by Israeli television in 2012, one of his students, Dr. Yitzchak Mandelbaum, a clinical psychologist, astutely summed up his discovery of the teachings of Rabbi Shagar as follows: "ידעתי שמצאתי את שלא ידעתי שחיפשתי," "I knew I had found what I didn't know I had been searching for." And so it has been for many who have incorporated his teachings into their worldview.

Perhaps Rabbi Shagar attained this heightened sensitivity through his own struggles and suffering. His mother went through the Holocaust. From this he learned that the world is often a bad, cold place offering no personal security. While he was serving as a soldier in the Yom Kippur War, his tank took a direct hit in battle with the Syrians; two of his yeshiva buddies were immediately killed, and he was badly burned – an event he hardly ever spoke of, but which raised in him questions of faith. As a student of the works of Rabbi Kook and Rabbi Naḥman of Breslov, he reportedly said Rabbi Kook lacked that gnawing pain of extreme religious doubt. Rabbi Naḥman, on the other hand, was suffused with doubts, helping Rabbi Shagar tackle his own questions.

This sensitivity to the inherent conflicts within modern Judaism endowed Rabbi Shagar with the tools to reach many young students seeking intellectual and spiritual renewal. His unique fusion of a fresh and existential reading of classical Jewish texts, contemporary thinkers, the great Jewish and non-Jewish philosophers, and Hasidism addressed the growing sense of alienation within the younger generation of modern religious students, a fact rarely admitted in the yeshiva world.

The Jewish religious establishment was allergic to the concept of deconstruction – the postmodernist mode of textual analysis that parses the critical gap between text and meaning. Rabbi Shagar, on the other hand, saw this approach as an opportunity for the student to be released from the shackles of religious cliché, ideology, and convention, and to relate to religion as an ongoing existential dialogue that is more than just an institution of formal laws. Whether addressing the depth of one's relationships, the concept of forgiveness, or romantic love, Rabbi Shagar's writing blends Jewish thought with the works of secular philosophers, encouraging his students to seek a more authentic spiritual truth. As Rabbi Shagar explained, study is not only about what the Talmud says, but about how it speaks to the individual student. Even more stunningly, while always disappointed when a student who did not find his place within this spiritual world left the path of observance, Rabbi Shagar maintained warm relationships with those who questioned and rejected.

For those who chafe against the broad, grand arguments and dogmatisms of the prevailing Orthodox doctrine: Take comfort in Rabbi Shagar's postmodernist melding of theories and his new paradigm of learning and understanding our Jewish texts. While Rabbi Shagar's approach encourages religious observance and a vibrant dialogue with tradition, it lacks the dogmatic security of previous generations. My exposure to the works of this great man did not lay to rest the bulk of my ongoing questions. It did, however, provide me with some solace and a modicum of harmony for the mind and soul.

I believe a new Jewish way of living is evolving. Where it will go, nobody knows. But the process is already well underway, and Rabbi Shagar's work provides seedlings for the sprouting of this Jewish way of life.

My generation failed in its mission of synthesis; by demanding a religious certitude based on fixed and rigid systems, we failed to integrate the realities of the modern world with the individual religious and spiritual needs of today's Jews. I hope the teachings of Rabbi Shagar will be assimilated into the mindset of the next generation of Jewish leaders, who will utilize these tools – along with the neglected and marginalized philosophies of other great modern Jewish thinkers – to disseminate a Judaism more relevant for the new era.

Aryeh Rubin
September 4, 2016
Rosh Chodesh Elul 5776
Aventura, Florida

Introduction

We are delighted to present to the English-reading public a selection from the works of Rabbi Shimon Gershon Rosenberg (Shagar), *zt "l*, a project of the Institute for the Advancement of Rabbi Shagar's Writings and Maggid Books. Rabbi Shagar's oeuvre, much of which has yet to be published, spans lectures (*shiurim*) on the Talmud, essays on halakhic issues, expositions on the festivals, lectures on Jewish thought (and especially Hasidism), and treatises on various philosophical themes and current events.[1] This volume contains translations of ten essays that constitute, to our minds, an optimal representation of Rabbi Shagar's groundbreaking spiritual approach. Six of them were taken from his major philosophical work, *Tablets and Broken Tablets*; two were published in his lifetime and included in the book *We Will Walk in Fervor*, and the remaining two come from his collections of expositions on the holidays

---

This introduction is based on the one appearing in Rabbi Shagar's *Tablets and Broken Tablets*, several chapters of which are reproduced in this volume.

1. At the back of this volume is a list of Rabbi Shagar's Hebrew publications to date, as well as two preliminary attempts to translate his work into English. This volume refers to works by Rabbi Shagar by their English titles.

(one on Ḥanukka and the other on Sukkot), which also contain wide-ranging theoretical treatises. Rabbi Shagar was born and lived in Israel, and his writings are very much a product of his surroundings. Thus, for this volume, we selected theoretical works that would, in our estimation, prove relevant to Diaspora Jews as they contend with the challenges to religious life posed by modernism and postmodernism. In some essays, we omitted passages liable to be lost on the non-Israeli reader.

Several weeks before Rabbi Shagar's passing, in Sivan 5767, a large crowd of his students and followers assembled for an evening of study and prayer, and in order to establish a committee for the publication of his writings. Unable to attend the event, the rabbi sent a letter to the participants that included the following:

> Guided by Hasidism, for many years I devoted the bulk of my efforts to developing a personal-existential discourse that by its nature appeals to the individual whose position is often in conflict with the demand to repair society. Yet, to my mind, the rectification of the personal must also bring about an elevation of the social realm. Hence my motivation to develop a Torah-driven alternative to the current cultural discourse, an alternative nourished by our tradition, in a manner that would appeal to as large a swath of Israeli society as possible, including the secular.
>
> What is more, I sought to create, within the national religious community, a significant Torah-based position that would provide a fitting solution for the religious and existential stirrings of our generations, and pose an alternative to the existing currents in that community. This attempt took place against the backdrop of the conflicts and contradictions faced by that community, of which I am a member, and which I often broached in my writing and lectures. I believe that through the efforts manifest in my writings, I have come a long way toward that longed-for solution, even if what I wrote still falls far short of perfection.

The word "and," so typical of the national religious movement – yeshiva *and* military service; yeshiva *and* academia; Torah *and* secular studies – does not represent an artificial synthesis, and certainly not, as some have alleged, a sort of idolatry by association.[2] It should be interpreted in the vein of Franz Rosenzweig, who described the "and" as the keystone that supports the entire edifice and imbues it with meaning.[3] That, to my mind, is the "straight line" of which the Maharal of Prague so often spoke.... [4]

Hence my efforts to blend and include a variety of schools of thought in my writing, even if they are not generally perceived as part of traditional Torah study. In that I was inspired by Rabbi Abraham Isaac Kook, whose legacy guides us all. I pray that my writing will constitute a notable contribution to the personal and national rectification so necessary today.

The highlight of Rabbi Shagar's theoretical work was his attempt to provide a religious and spiritual response to postmodernism. He contended that just as Rabbi Kook – and, in his own way, Rabbi Joseph B. Soloveitchik – endeavored to unearth the positive in modernity,[5] which to many people, including prominent thinkers, seemed an existential threat to the Jewish tradition, our generation would have to contend with postmodernism. He ruled out the prevailing stance among the spiritual leaders of Israel's religious community, who accepted the modern ideals "kashered" by Rabbi Kook – chief among them the virtues of Zionism – but refused to extend his approach to such pervasive

2. This common *ḥaredi* idiom (*avoda zara beshittuf*), originally a halakhic term referring to worshipping both God and idols, is applied to religious Zionism, which the ultra-Orthodox see as obligated both to Torah and to secular values like nationalism.
3. Franz Rosenzweig, *The Star of Redemption* (Madison: University of Wisconsin Press, 2005), 247.
4. See Maharal of Prague, *Be'er HaGola, be'er* 6, chap. 8; Maharal of Prague, *Tiferet Yisrael*, chap. 11.
5. The idea, based on Lurianic Kabbala, that sparks of holiness embedded in evil must be sifted out (*birur*) and raised up – in order to vanquish evil as well as form an important layer in the structure of holiness – is central to Kabbala and Hasidism. It is also at the core of Rabbi Kook's response to the spirit of modernity, especially atheism.

Western values as individualism, skepticism, and pluralism, all modern outlooks amplified by postmodernism. Rabbi Shagar took upon himself the task of being the vanguard of an attempt to adopt, albeit critically, those values as well.

The title of the book from which most of the essays in this volume were selected is *Tablets and Broken Tablets*, based on the famous midrash to the effect that the tablets shattered by Moses were laid alongside the second, whole tablets, inside the Ark of the Covenant.[6] This title expresses Rabbi Shagar's unique method: the intense subversion and shattering of many religious and social conventions – while adopting, to a certain extent, the deconstructive attitude of postmodernism – alongside an attempt to formulate an alternative approach to faith and education. That method stemmed from the counterintuitive conviction that postmodern deconstruction can purify and refine religious faith. Furthermore, as is clear from the letter quoted above, Rabbi Shagar did not think his work would be the be-all and end-all for this intricate issue. In many cases, he considered his writings fragments of tablets, perhaps fragments of vessels,[7] to be utilized by his successors in their efforts to develop and establish a Jewish worldview and educational approach for our generation. The importance of this book lies in its trailblazing boldness, its religious and intellectual potency, and Rabbi Shagar's luminous and profound spirit – all of which form a foundation for the new path entailed by the religious and spiritual realities of our generation.

Our sages said, "Anyone who cites a teaching in the name of the one who said it should envision the giver of that teaching as though he were standing before him."[8] Since the Torah cannot be considered independently of those who teach it, we have seen fit to sketch an outline of

---

6. "R. Yosef learned: 'Which you broke, and you shall place them [in the Ark]' (Deut. 10:2) – [The juxtaposition of these words] teaches us that both the tablets and the fragments of the tablets were deposited in the Ark" (Bava Batra 14b).
7. Hence the title of one of Rabbi Shagar's works, *Broken Vessels*.
8. Y. Shabbat 8a.

Introduction

Rabbi Shagar's personality and life story, especially for readers who were not acquainted with him in his lifetime.

Rabbi Shagar was born in 1949 to a religious family. His parents were Holocaust survivors, and he attested that the *Shoah* was always a powerful presence in his world. Raised on, and molded by, an innocent brand of Zionism, along with joy and pride in the establishment of a Jewish state in the Land of Israel, he was imbued with firm national-religious convictions. Still, in many of his writings he did not shy away from criticizing the national religious movement.

This basic stratum of religious Zionism was supplemented by immersion in the world of Torah – first at the Netiv Meir yeshiva high school, headed by Rabbi Aryeh Bina, *zt"l*, and later at the precursor of all *hesder* yeshivas, Kerem B'Yavneh, headed at the time by Rabbi Chaim Yaakov Goldvicht, *zt"l*. Rabbi Shagar was educated in the *haredi* method of Torah study, which was also prevalent at national religious yeshivas at the time. He was among the cream of the crop of the *hesder* yehivas, and in 1974 was invited to teach at Yeshivat HaKotel, a *hesder* yeshiva where he had studied after his military service (he served first in the paratrooper brigade and then in the armored corps). Two years later, he was ordained as a rabbi. He was a man of the Torah in his entire being, and strictly observant. He had great fondness and respect for the ultra-Orthodox world, and, as this book clearly attests, considered some of its attributes vital for the national religious community.

Still, already as a yeshiva student he began questioning the prevailing Brisker method of talmudic analysis as well as the classic national religious ideology. The crisis he had experienced in the 1973 Yom Kippur War – during which, as a young reservist, he lost two members of his tank crew and was himself seriously injured – further fueled his attempt to blaze a new trail in Torah learning. Even as a young teacher at HaKotel, he stood out for two innovations: an existential approach to the study of Talmud and Jewish philosophical works, and the study of hasidic literature. The two were intertwined, in that Rabbi Shagar was drawn especially to Hasidism's piercing, existential aspect. Meanwhile, he also became convinced that the various schools of academic research could greatly enhance the study of halakha and aggada, and even Jewish philosophy and mysticism. He realized that to fully actualize the three

xv

revolutions he had engendered – the existential, the hasidic, and the academic – he would require a new kind of yeshiva. Hence his involvement in the establishment of the Makor Chaim Yeshiva, founded by Rabbi Adin Steinsaltz in 1985; the Maale *beit midrash* in 1989; and Beit Morasha, founded by Professor Benjamin Ish-Shalom, the following year. At Beit Morasha, which set out to combine yeshiva-style Torah study with academic scholarship, Rabbi Shagar headed the *beit midrash*. There he honed his unique approach, fusing yeshiva methods with academic research and existential inquiry. It was during this period that he discovered postmodernist philosophy.

In the fall of 1997, Rabbi Shagar left Beit Morasha and founded, with his old friend Rabbi Yair Dreyfuss, the Siaḥ Yitzḥak yeshiva. It was important to him to implement his method within a yeshiva environment, to create an innovative program that would combine devotion to Torah study and spiritual striving with an atmosphere of freedom and intellectual curiosity. In fact, every chapter of this book is based on material he taught and wrote during the following decade (from 1997 until his passing in 2007), when he delved into postmodernism.

Immersion in the public sphere was a strain for Rabbi Shagar. He was an introvert, engrossed in a rich private world and utterly devoted to Torah study. He left thousands of computer files along with thousands of handwritten pages on a variety of Torah topics, mostly Talmud; he once told a student that he never delivered a lecture without spending at least ten hours preparing it. Yet he could not ignore the dilemmas of the time, voicing his opinions in lectures delivered in various public venues, as well as in the book *Broken Vessels*. Most of this volume is based on those lectures.

It is important to emphasize that Rabbi Shagar dwelled entirely in the tent of Torah. He never attended university and knew no foreign languages, yet he accrued an autodidactic education of remarkable breadth, based on a library he assembled for himself (featuring, among other tomes, translations into Hebrew of postmodernist works) and articles he collected. He read voraciously: philosophy (old and new), fiction (especially science fiction), history, sociology, and more. Yet his reading of theoretical works was creative (at times even homiletic). He did not consider himself a professional philosopher, and his familiarity with secular literature was limited to what was translated into Hebrew in his lifetime. Hence the futility of asking whether his portrayal of postmodernism, or of any other thought system, is "authentic" or "precise"; what mattered to him was how external ideas could enrich and challenge the religious world.

Rabbi Shagar passed away on 25 Sivan 5767, only a few months after learning he had cancer. In those final months, he appointed a committee and provided instruction regarding the publishing of his writings. It was very important to him that his thoughts on contemporary matters be published. Thus far, the committee has put out more than ten volumes of his works, including lectures on the holidays, halakhic treatises, and essays on Hasidism. In addition, the committee has set up a website to provide access to essays, recorded lectures, and other materials from his estate. It intends to complete the publication of all of Rabbi Shagar's writings in the coming years, with an emphasis on his inimitable Talmud lectures.

Rabbi Shagar was always immersed in study and writing, in spiritual and creative work, but he spent very little time consolidating his ideas into a cohesive system. Even the works published in his lifetime (with the efforts and coaxing of Rabbi Dreyfuss) were not assembled into book form by him; rather, he let his students edit his files. That is why the essays in this book were edited by a variety of editors (from among his many students), some in his lifetime and others after his death, based on drafts he kept on his computer. A note at the beginning of every essay provides the name(s) of its editor(s), along with a brief description of the raw materials – the lectures and drafts – that went into it and basic information regarding the circumstances in which it was composed.

We have also included notes on various terms used by Rabbi Shagar (especially kabbalistic terminology) as well as references to other works of his, most published posthumously.

We will now attempt to sum up the main arguments in this collection of essays.

As noted, the heart of the book is Rabbi Shagar's grappling with postmodernism and the cultural and spiritual changes it wrought. In chapter 5, he attempts to get at the foundations of postmodernism: the denial and deconstruction that come from the erosion of belief in any "grand narrative" and in the ability to perceive the truth. Rabbi Shagar distinguishes between "hard" and "soft" postmodernism: While the first leads to utter nothingness, the second does not deny the existence of truth and goodness, but claims that these values are not predetermined, but rather man-made; hence their relativistic nature. According to Rabbi Shagar, the first brand of postmodernism should generally be rejected. Yet he notes a surprising connection between it and the religious agnosticism discussed by, among others, Maimonides and Rabbi Naḥman of Breslov (both of whom figure prominently in his writing). Elsewhere, he grants an important role to hard postmodernism in the post-Holocaust context.[9] While postmodern nothingness can breed heresy, moral paralysis, and nihilism, its religious counterpart emphasizes the divine infinitude and human humility. It bears mention that the extreme of postmodernism's negative theology is only one aspect of Rabbi Shagar's outlook, which is characterized more by its search for immanence, the divinity indwelling in the human world.

Rabbi Shagar devoted most of his efforts to exposing the positive in soft postmodernism, which does not necessarily lead to nothingness in that it recognizes beingness – albeit as a human construct (which is thus dangerous in that it can engender relativism and even contempt for morals, norms, and responsibilities). To his mind, it is faith, of all things, that can redeem postmodernism by imbuing human constructs with new value and validity, as vessels for the divine light. Soft postmodernism can also foster a humility and tolerance capable of greatly enriching the religious outlook. The religious person's challenge in the postmodern world is to choose and believe in his path, and to trust his creative powers. Paradoxically, Rabbi Shagar argues, it is easier to maintain a religious lifestyle in a postmodern world. For while modernism

9. See Rabbi Shagar, "Muteness and Faith," in *On That Day*, 64–77.

was characterized by an onslaught against religion and faith – in light of philosophical and scientific discoveries that were perceived as absolute truths – postmodernism's skepticism casts religion as an option no less valid than others. The challenge for us as believers, of course, is to choose religion as the best option.

Rabbi Shagar develops these points in chapter 2. There he also posits a solution to a problem arising from soft postmodernism: In acknowledging that our values and conceptions are constructed, do we not relegate religion to the subjective realm? Inspired by the work of the influential psychoanalyst Jacques Lacan, Rabbi Shagar explains that faith belongs to the domain of the Real, where there is no difference between subjective and objective.

That domain is also mystical, and, indeed, one basic argument in this book is that postmodernism leads to mysticism, and that the concurrence of postmodernism and the various strains of New Age mysticism is no accident. Rabbi Shagar elaborates in chapter 7, emphasizing that Kabbala describes multiple worlds and aspects and can thus serve as a basis for life in a postmodern world where the psyche must contain syntheses and contradictions. Furthermore, postmodern nothingness can be congruent with the mystical and kabbalistic nothingness – indeed, in Kabbala, the highest *sefira* is *keter*, nothingness. Seen from this perspective, postmodern skepticism and relativism can translate into the sublime levels described by Kabbala, which enables us to think of the former as bettering the world, not degrading it. However, to prevent these lofty strata from shattering our basic world, with its simpler faith, religion, and mores, we must temper our fervent relativism and skepticism with more elementary kabbalistic aspects (*malkhut*, or kingship) that enable us to revalidate our certainty and dedication to a particular path as a decision that itself partakes of the divine. The equation between postmodernism and mysticism requires us, in the vein of Rabbi Kook, to see Jewish esoterica (*torat hasod*) as the foundation of religious thought in the postmodern age.

In chapter 6, Rabbi Shagar discusses one of the most acute problems raised by postmodernism: how to create an ethical society when we possess no ultimate yardstick for judging actions. Here, too, he argues that soft postmodernism provides adequate means to deal with the challenge. It does not necessarily lead to nihilism, because we can create a society with agreed-upon ethical norms, even if they are not predetermined but rather emerge from dialogue between all segments of society. Moreover, postmodernism does not rule out ethical action; on the contrary, it elevates it by portraying it as arising from the decisions of humans who require no external fulcrum upon which to prop their worldviews.

This ethical outlook does not clash with the basic conception of Judaism, according to Rabbi Shagar, because it too acknowledges that, at least until the Messiah's arrival, it exists in a variegated world. For the time being, Judaism has no aspiration to foist itself on the rest of humanity and, in any event, can make do with a complex message wherein, while believing fully in its truth, it is willing to compromise with those who believe in other, even contradictory paths. Chapter 10 elaborates on this matter, employing the idea of the remainder, as elucidated by the German Jewish philosopher Franz Rosenzweig. Rabbi Shagar posits that Jewish chosenness need not render us aloof and hostile to the rest of humanity; rather, it requires us to be the ultimate Other, constantly challenging the world order with our difference.

Chapter 4 does not deal with postmodernism directly, considering it instead as the culmination of a problem that has vexed religion throughout the ages (and Rabbi Shagar for many years): the place of freedom in the religious world. He describes the various incarnations of the idea of freedom, and shows that although freedom appears to clash with religion, it has in fact always been a cornerstone of Judaism. In this respect, too, postmodernism propels freedom to the most radical places, which, in the religious context, at once pose the largest threat and present the greatest promise. Rabbi Shagar argues that only an atmosphere of freedom can give rise to an authentic, profound religiosity.

Rabbi Shagar claims that the rise of postmodernism compels the religious person to let go of the modern attempt to "rescue" the religious world from its theoretical and practical conflicts with the modern world by offering up an interpretation of Judaism, or modernity, or both, that resolves the contradictions. He suggests that such interpretations cause both Judaism and modernity to become shallow, even sterile. It is postmodernism that may provide us with proposals for contending with these contradictions. In chapter 2, Rabbi Shagar proposes a new brand of compartmentalization that places faith in its own realm, one that he identifies with Lacan's Real, thus "rescuing" it from its clash with modernity. In chapter 3, Rabbi Shagar emphasizes the centrality of halakha as the Jew's way of life (or, put philosophically, based on Ludwig Wittgenstein's later work, as a religious "language game"), a lifestyle that encompasses both faith and tradition as integral aspects of the religious world. By maintaining these two ingredients, we can lead a rich religious life within the modern world, without relegating faith to the rack of philosophical apologetics.

Chapter 3 also features a rare, in-depth treatment of Reform and Conservative Judaism. Rabbi Shagar sings the praises of Orthodoxy, but not from the classic ideological and conservative perspective. To his mind, the Reform and Conservative movements lack two critical components. The first is what he terms the "difficult point," the total commitment, the self-sacrifice that sometimes takes precedence over comfort, cultural fads, and life's constraints. Second, both movements fail to apprehend the nature of halakha, which is not an ideology but rather a flowing of life. That flow is characterized by commitment to the past, to the source of holiness, and by imperviousness to the academic-critical gaze with which Reform and Conservatism (inspired by the nineteenth-century "science of Judaism" movement) examine halakha.

The existentialism adopted by Rabbi Shagar led him, as he wrote in the letter quoted above, to the individual and his world. For example, chapter 2 opens with the assertion that faith is a private language that percolates in the most intimate realms of one's psyche. Chapter 1, which is devoted to midrashim on the Binding of Isaac (and offers a glimpse of Rabbi Shagar's profound analysis of *Ḥazal*'s thought), demonstrates that faith need not be a rigid ideology; rather, it can be a personal, frank, and blunt grappling with the elemental gulf between human and divine.

Another aspect of Rabbi Shagar's work is the idea, brought into relief by postmodern discourse, that it is not us, as individuals, who create language (be it social or religious); to a large extent, language (formed by society) creates us. The question of the relationship of the individual and society was a cardinal one for Rabbi Shagar. Chapter 9 provides some of his thoughts on the matter, emphasizing the issue that troubled him most: how to build a society without denying the inimitability and choice of the individual. Rabbi Shagar was repulsed by outlooks that portrayed the individual as an organ of society, with the latter superseding agency and choice. To his mind, every community is an assemblage of individuals, but not in the sense propounded by economic liberalism, which can easily slide into alienation and the instrumentalization of society; rather, in the sense of establishing a genuine unity.

Another window into his conception of society can be found in chapter 8, which deals with the effects of the postmodern world on one of the most sensitive and painful subjects for the religious individual: sexuality and family life. Here, too, he highlights postmodernism's potential to facilitate loftier relationships through our growing awareness of the commercialization of romance, and by lending a quality of absoluteness to the random world of dating.

As stated, Rabbi Shagar did not consider his work the be-all and end-all. In fact, it seems he had an aversion to bottom lines. He saw himself as someone who provokes thought, subverts outmoded conventions, and opens up new vistas and possibilities for holiness and divine worship. Thus, this book should be treated not as a systematic program for religious life in a postmodern world, but rather as a trailblazing work that, to our mind, is unique in the landscape of Jewish philosophy and of great importance for Judaism in the twenty-first century.

This book invites the reader to engage with its thought processes in a penetrating manner and to ask questions. For instance: Are the ideas raised by Rabbi Shagar, a man immersed in the Torah world, relevant to young people living in a far more secularized world? Are the traditionalism and intimacy that he held in such high esteem still accessible to a young generation in whose world Western culture is the dominant force? The rabbi was aware of these difficulties. He was never certain that he had established the optimal balance between openness and isolationism, certainty and doubt, yet it was clear to him, as it is to us, that the directions he highlighted are essential to striking such a balance.[10] With his keen eye, discerning heart, and broad mind, he added fundamental questions to the spiritual agenda of Modern Orthodoxy – formulating them sharply and profoundly, without dressing them up – and even proposed new philosophical directions and spiritual paths. These emanated from the depth of the soul of a true man of God, devoted to Him with every fiber of his being and prepared to give his life in his quest for truth.

We invite the reader to embark on a spiritual journey with Rabbi Shagar. His is a unique blend of a Torah vocabulary – informed by so many and varied Jewish sources – and the postmodern discourse, giving rise to a new religious language. Understanding requires patience, openness, and a willingness to delve deep; we hope that readers who accept the invitation will enrich and strengthen their religious and spiritual world.

We would like to express our appreciation to the editors of the various chapters in their various versions: Rabbi Yair Dreyfuss, Odeya Zuriely, Yishay Mevorach, Dr. Itamar Brenner, and Dr. Eitan Abramowitz; to the head of the publication committee, Rabbi Shimon Deutsch, for his deep involvement; and to Miriam Rosenberg, Rabbi Shagar's widow, who assisted in many ways, including by finding the raw materials from which the book was edited. Many thanks, too, to Rabbi Reuven Ziegler and Tomi Mager of Maggid Books for their fastidious and devoted treatment of the manuscript, and special, heartfelt thanks to Elie Leshem, who translated the book with judiciousness and skill, managing to convey Rabbi Shagar's profound and complex thoughts in English. Translations of source material in this book are the work of the translator unless

---

10. Rabbi Shagar's own conceptions frequently changed with the times and with the development of his theories. Thus, we should take into account that, had we merited his continued presence among us, he likely would have reexamined his words and, on various issues, diverged from the ideas presented here.

indicated in the reference. Dr. Moshe Simon-Shoshan skillfully edited the translation; Robert Milch and Judy Lee proofread it. Thanks also to Dr. David Landes for reviewing the translation and providing important input. Finally, our gratitude to Aryeh Rubin and the Targum Shlishi Foundation for underwriting the translation and to Rabbi Prof. Shalom Carmy for contributing the afterword.

Dr. Zohar Maor
Managing Editor of Rabbi Shagar's Writings
Shevat 5777

Chapter One

Uncertainty as the Trial of the Akeda

The *Akeda* (Binding of Isaac) is one of the most significant events in Jewish history. On the one hand, it shaped the core Jewish values of sanctifying God's name and of self-sacrifice. On the other hand, it raises difficult questions regarding the relationship between divine commandment and human ethics. That is why interpretations of the *Akeda* are not restricted to deliberations among Torah scholars. The trial of the *Akeda* has become a reality of Jewish life throughout the generations. I would like to begin by surveying the approaches of several modern thinkers to the *Akeda*. I will then focus on a sampling of midrashim, to see what disturbed Ḥazal about the story of the *Akeda* and what did not, what answers they found to their questions, and how the *Akeda* was perceived in their world.

First published during Rabbi Shagar's lifetime in A. Weitzmann, ed., *The Old Will Be Renewed: Philosophy and Thought from a Renewed Angle* [Hebrew] (Jerusalem, 1999), 68–91. It was re-edited by Dr. Zohar Maor after the author's death and included in *We Will Walk in Fervor*, 111–24.

QUESTIONS ABOUT THE *AKEDA*

In the world of modern philosophy, the *Akeda* raises several key questions. The first, elucidated by Kierkegaard, became the foundation of his famous interpretation of the *Akeda*. What is the distinction between what he terms the religious, which at its core is an appeal to the individual, and the ethical, which considers the individual as part of a collective? In the broader context, the question is whether man must carry out a commandment that is unethical. Is man permitted to become a criminal in the name of faith? For Kierkegaard these issues define the trial of Abraham.[1] The prevalent outlook in the Modern Orthodox world is that God stands above ethics. This idea was emphasized by Yeshayahu Leibowitz, who would often call attention to the gap between human ethical values and the divine law, to which man can relate only through obedience. To his mind, the meaning of the *Akeda* is that ethics is irrelevant to the religious world.[2] Obedience is an equally central component of Rabbi Soloveitchik's thought. To him, the *Akeda* means man must subject his will to the divine will, for the purpose of the religious act is to reveal holiness, God's transcendence, in the world. Unlike Leibowitz, however, he sees obedience as cutting against man's natural impulses, but not against ethics. As a student of Maimonides, who asserted that "in every passage [the sages] state clearly that for Him, may He be exalted, justice is necessary and obligatory,"[3] he maintains that God would never commit an injustice. Drawing from the philosopher Hermann Cohen, Rabbi Soloveitchik identifies the ethical imperative with God's attributes of action.[4]

1. Søren Kierkegaard, *Fear and Trembling* (Cambridge: Cambridge University Press, 2006); Yehuda Shaviv, "Mitzva Versus Morality: The *Akeda*" [Hebrew], *Megadim* 1 (Nisan 5747): 9–17; Hannah Kasher, "How Could God Command Us to Perform Such an Abomination? Rabbi Joseph ibn Kaspi's Critique of the Binding of Isaac" [Hebrew], *Et HaDaat* 1 (1997): 39–47.
2. Yeshayahu Leibowitz, *Judaism, Human Values, and the Jewish State* (Cambridge: Harvard University Press, 1995).
3. Moses Maimonides, *The Guide of the Perplexed*, trans. Shlomo Pines (Chicago: University of Chicago Press, 1963), III:17.
4. Pinchas H. Peli, *Soloveitchik on Repentance* (Ramsey, NJ: Paulist Press, 1984), 245–48.

Rabbi Abraham Isaac Kook espouses a different point of view.[5] He rejects the notion of a contradiction not only between ethics and religion, but also between nature and religion. The *Akeda* thus constitutes decisive proof of the harmony between a father's natural love for his son and God's true commandment, between the general and the particular. His interpretation of the *Akeda* is antithetical to that of Kierkegaard. An entire generation in Israel was raised on this harmonizing idea, and we are still eating its fruits.[6] But can we find another approach in *Ḥazal*, one that calls for rebellion, insubordination, or at least protest?

The second question that arises in the context of the *Akeda* is not that of humans' obeying an ostensibly unethical divine command, but that of the very injustice of God's ordering a trial involving the sacrificing of one's son. Can God act unjustly? The question begs comparison to Job, whose ordeal was caused by Satan. Would it be correct to assume the same of the *Akeda* and similar cases?

The comparison to Job is quite problematic. *Ḥazal* teach that "Job sought to overturn the platter"[7] and "he rebelled against his suffering."[8] According to a straightforward reading of the biblical text, his protest is accepted by God. He says to Job's friends: "You have not spoken of Me the thing that is right, as My servant Job has" (Job 42:7). It would appear that Abraham's reaction is identical to that which Job's friends demand of him, but while they are admonished by God, Abraham is praised. What, then, is the relation between Abraham and Job? Several midrashim draw comparisons, and we will get to one of them soon enough, but first we must mention an extreme, thorny statement by R. Yoḥanan:

> Greater praise is accorded to Job than to Abraham. For of Abraham it is written, "For now I know that you fear God" (Gen. 22:12), whereas of Job it is written, "That man was perfect [innocent] and upright and one who feared God and eschewed evil" (Job 1:8).[9]

5. Rabbi Abraham Isaac Kook, *Olat Re'iya* (Jerusalem: Mossad HaRav Kook, 1963), pt. 1, 84–98.
6. See *Tablets and Broken Tablets*, 161.
7. Bava Batra 16a.
8. *Pesikta Rabbati* 47.
9. Bava Batra 15b.

R. Yoḥanan contrasts fear of God with innocence, and upright-
ness with eschewing evil, as if there is a fear of God that is not innocent,
an eschewing of evil that is not upright. His words are astonishing not
only due to our tendency to identify these traits with one another, but
also because Job is portrayed as having been awarded loftier praise than
Abraham.

The third question returns to the issue of humans' following an
apparently unethical divine command. How can a person be sure such
a command really comes from God? Can man ever attain absolute certainty as to the will of God? The *Rishonim*, including Maimonides, used
the *Akeda* to prove the objective certainty of prophecy. Abraham would
never have been willing to slaughter his son, they posited, were he not
absolutely certain of the authenticity of the divine command.[10] In many
ways, such a portrayal of the ordeal renders it irrelevant to us, for we have
not been granted the privilege of prophecy, and God does not speak to
us as He spoke to Abraham. But does the ordeal of the *Akeda* in fact pre-
sume Abraham's sense of certainty as a prophet? The Midrash suggests
that this is not necessarily the case:

> As [Abraham and Isaac] were walking, Satan appeared to Abra-
> ham and said to him, "Old man, are you out of your mind? You're
> going to slaughter the son God gave you at the age of one hun-
> dred?! It was I who deceived you and said to you, 'Take now
> [your son]....'"[11]

---

10. *Guide of the Perplexed* III:24.
11. Solomon Buber, ed., *Midrash Aggada* (Vienna, 1894), *Vayera* 22. See the criticism
of Kierkegaard in the essay "On the Suspension of the Ethical," in Martin Buber,
Eclipse of God: Studies in the Relation Between Religion and Philosophy (Princeton:
Princeton University Press, 2016), 100: "Where, therefore, the 'suspension' of the
ethical is concerned, the question which takes precedence over every other is: Are
you really addressed by the Absolute or one of his apes? ... Ours is an age in which
the suspension of the ethical conscience fills the world in a caricatured form. The
apes of the Absolute, to be sure, have always in the past bustled about on earth. Ever
and ever again men are commanded from out of the darkness to sacrifice their Isaac.
Here the sentence is valid, 'That which the Single One is to understand by Isaac, can
be decided only by and for himself.' But stored away in men's hearts, there were in all
those times images of the Absolute, partly pallid, partly crude, altogether false and

In some midrashim, *Ḥazal's* approach is far from simplistic, eschewing the view that God's voice is clearly apprehensible and that the focal point of the ordeal is Abraham's willingness to obey it. The question of Abraham's capacity to know whether it is indeed God's voice speaking to him – and that he must obey – or whether it is Satan's, is posed in all its starkness. Perhaps *that* is the essence of the ordeal – the ability to distinguish between the two voices. From an ethical standpoint, Abraham is commanded to commit a crime, precisely the kind of crime against which he has railed his entire life. Moreover, the victim is to be his "only son," whom he loves, the sum of his hopes and his purpose. Such an action must spring from an absolute certainty that the commanding voice is indeed God's. The question of conviction thus emerges in all its harshness.

The Talmud raises a similar question regarding the story of the false prophet Zedekiah the son of Chenaanah. The Book of Kings tells of how Zedekiah prophesied to the king of Israel that he would be victorious in his battle against the king of Aram. The Bible reveals that this prophecy was in fact sent by God through a spirit (identified by the rabbis as that of Naboth) in order to deceive the king of Israel. With regard to this account, the Talmud asks:

> But what [else] could [Zedekiah] have done, seeing that the spirit of Naboth had deceived him, it is written, "And the Lord said: Who shall persuade Ahab, that he may go up and fall at Ramoth-Gilead? And there came forth a spirit and stood before the Lord, and said: I will persuade him. And [the Lord] said:

---

yet true, fleeting as an image in a dream yet verified in eternity. Inadequate as this presence certainly was, insofar as one bore it concretely in mind, one only needed to call on it in order not to succumb to the deception of the voices. That is no longer so…since the image-making power of the human heart has been in decline so that the spiritual pupil can no longer catch a glimpse of the appearance of the Absolute.… False Absolutes rule over the soul.… Everywhere, over the whole surface of the human world – in the East and in the West, from the left and from the right, they pierce unhindered through the level of the ethical and demand of you the 'sacrifice'… in the realm of Moloch honest men lie and compassionate men torture. And they really and truly believe that brother-murder will prepare the way for brotherhood! There appears to be no escape from the most evil of all idolatry."

You shall persuade him and prevail also; go forth and do so" (I Kings 22:20).[12]

The Talmud's answer is interesting: "R. Yoḥanan said:...He should have scrutinized [the predictions of the assembled prophets], even as R. Yitzḥak said: The same communication is revealed to many prophets, yet no two prophets prophesy in the identical phraseology." It is a Kierkegaardian answer: A true prophecy is revealed to the individual as authentic, and it cannot be duplicated or imitated. The very fact that several prophets prophesied in the style of Zedekiah should have made him doubt the prophecy's authenticity. The general, the social, is infected with lies.

Another question relates to the essence of the ordeal. This is a major aspect of the *Akeda,* and I will not address it at length. Ḥazal present many contradictory approaches to the ordeal, of which we will cite two. The first is in Sanhedrin. Commenting on the opening words of the *Akeda* story, "After these words" (Gen. 22:1),[13] the Talmud states, "R. Yoḥanan said in the name of R. Yose b. Zimra: After the words of Satan."[14] Abraham's ordeal is explained along the same lines as Job's: Both were initially goaded by Satan. The ordeal is seen as an "act of Satan" and thus evil. In this context, it is worth mentioning another statement of R. Yoḥanan's: "Were it not expressly stated in Scripture, we would not dare say it: [God is made to appear] like a man who allows himself to be persuaded against his better judgment."[15] In effect, the ordeal is unjustified, something God was incited to do.

Other midrashim maintain that either Abraham or Isaac, eager to demonstrate devotion to God, sought an ordeal. The ordeal is thus the ultimate religious act. The Talmud attributes this opposite approach to R. Levi:

---

12. Sanhedrin 89a.
13. [Ed. note: The Hebrew word *devarim,* rendered here as "words," can also mean "things." In context, the simple meaning of the phrase in question is "After these things," i.e., after the events of the previous chapter. Other midrashim indeed understand the text this way. Two such midrashim are quoted below.]
14. Sanhedrin 89b.
15. Bava Batra 16b.

R. Levi said: After Ishmael's words to Isaac. Ishmael said to Isaac: "I am more virtuous than you in good deeds, for you were circumcised at eight days [and so could not prevent it], but I at thirteen years." "On account of one limb would you incense me?!" he replied. "Were the Holy One, blessed be He, to say to me, 'Sacrifice yourself before Me,' I would obey." Straightaway, "God did test Abraham" (Gen. 22:1).[16]

In framing Isaac's words as a response to a challenge from Ishmael, R. Levi's statement also emphasizes the struggle against the nations. The motif of martyrdom is pronounced in the following midrash as well:

"After these things" – after the ponderings that transpired on that occasion. Who pondered? Abraham, who said to himself, "I have rejoiced and caused all others to rejoice, yet I did not set aside a single bull or ram for the Holy One, blessed be He." Said God to him, "It was so that if We command you to offer your only son, you will not dither."[17]

SATAN, AND ABRAHAM'S MISGIVINGS

Many midrashim feature a conversation between Satan, Abraham, and Isaac.[18] The purpose of these midrashim is to provide a backdrop and context for the conversation between Isaac and Abraham:

...so they went both of them together. And Isaac spoke unto Abraham his father, and said, "My father." And he said, "Here am I, my son." And he said, "Behold the fire and the wood; but where is the lamb for a burnt offering?" And Abraham said, "God will provide the lamb for a burnt offering, my son." So they went both of them together. (Gen. 22: 6–8)

---

16. Sanhedrin loc. cit.
17. Genesis Rabba 55:4.
18. See *Midrash HaGadol* on Gen. 22; *Tanḥuma* (ed. Solomon Buber), *Vayera* 46. On these midrashim, see Jacob E. Ephrathi, *The Trial of the Akeda: A Literal Interpretation of the Biblical Text and Its Literature* [Hebrew] (Petaḥ Tikva: Agudat Bnei Asher, 5743), 197 ff.

This conversation is characterized by intimacy and much tenderness. The words "father" and "son" are used repeatedly as terms of address, and it is clear from the text that beyond the explicit conversation is a covert dialogue about the unfolding *Akeda*. The verses allude to intense internal tumult throughout the exchange, such as in the verses that say, "they went both of them together," and in Abraham's response: "God will provide the lamb for a burnt offering, my son." Yet the Torah, as is its wont, is restrained in its description of these occurrences, a restraint that thickens the plot with meaning and retains its depth. *Ḥazal* raise questions about the conversation: Did Isaac realize what was about to transpire and appeal to his father's mercy? What was Abraham's answer? The ostensible meaning of his response is that God will provide the sacrificial lamb. The additional phrase "my son," an expression of mercy, more than hints at the identity of the intended sacrifice. Still, the sentence is ambiguous. Did Abraham conceal from Isaac the true purpose of their journey?

Ḥazal see Isaac as a willing participant in the sacrifice, as implicit in the repetition of the phrase "they went both of them together." Satan's presence is a device for the portrayal of Abraham's and Isaac's internal dialogues and thoughts leading up to the *Akeda*.[19]

Several midrashim suggest that Satan is inside Abraham, and that the dialogue between them expresses Abraham's stream of consciousness. "Satan [and] the evil inclination ... are one," the sages taught.[20] This approach is apparent in the *Midrash Tanḥuma*:

> Satan appeared before him on the road in the guise of an old man and asked, "Whither are you going?" Abraham replied,

---

19. It appears that these midrashim developed out of interpretations of the last part of the passage, "God will provide" (for instance, see the statement by R. Shimon b. Yoḥai in *Pirkei DeRabbi Eliezer 30*), and the first part, which describes Isaac's address to his father. The *Pesikta Rabbati*, for example, describes Satan speaking only to Isaac. Academic scholars have pointed out that the later midrashim are more simplistic and tend to dull the radical edge of their precursors, yet several of these later texts display a keen psychological eye and an unflinching willingness to see things through.
20. Bava Batra 16a.

"To pray."... Satan departed from him and appeared at Isaac's right hand in the guise of a youth. He inquired, "Where are you going?"[21]

Satan appears to Abraham "in the guise of an old man" and to Isaac "in the guise of a youth" – each according to his own identity. To put it in Freudian terms, we might say that he is a projection of their inner worlds. The misgivings, then, are Abraham's own.

The Talmud strings together several early midrashim (also quoted in the *Midrash HaGadol*) to form a sustained, charged dialogue between Abraham and Satan. It is a riveting and very instructive exchange in light of the aforementioned questions about the *Akeda*:

> On the way Satan came toward him and said to him, "Because He tried you with one thing, will you be weary? ... Behold, you have instructed many, and you have strengthened the weak hands. Your words have upheld him who was falling, and you have strengthened the feeble knees. But now it is come upon you, and you are weary" (Job 4:2–5). He replied, "I will walk in my integrity" (Ps. 26:11). But [Satan] said to him, "Is not your fear of God your confidence?" (Job 4:6). "Remember," he retorted, "I pray thee, whoever perished being innocent?" (4:7). Seeing that he would not listen to him, [Satan] said to him, "'Now a word was secretly brought to me' (4:12). Thus have I heard from behind the curtain: The lamb for a burnt offering, but not Isaac for a burnt offering." He replied, "It is the penalty of a liar that even should he tell the truth, no one listens to him."[22]

First, we must point out that the conversation is composed mostly of statements made by Eliphaz in his first address to Job. This insight takes us right to the heart of the problem: Abraham's behavior is diametrically opposed to Job's. "Job sought to overturn the platter," Ḥazal said; in effect, he rebelled against God. His friends regale him with

---

21. Samuel A. Berman, trans., *Midrash Tanḥuma-Yelammedenu: An English Translation of Genesis and Exodus* (Jersey City, NJ: Ktav, 1996), 144 (*Vayera* 22).
22. Sanhedrin 89b.

religious platitudes, but apparently God prefers Job's integrity over his friends' virtue, which is deemed a sin. And what of Abraham? He seems to conduct himself according to the same sinful maxims espoused by Job's friends. The author of the midrash puts Eliphaz's words – "Because He tried you with one thing" – in Satan's mouth, but reverses their meaning. While Eliphaz demanded obedience from Job, the midrash reads his statement as a reflection of Job's actions: rebellion and protest over the injustice done him. The subversion of Eliphaz's utterance implies that the fear of God he demands of Job leads to a conclusion that's the opposite of the one he proffers. The correct conclusion is Job's, borne out by Eliphaz's own argument. It is a twofold paradox: Eliphaz's words are put in Satan's mouth with a subverted meaning, while their original meaning calls for the exact same behavior practiced by Abraham. What can we learn from this paradox? Here is Rashi:

> "Because He tried you with one thing, will you be weary?" – Should He who loves you have tried you with a thing that wearies you and eradicates your progeny?!

> "Behold, you have instructed many" – You revived the entire world with your teachings, and now He comes to weary and frighten you?!

According to Rashi, this is a protest over God's very demand of Abraham. Yet the words of the *Midrash HaGadol*, which are likely the source of the midrash in the Talmud, have different implications:

> And it is of him that the verse says, "Because He tried you with one thing, will you be weary?" This verse speaks of Abraham our forefather. For when God said to him, "Slaughter your son and make an offering of him before Me," he immediately resolved to slaughter him. On the way, Satan came toward him and said to him .... "Couldn't an old man like you misinterpret such a thing? [God] sought only to deceive and weary you, for the Torah writes, 'Whoever sheds man's blood, by man shall his blood be shed' (Gen. 9:6), and yet you erroneously intend to slaughter

your son?! Even if you say, 'It was You who instructed me,' He will say, 'Who can bear witness against Me?' Even if you had witnesses, a slave cannot testify against his master, and even if he does, his testimony is void. Change your mind!" [Abraham] replied, "I will not heed your request that I disobey the will of my Father in heaven, for it is said, 'If one venture a word unto thee, will you be weary?'"[23]

This version of the midrash gets to the heart of the dilemma, which has two aspects to it: the conflict between the ethical-religious imperative forbidding murder and God's commandment to slaughter Isaac, and the uncertainty as to the nature of the trial. Could it be that Abraham was tested not regarding his ability to obey God's commandment, but rather regarding his ability to disobey? What if Satan assumed the voice of God to deceive Abraham? The argument here is that even if it truly is God's voice demanding the slaughter of Isaac, it is open to multiple interpretations. Abraham has no way of determining whether God truly wants him to sacrifice his son, or whether His commandment is a ploy. The *Midrash HaGadol* subverts Eliphaz's invocation of the fear of God by reading it as a call for rebellion – one that, compounding the irony, reflects God's true will. Eliphaz stands for a religious argument: Man must heed the Torah's imperative; the written code reigns supreme. But it is precisely that demand which, according to the midrash, can lead man astray from God's true intentions. By transplanting Eliphaz's statement in this new context, the midrash ingeniously gets at the core of the religious problem.

Satan's argument is that, in this instance, Orthodoxy's very demand for obedience and fear of God necessitates rebellion: Through ethics, the imperative of conscience, the true fear of God is revealed. Thus, God is trying Abraham to see if he will obey. Abraham can no longer fall back on his usual line of defense, can no longer say, "God willed it," and lay the responsibility on a higher legal authority, including God Himself. Satan claims that Abraham will not be eligible to testify, and the responsibility will, of necessity, devolve upon him.

---

23. M. Margulies, ed., *Midrash HaGadol* (Jerusalem: Mossad HaRav Kook, 5747), pt. 1, 346.

Does the midrash, in reading Job's friends' plea for obedience as Satan's call for defiance, imply that the argument, which turns religiosity on its head, is an act of Satan? The answer is unclear, for both the original comments and their subversive interpretation are rejected by God, leaving us to wonder which voice is God's and which Satan's.

Abraham's response is based on a verse in Psalms: "I will walk in my integrity (*temimut*)." Integrity, in the sense of moral soundness or innocence, is the answer to the doubts raised by Satan. We must read on in the Talmud if we are to understand the bite of its account.

Later, the midrash once again puts Eliphaz's words in Satan's mouth – "*Halo yiratkha kislatekha*" – but again subverts their meaning. The word *kislatekha*, in its original context, connotes confidence or hope. The simple meaning of the verse is thus, "your fear of God is your hope." But this midrashic reading of the verse plays on another meaning of *kislatekha*, "folly," so that the verse can also be read as "your fear of God is your folly."[24] By conflating "hope" with "folly," Satan's harangue ridicules Abraham for his naïveté, his folly and blindness to reality. The believer's utopian hope is naught but silliness that flies in the face of reality, Satan asserts.

Abraham's response is drawn from Eliphaz's own statements further on in the text: "Remember, I pray thee, whoever perished being innocent?" What is the meaning of this answer? Ostensibly, Abraham is steeling himself with simple faith, arguing that it is inconceivable for the innocent to perish. Abraham evokes the arguments of Job's friends, which were rejected by God. What does this mean?

One thing sets Abraham apart from Job's friends: his integrity. Their opinion, in and of itself, may not be false, but it is true only if uttered with integrity. The problem with their religious stance is that it is not expressed with integrity. The fact that the author of the midrash carves up Eliphaz's address, putting some words in Abraham's mouth and others in Satan's, proves that both reactions are appropriate; neither can be rejected – it all depends on the context in which they are uttered.

---

24. The source of this reading is *Midrash HaGadol*, which cites R. Shimon b. Lakish paraphrasing this verse as *yirat shamayim shebakh, kesilut*.

In the context of our discussion, there is certainly an accusation leveled at Job's friends: namely, that they lack integrity. In effect, Abraham, in addition to being a true innocent, is also a true rebel. In Abraham, integrity – typically the foundation of a commonplace religious stance, like that of Job's friends, who automatically justify God's actions – rises to the level of true belief, which does not set aside ethical and other considerations in obeying the divine imperative.

But there appears to be another aspect of Abraham's response to Satan. Abraham truly believes that the innocent cannot perish. His fear of God, which Satan derides as "folly," is the source of his confidence. He believes there will be a divine solution to the problem. It is a paradoxical faith, but one in which Abraham is fully invested. This emerges further along in the midrash: Realizing that he cannot dissuade Abraham from proceeding with the *Akeda*, Satan nevertheless attempts to prevent him from passing the test by revealing its "happy ending," which pulls the rug out from under the trial.

Here, too, Satan simply echoes Abraham's own thoughts, playing on his statement to Isaac that "God will provide the lamb for a burnt offering, my son." Is Abraham truly prepared to slaughter Isaac, or is he constantly hoping against hope that he will ultimately not have to go through with it? Satan raises Abraham's hopes, thus rendering the trial moot.

What is Abraham's response to Satan? The midrash remains ambiguous: "It is the penalty of a liar that even should he tell the truth, no one listens to him." On the face of it, Abraham knows that Satan is speaking the truth, but for some reason he is unwilling to heed it. His integrity lies in proceeding in earnest, and thus he does not allow the thought of "Where is the lamb for a burnt offering?" to enter his mind. The religious belief in a happy ending, distant as it may seem, could corrupt the experience and meaning of passing the test, so Abraham takes an innocent approach to that as well.

The lesson is clear: A conceited, all-knowing religious stance renders the trial, and with it the entire religious endeavor, a sham. The trial, along with a religious lifestyle and a connection to God, can exist only in the context of a humble personality that is content in not knowing. A conceited stance stems from pride, and it is the voice of

Satan. The trial will forever be associated with a subject who by nature is in the dark. The objectivization of the religious trial invalidates it. Hence Abraham's response to Satan: Although he is aware of the objective truth, he does not allow his knowledge to detract one whit from the gravity of the trial.

In summarizing the midrash in the context of our discussion, we can say that it offers a twofold argument against the trial: first, that the normative ethical imperative proscribes Abraham's intended action; second, that one can never attain certainty as to the nature of the trial. What is God's true will – that man obey His directive, or rebel? How are we to know, if every divine utterance is open to multiple, sometimes opposing interpretations? The midrash's answer is integrity. Yet the implied conflict between Job's response and Abraham's teaches us that such integrity does not have a single fixed vector. In the context of a trial, protest is a legitimate religious response, on par with obedience.

PROTEST AND OBEDIENCE

But what is the nature of such a protest? Several midrashim can be described as "midrashim of protest." This protest is sometimes placed in Abraham's mouth. For instance, here is a midrash from Genesis Rabba:

> "The Lord tests the righteous" (Ps. 11:5) – that is Abraham, for it is written, "And it came to pass after these things that God tested Abraham" (Gen. 22:1).
>
> R. Avin opened: "Inasmuch as the king's word has power, and none say to him: 'What are you doing?' (Eccl. 8:4)." R. Avin said, "It is like a rabbi who instructs his students and says, 'You shall not judge unfairly' (Deut. 16:19), yet he judges unfairly; 'you shall not show partiality' (ibid.), yet he shows partiality; 'neither shall you take a bribe' (ibid.), yet he takes bribes; 'You shall not lend with interest' (23:19), yet he lends with interest."
>
> One student said to him, "Rabbi, you instruct me not to lend with interest, yet you lend with interest. Is it permissible for you and forbidden for me?"

The rabbi replied, "I am saying that you must not lend with interest to a Jew, but you may lend with interest to an idol worshipper, for it is stated, 'To a foreigner you may lend upon interest; but to your brother you shall not lend upon interest' (Deut. 23:20).

So, too, Israel said before the Holy One, blessed be He: "Master of the universe, You wrote in Your Torah, 'You shall not take vengeance or bear any grudge' (Lev. 19:18), yet You take vengeance and bear a grudge, as it is written, 'The Lord avenges and is full of wrath; the Lord takes vengeance on His adversaries, and He reserves His wrath for His enemies' (Nahum 1:2)."

The Holy One, blessed be He, replied, "I wrote in the Torah, 'You shall not take vengeance or bear any grudge against the children of your people,' but I take vengeance and bear grudges against idol worshippers: 'Avenge the Children of Israel' (Num. 31:2)."

It is written, "You shall not test the Lord" (Deut. 6:16), and "God tested Abraham."[25]

On the face of it, there is a problem with the midrash. The opening is not connected to the rest, including the conclusion. The midrash asks why the Torah forbids us from testing God when God himself tests Abraham. Yet the explanation – that a distinction is drawn between Jews and non-Jews – does not answer the question. The ordeal of the *Akeda* was endured by Abraham. Indeed, other versions of the midrash omit the ending about Abraham.[26] Nevertheless, how can we explain the fact that the midrash still opens with the *Akeda*? It appears that the midrash was initially composed not as a commentary on the *Akeda*, but on the revenge campaign against Midian. R. Avin's explanation neither solves the problems of the *Akeda* nor answers the student's question. However, in citing this midrash in the context of the *Akeda*, the editor of Genesis Rabba transforms it into a twofold protest: against the ordeal

---

25. Genesis Rabba 55:3.
26. Ephrathi, *Trial of the Akeda*, 64.

itself, but also against R. Avin's attempt to reconcile doubts about God's conduct. The irony is compounded by the verse that follows one of the verses quoted by the midrash: "Whoever keeps the commandment shall know no evil thing; and a wise man's heart discerns time and judgment" (Eccl. 8:5).

Such midrashim are expressions of protest, not rebellion. They do not challenge the demand for obedience. Abraham must obey a divine imperative that, arbitrary as it may be, is the word of the King. Furthermore, the midrash may imply that arbitrariness is the expression of the Monarch's kingship and authority.

Ḥazal never call for rebellion and insubordination. Nonetheless, one is under no obligation to turn a blind eye to an injustice, even a divine injustice. It is precisely through the act of protest that one expresses religious fervor and, perhaps, retroactively justifies one's obedience.

Midrashim also make the opposite claim, and, like Maimonides, opine that all trials must stem from divine justice. One example is the following passage from Tractate Taanit:

> And it is further written, "Which I commanded not, nor spoke it, neither came it into My mind" (Jer. 19:5). "Which I commanded not": This refers to the sacrifice of the son of Mesha, the king of Moab, as it is said, "Then he took his eldest son, who should have reigned in his stead, and offered him for a burnt offering" (II Kings 3:27). "Nor spoke it": This refers to the daughter of Yiftaḥ. "Neither came it into My mind": This refers to the sacrifice of Isaac the son of Abraham.[27]

---

27. Taanit 4a. Another midrash questioning the morality of the *Akeda* has been preserved in a Yemenite manuscript: "The Holy One, blessed be He, replied, 'And behold, behind him a ram' (Gen. 22:13). The sages said: 'He who answered Abraham on Mount Moriah said, 'God will provide the lamb,' 'And behold, behind him a ram.''" Cited in Rabbi Menaḥem Mendel Kasher, *Torah Shelema* [Hebrew] (Jerusalem: Mekhon Torah Shelema, 5752), vol. 1, chap. 22, 97. In response to the divine imperative, Abraham prays to be delivered from the need to uphold it. It is a prayer to God for protection from God. That is how the midrash explains the mishna in chap. 2 of Taanit: "He who answered Abraham on Mount Moriah, He shall answer you"

It is important to note, however, that the argument relates to the morality of God – whether it is conceivable that He would act arbitrarily or (as we will see) come under Satan's sway. There is no argument regarding the imperative that man obey. We should thus distinguish between the two perspectives: that of God and that of man.

The questions of obedience and divine justice receive intensive treatment in several additional midrashim, including the aforementioned one in the *Tanḥuma*:

> The old man [Satan] responded, "…I was present when the Holy One, blessed be He, ordered you to take your son. Why should an old man, who begets a son at the age of a hundred, destroy him? Have you not heard the parable of the old man who destroyed his possessions and then was forced to beg from others? If you believe you will have another son, you are listening to the words of the seducer. Furthermore, if you destroy a soul, you will be held legally accountable for it." Abraham answered, "It was not a seducer, but the Holy One, blessed be He, who told me what I must do, and I shall not listen to you."[28]

Satan's arguments are clear: Abraham's actions fly in the face of both mitzva and morality, and they belie his own yearning for sons. Most critically, Satan declares that the word of God is in fact his own. "I was present," Satan says. The divine imperative emerged from a seduction. The comparison to Job is obvious – there too the trial was an act of seduction. But what are we to make of Abraham's response? "It was not a seducer, but the Holy One, blessed be He," he asserts. Is this a straightforward denial of Satan's claim? Indeed, such was the case with Job, who was unwilling – with good reason, it turned out – to accept his calamities at face value, as an expression of God's justice. Let us turn to another midrash:

(see Rabbi Kasher's explanation in *Torah Shelema*). Abraham's statement that "God will provide" is interpreted by the mishna as a prayer. The trial is not itself an ideal, and the response to its injustice is prayer.

28. Berman, *Midrash Tanḥuma-Yelammedenu*, loc. cit. Emphasis added.

"And Isaac spoke unto Abraham his father, and said, 'My father'" (Gen. 22:7) – Samael [Satan] came to Abraham our forefather and said, "Old man, have you lost your mind?! Do you truly intend to slaughter the son given you at the age of one hundred?" "Indeed so," he replied. Samael said, "And will you be able to stand it if He tests you even more? 'Because He tried you with one thing, will you be weary?'" Abraham said, "Even more so." Samael replied, "Tomorrow He will call you a murderer and say you are culpable for shedding your son's blood!" Said Abraham, "Indeed so."[29]

The plot thickens. The midrash is clearly interpreting and expanding on R. Shimon b. Yoḥai's homily in the *Midrash HaGadol*. The verse "Because He tried you with one thing, will you be weary?" is interpreted as: Is Abraham capable of withstanding larger trials? Is there no limit to obedience? Will he comply with any command? Were Abraham to answer that there were some commands he could not carry out, he would be giving Satan an opening to convince him to disobey the command to sacrifice his son. Satan presses on, saying, "Tomorrow He will call you a murderer." Here, too, is a powerful assertion: The arbitrariness of God's will, as it is brought to bear on the *Akeda*, is boundless. Abraham's response, "Indeed so," indicates that he is prepared to endure anything – even the arbitrariness of God's will. Abraham, the midrash says, is prepared to forgo even the small consolation of the assurance of God's love, along with the belief in His justness.

"Indeed so" expresses a resolve that goes beyond commonplace obedience. An obedience motivated merely by submission, dedication, and a desire to fulfill the letter of the law cannot produce such a reaction. How can Abraham be motivated by obedience when obeying could itself constitute a transgression of God's will? His is an absolute, unconditional commitment, his love of God so complete that he remains undeterred even by the prospect of God's accusing him of murder after the fact. The answer that this midrash provides to the question of doubt differs from the previous ones. It expresses Abraham's unremitting dedication, his willingness to forfeit everything – not just his ethics but even his very

---

29. Genesis Rabba 56:4.

religion – which is his only path to unqualified devotion, if not utter certainty. In any event, it appears as though Abraham's insistence on the divine origin of the imperative to slaughter his son can be facilitated only by the seed of doubt planted by Satan. This is what sets it apart from ordinary obstinacy, especially if we read Satan as a manifestation of Abraham's own misgivings. Intransigence that does not take doubt into account is meaningless and false.

Chapter Two

My Faith: Faith in a Postmodern World

FAITH BEYOND WORDS

I wish to describe the religious worldview of an Orthodox Jewish believer. This outlook neither represents nor characterizes a conventional Orthodox worldview, and that is no accident: I do not consider myself an ambassador for a certain person or group; to me, faith is a private language.

In one of his talks, Rabbi Naḥman of Breslov relates the following teaching:

> "For I know that the Lord is great and that our Lord is above all gods" (Ps. 135:5). King David, may peace be upon him, said,

Compiled from notes recorded in Sivan 5764 in preparation for a lecture. The compilation was not published in the author's lifetime and was edited after his death by Dr. Itamar Brenner and Dr. Zohar Maor for publication in *Tablets and Broken Tablets*, 407–26. Turning the text into an essay required extensive editing, and excerpts from other writings were added for clarity. The drafts comprised two sections, one relatively organized and the other more fragmentary, reflecting on the theme of faith. During the editing process, the decision was made to retain certain fragments and include them as footnotes.

"For *I* know," with the emphasis on "I." For the greatness of the blessed Creator cannot be imparted to one's fellow, and even in affirming it to oneself, one can only draw from the influence and insight one has received on that very day. One cannot affirm the Lord's greatness to oneself with the influence and insight of the previous day. Thus he said, "For I *know*," emphasizing "know," for it is utterly indescribable.[1]

In effect, according to Rabbi Naḥman, not only is faith not a public language, it is not a language at all. That is why it is so difficult to fully depict one's faith. Something will always remain unspoken, a mystery and intimacy that cannot and should not be revealed, for baring it would violate the intimacy of faith. This is not to gloss over the communal aspect of faith, which is by nature a public language as well; however, the collectivity of faith is the second stage, not the first.

The assertion that faith is a private language goes against both the prevalent attitude in Israel's religious Zionist community, which sees faith as collective (according to such an attitude, it is one's membership in the Jewish people that establishes one's connection to God), and the view – shared by modern thinkers such as Yeshayahu Leibowitz – that emphasizes the normative aspect of Judaism and sees the Torah as something of a categorical imperative placed upon man.[2]

---

1. Rabbi Naḥman of Breslov, *Siḥot HaRan* 1. Rabbi Naḥman proceeds to quote the Zohar's commentary on the words "Her husband is known at the city gates" (Prov. 31:23), which states, "Each according to what his heart imagines" (Zohar, *Vayera* 103b).

2. Although for Leibowitz the other side of the coin was one's personal decision to submit to the yoke of the kingdom of heaven (*ol malkhut shamayim*), this was a decision to accept the yoke of the commandments (*ol mitzvot*): "Faith is an expression of the commandments, but the commandments are not an expression of faith" (Yeshayahu Leibowitz, *Torah and Commandments in Our Time* [Hebrew] [Tel Aviv: Schocken, 1954], 11. His system is further elucidated in his *Judaism, Human Values, and the Jewish State*). I see the relationship between belief and religious practice differently. The Mishna states, "R. Yehoshua b. Karḥa said, 'Why does *Shema* precede *Vehaya im shamoa*? So that one may accept the yoke of the kingdom of heaven first, and after that accept the yoke of the commandments'" (Berakhot 2:2). I read this mishna to mean that the acceptance of the yoke of the kingdom of heaven is not

True, we are not born into a vacuum, nor do we create ourselves. This is true in any cultural context, doubly so when it comes to
faith. Indeed, the covenant entails assimilation into the community –
it is what imbues the covenant with meaning. But on its own, this
assimilation – deciding what and what not to do, what and what not
to believe; assuming responsibility; standing before God – is personal,
immediate, and utterly private. The freedom to be private is a prerequisite of faith, and the only thing that can lead, on the next level, to honest,
genuine dialogue between believers.

Hence, what I am trying to describe here is not a philosophy or
outlook regarding faith. Philosophies and outlooks are, in this context,
nothing but rationalizations – apologetics, even – whose sole role is to
justify what has already been arrived at, and which must thus be regarded
with a certain wariness. They are not the substance of faith but explanations for it; thus, they are ancillary to it and always involve a degree
of duality. To paraphrase the opponents of Maimonides and his school,
who stated that a God whose existence must be proven is no God at all,[3]
I offer the absurd assertion that a believer who requires an intellectual
proof for his faith is no believer at all.[4]

There is no proof of faith, and no certainty of faith to be gained
with a proof. In any event, proofs do not impact our existence like a gun
pointed at one's temple; they do not touch upon the believer's inner life.[5]
That is why, when it comes to faith, I prefer to use terms such as "occurrence" and "experience." God's presence in my prayers is as tangible
to me as the presence of a human interlocutor. That is not a *proof* but

---

merely a decision to act according to one's faith, but a decision of faith itself, which
is a prerequisite for all duty.
3. See, for instance, Rabbi Hasdai Crescas, *The Light of the Lord* [Hebrew] (Jerusalem:
Rabbi Shlomo Fisher, 5750), 9–12, 94–98.
4. See the quotation from Freud in Avi Sagi, *Tradition vs. Traditionalism: Contemporary
Perspectives in Jewish Thought* (New York: Rodopi, 2008), 5 – "The paradox of tradition
is that once it has been spoken the tradition is no more what its spokesmen claim it
to be" – and Sagi's comments there.
5. Compare Maimonides' statements, in various contexts, implying that miracles, being
external proofs, cannot be the foundation of sustainable internal resolve. See *Mishneh
Torah*, Laws of the Foundations of the Torah 3:24, 32. For more on this point, see
Rabbi Shagar, *A Time of Freedom*, 81–82.

rather an immediate experience. Similarly, I do not assert that the sight of someone standing in front of me is proof of the person's existence. That would be foolish: After all, I *see* you.

But try as I might, I cannot refrain entirely from rationalization and apologetics. In fact, as soon as I put things into words, I am ensnared by the same fallacy. The price of language is duality, and, in the context of faith, unreality.[6] Even what I am about to present here constitutes speech about faith; hence, it is a pale simulacrum. Faith does not reside in words, and certainly not in any exposition or essay. The language of faith is the first-person address of prayer. It is not speech about something, but rather activity and occurrence. That is why there will always be a gap between the words and what they aim to represent.

This is not to minimize rationalizations; to my mind, rationalism is a sacred task, without which "men would swallow each other alive."[7] Barring a shared rational platform, society cannot exist, because rationalism, despite being "speech about," is a prerequisite of communication and understanding among people. Let us imagine a world where every individual "shall live by his faith" (Hab. 2:4), conducting himself solely according to his own inner convictions. Such a world would quickly degenerate into one where man would *kill* by his faith. Yet when we discuss faith in the personal context – the existential, not the social – rationalization is the source of the gap I am trying to bridge.[8] Having clarified that, I will attempt to describe the difficulties faced by believers in the modern world, and how they can cope.

---

6. See Alain Vanier, *Lacan* (New York: Other Press, 2000).
7. Mishna Avot 3:2.
8. Rabbi Yaakov Moshe Ḥarlap, one of Rabbi Kook's most prominent students, claimed that while Greek philosophy's quest for truth was founded on doubt, the basic postulate of Maimonides' philosophy was faith. He saw philosophizing as merely a tool with which to lend intellectual rigor to faith. See Ḥarlap, *Mei Marom on The Eight Chapters of Maimonides on Ethics* [Hebrew] (Jerusalem: Beit Zevul Yeshiva, 5742). I am unsure whether Rabbi Ḥarlap was correct regarding Maimonides himself, but when it comes to faith and intellect he was certainly correct. See also Rabbi Shagar, *Expositions on Likkutei Moharan*, vol. 2, 52–53.

FAITH AND SCIENCE: TWO DIFFERENT WORLDS?

The philosopher Ludwig Wittgenstein sought to explain the following phenomenon: "*Very* intelligent and well-educated people believe in the story of the Creation in the Bible, while others hold it as proven false, and the grounds of the latter are well known to the former."[9] Do such believers believe in the biblical story of Creation just as, for instance, they believe the earth is a sphere that orbits the sun?[10] As we will establish below, Wittgenstein himself distinguished between these two types of "faith," although the tension between faith and the scientific outlook yet remains.

Our view of the world, as modern human beings, is dominated by science, which has created one of the most profound conflicts with Jewish faith. More accurately, the main problem is not the scientific worldview itself, but its hidden underpinnings, which are steeped in values and basic premises that are at odds with, and fundamentally different from, religion. One example is the belief in a set of laws that contradicts the belief in divine providence; another is science's sense of dominating the world, which is fundamentally opposed to the sense of dependency that the believer is meant to experience. Thus, science cannot be presented as a neutral worldview with no bearing on the religious outlook, as Leibowitz tried to do.[11]

However, the problem of faith in our time is linked not only to the natural sciences, but also – perhaps primarily – to the social sciences and the humanities: history, sociology, psychology, and the like. These uncover the motivations, point to the conditionings, describe the development, and form a historical-social-psychological story of man and the world that diverges from the one related by religion. Freud, for instance, considered faith a psychological need, a neurosis, an outcome

9. Ludwig Wittgenstein, *On Certainty* (New York: Harper & Row, 1972), 43e.
10. Moshe Halbertal develops an argument similar to Wittgenstein's and, following his example, posits various models and modes of "faith." See Halbertal, "On Belief and Believers," in *On Faith: Studies in the Concept of Faith and Its History in Jewish Tradition*, ed. Moshe Halbertal et al. [Hebrew] (Tel Aviv: Keter Press, 2005).
11. See Yeshayahu Leibowitz and Joseph Agassi, *Conversations Concerning the Philosophy of Science* [Hebrew] (Tel Aviv: Ministry of Defense, 1996).

of conditionings and emotional urges,[12] while Marx saw it as no more than a social construct, an ideology furthering the interests of the ruling class, a mere "opiate of the masses."[13]

We are immersed in these outlooks, which inform our worldviews, the deepest, most hidden preconceptions of our personalities. How can they coexist with traditional faith?

I like to refer to the prevailing modernist method of maintaining religious faith – in the face of the deep chasm between it and the world in which the modern believer lives – as the "two-world approach."[14] This approach establishes a boundary between the internal and the external, between one's faith and the world in which one resides. On the face of it, the Torah belongs to a different world, a world of values, and has no bearing on this one, where science reigns supreme.

That is the mainstream Orthodox position, and it is shared by many contemporary Orthodox Jews, including several of the most prominent ultra-Orthodox ideologues and their adherents, and, to a certain degree, modern thinkers such as Rabbi Joseph B. Soloveitchik[15] and Professors Leibowitz and Eliezer Goldman. At its core is an attempt to fend off modernism's criticism by isolating faith from the world and its values.[16] It is an extremely dualistic approach. Leibowitz's faith in a world that conducts itself according to the laws of nature, as described by science, was no less powerful than his religious belief. To him, Jewish faith, like all other values, exists on an entirely different plane. It does not teach us a thing about the material world and has no bearing on the world of phenomena. It exists as the domain of freedom, and its significance lies in the observant Jew's commitment to the halakhic lifestyle. The rebellion of man, taking his liberty into his own hands, the human autonomy that often contradicts faith – to his mind, these were the very

---

12. See Sigmund Freud, *The Future of an Illusion* (London: Hogarth Press, 1928).
13. Karl Marx, *Early Writings* (London: Penguin Books, 1973), 212–15, 222–26, 243–45.
14. For more on the "two-world approach," see *Tablets and Broken Tablets*, 152–54.
15. Compare Rabbi Shagar, *On That Day*, 163.
16. According to the two-world approach, in many instances faith is not perceived as a substantive assertion about reality. Take, for instance, the debate about the Messiah and messianism: The coming of the Messiah, "though he may tarry," is a cardinal article of Jewish faith, but it demands no political or other real-world action.

sources of faith, a freedom to side with belief, perhaps even manufacture it. This is certainly a striking point of view,[17] in that it accepts the yoke of the kingdom of heaven for the sake of heaven, while forgoing all the benefits and promises vouchsafed by religion. According to Leibowitz's approach, for example, I am enjoined to pray independently of the question – which, pertaining to phenomena, is divorced from faith – of whether prayer affects the world, or even whether one can influence the course of natural events. Goldman, meanwhile, says the commandment is normative: God enjoined us to examine our actions and repent when facing calamity. To his mind, whether or not our actions caused the calamity is immaterial.[18]

Yet the price of this dichotomous path is unbearably high. It pulls the rug out from under basic articles of faith – or, at the very least, strips them of their traditional interpretations – such as belief in providence and in the immortality of the soul, and even in the value of prayer. Since these beliefs contradict the scientific outlook, they are designated as norms of halakhic conduct and nothing more. For example, according to the traditional Jewish outlook, calamities are a cue for repentance; however, the two-world approach is almost entirely divorced from the belief

---

17. Sometimes, when I read modern thinkers such as Leibowitz, I am struck by the sublimity of the faith embodied in their words. It is a faith so untenable and illogical, so divorced from common sense, that I ask myself why they believe. Indeed, these erudite, lucid, rational people, these perspicacious men of science and philosophy, often arrive at conclusions that I find absurd. They engage in astounding intellectual acrobatics, deploying elaborate and sophisticated philosophical arguments to defend their religious convictions. But to what end? My conclusion is simple: Their faith is profound and powerful. I don't know if they even want to believe, but it seems that belief wants them, and in any event, they are unable to break free of it. But speaking objectively, as an outside observer, such an absurd faith is unjustifiable.

    Oftentimes, the answers provided by these thinkers are weaker than the questions. My conclusion is that faith is a force more powerful than they. Shall I posit a psychological, sociological, or other disparaging explanation? Or perhaps their intellectual capacities are insufficient to reflect the deep truths inherent in them? Faith is self-acceptance, and since I accept myself, I wish to believe in their faith as well. In any event, my approach to faith is not rational.

18. See Eliezer Goldman, *Expositions and Inquiries* [Hebrew] (Jerusalem: Magnes Press, 1996), 346–60; and *Judaism Without Illusion* [Hebrew] (Jerusalem: Shalom Hartman Institute, 2009).

that calamities are caused by sin and that repentance can bring salvation, for neither sin nor repentance has the power to affect the natural order.

The less deliberate approaches, such as that of the ultra-Orthodox Haredim, compartmentalize so as to prevent the scientific outlook from seeping into the world of belief, which must conduct itself as in the days of yore. They allow science only as a technical, external tool, while the implications of the spirit of science, and any of its conclusions that contradict belief, are ignored. But because it is so difficult to remain innocent in our sophisticated world, *haredi* Judaism is often forced to barricade itself behind fundamentalist views – fundamentalism being faith's reaction to the encroaching modern world – which distort its core beliefs.

How, then, do I believe?[19] How can my belief exist against a backdrop of modernity, and despite my criticism of the two-world approach?

The truth is that I, too, favor a two-world approach. But I do not pit a world of phenomena against a world of ethics and practical reason; nor do I posit a scientific world and one of halakhic or moral norms. Rather, I speak of two worlds that are both ontologically real, even if each possesses a competing definition of reality. Moreover, as in the thought of Immanuel Kant, only God can unite them.[20] One could divide the two worlds into the world of duality, in which we reside and which science seeks to explain, and the world of unity, which sustains faith. To my mind, these are parallel worlds, not unlike the parallel universes

---

19. Despite the challenges posed by the scientific worldview, there is nothing untenable about religious belief. On the contrary: Faith has deep roots in human existence, deeper even than scientific and cultural consciousness. Faith is a fundamental attribute of humanity. The sense of meaning that one experiences in life, the values for which one is prepared to give one's life, the people one loves, the profound connection with others (which, admittedly, is rare), suffering and happiness – these are proof not of God's existence but rather of God's very presence. They cannot teach us a thing about anything external to them; rather, they are themselves holiness. Prayer and the Sabbath, Yom Kippur and the mitzvot, are where I encounter a tangible and present holiness. Questions such as "Is this the only way to encounter holiness?" or "Is this the only kind of holiness?" are meaningless and of no concern to me. The certainty of faith lies in these realms, whence the believer draws his trust in God.

20. As opposed to Hermann Cohen's conception of reality, this reality is not the reality of the idea, but rather an actuality of this world. See Cohen, *Religion of Reason Out of the Sources of Judaism* (New York: Frederick Ungar, 1972), 367.

described in science fiction. Here we require a mysticism centered on various worlds existing side-by-side in multiple dimensions. Indeed, Rabbi Kook writes that mysticism is the heart of the religious world. Postmodernism, which also speaks of multiple worlds, may enable and perhaps even encourage such an outlook.

While the *haredi* attitude posits that the innocence required of the believer means denying the world (like the Eastern mystical traditions that consider spirituality the true reality and see the material world as an illusion), the outlook I am propounding considers awareness of the world, and the conscious choice to believe nonetheless, as the true innocence. The believers I wish to describe exist within a scientific causal system and are fully aware of their personal and historical conditioning, as well as of the evolution of the idea of faith over the centuries. In other words, they are cognizant of external – historical, sociological, and psychological – interpretations of religion. They are not blind to the many critiques of religion; nor do they rule them out. Yet they choose to lead a stringent halakhic lifestyle. They do not ignore the contradictions; that would constitute willful ignorance. Rather, they resolve to remain in both contradictory worlds: that of reality and that of faith.

As a basis for this two-world approach, let us consider a passage on miracles by the Maharal of Prague. The Maharal is known for establishing that there is order to miracles, stating that "just as there is a natural order to the world, so too is there an order to miracles … for just as it is fitting that the world is conducted according to its nature and laws, so too is it fitting for the Jewish people, in light of its cleaving to a separate world, to have a system of miracles." A miracle, he continues, is the result of a separate order infiltrating everyday reality:

> They said, "Ten miracles were performed for our fathers in the Temple," and one of them was that "though the worshipers stood pressed together, they could freely prostrate themselves" (Mishna Avot 5:8). This, too, seems an impossibility to the philosophers. … Yet, according to the words of the true sages, it does not constitute a departure from nature. For anything that is miraculous or a wonder is not of nature at all and thus cannot be said to depart from nature when it is in contradiction with it.

Rather, it is unnatural to begin with. That is why they had ample space to prostrate themselves: It was wrought by a separate world, whence miracles come into this world, and where everything is spacious. It was as if they departed the natural world to stand in a world that is not natural.[21]

The world of faith, like the world of miracles, and like God Himself, is a different stratum of reality – as Maimonides describes it, "He exists, but not through an existence other than His essence." Reality, in its regular sense, is not identical to the divine essence, Maimonides teaches; to God, reality is merely an attribute.[22] Rabbi Shneur Zalman of Liadi formulated it as the difference between "upper knowledge" (*daat elyon*) and "lower knowledge" (*daat tahton*). From the perspective of lower knowledge, the reality of God is less perceptible and is conceived of as *ayin*, or nothingness. From the perspective of upper knowledge, however, the situation is reversed, and the reality of the material world becomes *ayin*.[23] Modern philosophers have made similar distinctions. Hegel differentiated between the actual and the real, while Heidegger differentiated between all being and the Being (*das Sein*) that enables it.[24] Reality is not necessarily the most real mode of existence; dreams, for example, often contain far more reality and truth value than objective facts.[25]

---

21. Maharal of Prague, *Gevurot Hashem*, second introduction. Compare the duality he delineates to Rabbi Moshe Hayim Luzzatto's description of God's two modes of governance, that of the law and that of unity. See especially Luzzatto, *Daat Tevunot* 51–52.
22. *Guide of the Perplexed* I:57. Hasidism distinguishes between the *Yahid*, or Single, which is equivalent to the *sefira* of *keter*; and the *Ehad*, or One, equivalent to the *sefira* of *hokhma*.
23. Rabbi Shneur Zalman of Liadi, *Likkutei Torah*, Va'ethanan 6a ff.
24. Herbert Marcuse, *Hegel's Ontology and Theory of Historicity* (Cambridge: MIT Press, 1987); George Steiner, *Martin Heidegger* (Chicago: University of Chicago Press, 1991), 34–35.
25. If we had been present at Mount Sinai for the Giving of the Torah, what would we have seen? It is an unanswerable question. Not only could we not have been there because we live in the present rather than the past, but also, even had we been there, we would not have been ourselves. But the impossible answer to the impossible question is that we would not have seen a thing. The Maharal taught, regarding the sun standing still in Gibeon during Joshua's conquest of the Land of Israel (see *Gevurot*

Employing Freudian terms, we may ask: Who says we must submit our worldview to the "reality principle" that's behind the scientific approach? Is not the fantasy that characterizes the pleasure principle far more real? Rabbi Kook wrote, "From the perspective of holiness, reality is free of exaggeration – anything that can be perceived or imagined indeed exists. That was the guiding principle of the Kalamists, which was rejected by Scholastic philosophy on the grounds that it was indemonstrable."[26] Faith resides in the realm of the fantastic, which is no less real – more real, in fact – than the scientific world.[27]

Wittgenstein asserted that "it is not *how* things are in the world that is mystical, but *that* it exists."[28] It is my understanding that his statement refers not to the physical-scientific world, but to a different one. Mysticism is the apprehension of a transcendent reality; it is faith. In hasidic tradition, this faith is often identified with the sense of wonder[29]

Hashem, second introduction), that miracles occur only for those who are on a lofty spiritual level. As Rabbi Simḥa Bunim of Peshischa taught, after a miracle occurs it is no longer accessible, and one can encounter it only through the Torah. See *Midrash Simḥa* (Jerusalem: 5735), pt. 1, 130.

26. Rabbi Abraham Isaac Kook, *Orot HaKodesh* (Jerusalem: Mossad HaRav Kook, 5745), vol. 1, 212.

27. See Rabbi Shagar, "The Torah of the Land of Israel," in *On That Day*, 147–50.

28. Ludwig Wittgenstein, *Tractatus Logico-Philosophicus* (London: Routledge & Kegan Paul, 1961), sec. 6.44, p. 73.

29. A sense of wonder at our very existence brings us into contact with it, and through a sense of wonder at the existence of the world, we come to grasp life as a marvel. That is the only mysticism permitted by Wittgenstein; anything else is fated to crash against the barrier of language. This experience of wonder imbues our lives with sublime meaning, casting us as creatures of eternity. The Hasidim taught that the letter *aleph* is a permutation of the Hebrew word *peleh*, or "marvel," and contains God, the *Aluf*, or "Master," of the universe. Wonder is the beginning of faith, as Rabbi Mordekhai Yosef Leiner of Izbica wrote of Abraham: "…it was a great wonder in his eyes, and pondering who could create this disturbed his soul. Then the master of the city glanced upon him, meaning that the Holy One, blessed be He, answered him, 'Do you not see by yourself that the whole world is not stumped by this difficulty, and there is not one among them who considered asking who made this[?] Yet for you it is a wonder. From the very infuriation of your heart you may estimate that certainly there must be a Creator who suffers the entire world, and permeates the entire world, and He is the one who awakened your heart to this.' And this is the specific use of 'upon [him],' meaning that from [his] very question [he himself]

that comes with glimpsing the world of miracles, of the fantastic, which lies behind the curtain of everyday reality,[30] beyond nature.[31]

FAITH AND THE REAL

In order to flesh out the sense of my two-world approach, I will attempt to elucidate the unique characteristics of the world of faith.[32]

Is my faith subjective? To my mind, the question bespeaks a dichotomy between the subjective and the objective that is dissolved by faith, and is best approached using the terminology of the psychoanalyst Jacques Lacan.

Lacan delineates three orders: the Real, the Imaginary, and the Symbolic. The Real characterizes the state of the newborn child, which does not experience itself as confined to an identity or body, but instead is an amalgam of organs, energies, and urges. Since it is undefined, it is also unbounded and cannot differentiate between itself, its mother, and its surroundings. As a developmental stage, the Imaginary denotes a state of duality, when the infant first experiences a gap between itself and its mother. Lacan identifies this stage with a process wherein the child forms an identity based on its mother's relationship to it. The Symbolic stage establishes a world of separate objects, and introduces language and rules. Because language is tied in to a reality of boundaries and differentiations, it is necessarily subsequent to the Real, where there can be no duality, especially between subject and object. It is "the life substance in its mucous palpitation,"[33] before all symbolization and

---

managed to come up with a sufficient answer." Betsalel Philip Edward, trans., *Living Waters: The Mei HaShiloach* (Lanham, MD: Rowman & Littlefield, 2004), 35–36.

30. The smile of a child is a manifestation of God's existence.

31. See Hillel Zeitlin, *On the Border Between Two Worlds* [Hebrew] (Tel Aviv: Yavneh, 1965), 25–26; *A Time of Freedom*, 132–36.

32. [Ed. note: See Rabbi Shagar, *In the Shadow of Faith*, 78–83; *On That Day*, 256–58, 263. Rabbi Shagar's identification of faith with Lacan's Real is built upon a creative reading of the latter.]

33. Slavoj Žižek, *Enjoy Your Symptom! Jacques Lacan in Hollywood and Out* (New York: Routledge, 1992), 22. See also Dylan Evans, *An Introductory Dictionary of Lacanian Psychoanalysis* (London: Routledge, 1996), 162: "'The real is absolutely without fissure.' It is the symbolic which introduces 'a cut in the real' in the process of signification: 'it is the world of words that creates the world of things – things originally confused

interpretation. The stripping of reality of all interpretation, "when the words suddenly stay out"[34] and only the thing-in-itself remains, enables the encounter with this dimension. Human consciousness, with its dualism of subject and object, opens up a chasm between the world of beliefs and the outside world. Hence my assertion that faith is presence, activity. I have deliberately avoided the word "experience," which perpetuates the schism between subject and object. Faith can arise only from a pre-differentiated world; only thus can it retain its connection to reality. As we have established, however, that reality is not the scientific, dichotomous one, but rather the reality of the Real.

Faith, in light of Lacan's terminology, can thus be described as being rooted in the Real, in the prelinguistic, where the subject is yet to be differentiated from the object; in other words, it is rooted in the mystical. And truly, my faith is mystical; it is a wordless, letterless faith. It is my lot to believe without telling others (in this context, I am an Other) that I believe, much as the kabbalists cleaved to the Almighty with *ovanta deliba*, "the understanding of the heart."[35] This psychological technique or practice precedes language and grants it its vitality. In its second phase, belief manifests as a life of faith. It is compelled to function in a world of duality, and if I overlook its origins in the Real (for instance, by trying to demonstrate its objective truth), I destroy it.

Keeping all this in mind, we can describe, I think, two contradictory paths to religious faith. The first is a return to innocence, to self-acceptance: "I am what I am." Faith is where one accepts one's identity. In hasidic terms, this psychological practice is called *hitbatlut*, or self-surrender. It is vindicated in the realization – much like the one propounded by existentialist philosophers – that one was cast into the world; we did not create ourselves, and only self-acceptance can facilitate a life of authenticity and an encounter with the Real.

---

in the *hic et nunc* of the all in the process of coming-into-being'... It is 'that which resists symbolization absolutely.'"

34. Žižek, *Enjoy Your Symptom!* 23.
35. The idea of *ovanta deliba* originated with Ḥasidei Ashkenaz. For a discussion of the term, see Joseph Isaac Lifshitz, "*Ovanta DeLiba* and Infinity: On the Tension Between Subjective and Objective Perception of God" [Hebrew], *Daat* 62 (2008): 27–50.

A dog is a dog. It can be nothing else. Thus, in a certain sense, it possesses, to use a Maimonidean term, "necessary existence." Its existence is as the Creator intended it. But man possesses awareness, reflexivity, which is why he leads a dichotomous existence, apart from reality. Unlike the dog, he can question his own existence. That is why faith, to borrow a term from the German philosopher Johann Gottlieb Fichte, is "self-positing."[36] Faith, in this sense, is self-acceptance, meaning the acceptance of one's life as part of reality, of God's will. There's a fine line between such a faith and the pronouncement that the kabbalists considered original sin: *Ana emlokh*, "I shall rule!" This is the will to kingship, or in this case the tendency to turn oneself into the yardstick of reality. Self-acceptance is faith only when it is not infected with hubris, when it arises out of *hitbatlut*: unity with God.

The second path is the opposite one. It is a path of choice, of creativity. Its point of departure is not identity but freedom, such as ethical freedom, which does not rely on facts but rather establishes them. It conducts itself, as Kant taught us, not according to what is, but according to what ought to be. It is, to my mind, a loftier path than that of self-annulment, of being what one is: It does not require the inspiration that comes with self-surrender (which is, paradoxically, self-affirmation and not self-negation), but creates its own existence by the Godlike powers of creation *ex nihilo*. It stems from a postmodern consciousness that denies the self and authenticity posited by the existentialists. Here faith is a choice in the full sense of the word: establishing, rather than abiding by, the rules of the game.[37]

These ideas can be demonstrated through the issue of providence. In what sense do I believe in divine providence? Do I believe, for example, that a person who slips on a banana peel is being punished because one of the mezuzas in his house is defective? Although some reject such a view of providence – Maimonides, for instance[38] – many

---

36. See Frederick Neuhouser, *Fichte's Theory of Subjectivity* (Cambridge: Cambridge University Press, 1990).
37. In any event, it is conceivable that such a construction, too, can be approached only through inspiration, and perhaps even vessels, techniques, and philosophies. For more, see below, chap. 5.
38. *Guide of the Perplexed* III:17.

Orthodox Jews think that to believe in divine providence is to posit a system of causality that competes with the natural world, one whose mechanism is reward and punishment, and the kind of petty reckonings often invoked by some rabbis.

In rejecting such a conception, must we adopt Goldman's opinion that providence has only normative implications, meaning that we are under a halakhic obligation to treat calamities as punishments for our sins and repent, and to treat positive occurrences as gifts from God that require our thanks? I think not, as such an approach does away with the basic religious significance of providence: the perception of God's guiding hand in reality. My contention is that providence is evident not in everyday reality, but rather on the level of the Real. Instead of offering a competing model of cause and effect, providence operates on the hermeneutical level, requiring me to ascribe meaning to the things that happen to me.[39] However, what removes any vestige of subjective interpretation from it is the level of the Real, where there is no external reality that I, as a subject, interpret, where reality and I are one. Everything that occurs in the world is a revelation of God that expresses something. God is not only an external supervisor, about whom we ask, "Why?" Rather, He is the vitality of all things, and the question we must ask is "What is He saying to me?" By facilitating a plurality of languages and perspectives, postmodernism can enable us in this context, too, to exist in two worlds: the scientific-causal world, on the one hand, and the world of meaning, which is also the world of faith and providence, on the other.[40]

Here is an example from something that happened to me this morning: Our boiler cracked and the house flooded. Was it providence? Maimonides asserts that we must examine our actions when a calamity occurs – it may have been fairly minor, as calamities go, but it was annoying nonetheless. However, such an examination means asking myself not why it happened, but rather, "What does it mean?" To ask why something happened is to search for a cause, but I already

---

39. This distinction can itself be considered an expression of the two-worlds approach discussed above.

40. In hasidic terminology, this suspension of one's causal point of view might be termed *bittul hayesh*, "the nullification of being."

know the cause: Over time, the heating element became encrusted in limescale and rust, forming a crack, perhaps because I had failed to maintain it correctly. Yet when I asked myself, "What does it mean?" I had a revelation: Perhaps I hadn't given enough *tzedaka*. Maybe I should repent, I thought. But can that truly be the meaning of a calamity? Such interpretations would be utterly arbitrary if not for the sense of certainty that accompanies them. The event merges with other occurrences, snippets of thoughts, impressions, and more. It strikes one as a revelation; an epiphany even. Unlike the newspapers' unrelenting interpretations of the events that befall us, this one does not grasp at external reasons. It is a revelation not of my own design; rather, it grasps me.

Such a revelation is analogous to the creative process, or the experience of studying a passage in the Talmud. The text lies before me, a heap of ideas, thoughts, and assertions that do not coalesce into a clear, meaningful picture – until lightning strikes and an idea germinates, and all the details cohere around it. That clarity yields internal conviction.

Such a sense of certainty does not negate the fact that faith often resides in the realm of doubt, due to the gap between the world of faith and the world of duality, where, at the end of the day, we reside.

FAITH AS POSSIBILITY

Do I believe in the Redemption? Yes, but what does that mean? Will I have the privilege of witnessing it in my lifetime? Probably not – I'm pessimistic by nature – but I do await the Messiah's arrival every day. Perhaps he'll come – who knows. Sometimes good things happen; sometimes God shines His countenance on us.[41]

My belief is that there is a chance, utopian as it may be, for the Redemption to come about. Although it is unrealistic in the current state of affairs, the possibility's very existence transforms my life,

---

41. I pray, but am I certain that my prayer will be answered? I am unsure. Neither do I know that it *won't* be answered. But prayer certainly has an effect, someone hears it. We say it is God, but God is just a word, meaningless without context. If I perceive God as something external to me, then I have diverged from the Real. I believe in a profound, higher, transcendent self. God exists where such a self exists. (In this sense, faith is susceptible to psychological reductionism when it is elevated to the Real.)

making it, like the dream, more real. As Rabbi Kook wrote in his critique of Maimonides,[42] possibility is also reality. In light of this conception of the Redemption, one can posit a new reading of Maimonides' well-known words:

> The Messianic Era. We are to believe as fact that the Messiah will come and not consider him late. If he delays, wait for him (Hab. 2:3); set no time limit for his coming. One must not make conjectures based on Scripture to conclude when the Messiah will come. The sages said, "May the Spirit depart from those who calculate the end-time" (Sanhedrin 97b). One must believe that the Messiah will have more station and honor than all the kings who ever lived, as all the prophets from Moses to Malachi prophesied. Whoever doubts this or minimizes it denies the Torah, which testifies to it explicitly.[43]

When it comes to the Messiah, the cardinal thing is to believe in his greatness and that he will come and not be tardy, and to believe that one must love and pray for him. Essentially, to believe in the Messiah and Redemption is to believe that there is Redemption, that such a mode of being exists. It is a utopia manifested as an absent reality, and it is as an object of yearning that it influences reality.[44]

This is also true of faith in general. Belief does not necessarily depend on certainty, and its domain of the Real cannot necessarily be brought to bear on our everyday lives. In certain cases, the "maybe," or the belief in the possibility of a thing, is also faith in its fullest sense.[45] The

---

42. See quotation above from Rabbi Kook, *Orot HaKodesh*.
43. Maimonides' Introduction to Mishna Sanhedrin, chap. 10; translation from Isadore Twersky, *A Maimonides Reader* (New York: Behrman House, 1972), 422.
44. See Rabbi Shagar, "The Kingdom to Come," in *On That Day*, 140–44.
45. Where are my parents? I yearn to speak to them. These very yearnings; the brush with profundity; existence, along with its fears and disappointments – all are laden with the meaning that is the revelation of God. Where are they? Will I have the privilege of meeting them again? I believe so. But what does it mean? How can such a meeting come about? I tend to believe that life after death is an entirely different mode of existence. The dead pass on, death is a reality, and yet an intimacy is maintained between the dead and the living because, on a certain level of existence, the dead

very belief in a positive option transforms one's sense of life. For example, I do not have to be happy at any given moment in order to believe. The mere faith that I *can* be happy, that it is possible, is enough to facilitate my experience of God's presence. I have often found that what transforms people's lives is not so much a certainty regarding the religious world as a sense of possibility, a "maybe" that manifests as a realistic option and excites them, infusing them with feelings of liberation and redemption. This sense, on its own, is to them proof enough of the truth at the root of the "maybe."[46]

FAITH AND TRADITION

Despite all of the above, my faith is Orthodox. I believe in halakha and the halakhic lifestyle. Orthodoxy is a condition for maintaining the Absolute and its representations in our lives, bringing God's presence, the *Shekhina*, down into the lower realms, and elevating matter itself. Faith must manifest in one's day-to-day existence. A genuinely religious life is predicated on a connection with tradition, on a sense of obligation to tradition that, to my mind, is the essence of Orthodoxy.[47] In this context, I identify with the approach of Rabbi Kook, who, while asserting that Judaism is founded on esotericism, fully acknowledged that the word for the Jewish mystical canon, Kabbala, literally means "receiving" and "tradition":

> The esoteric logic is the freedom of Israel, meaning the soul of Israel. For it is a single soul, nourished by the nation of Israel's dew of life, that contemplates and imagines in keeping with its nature, and with all those elements that caused it to contemplate all the grand occurrences that are unique to Israel and its history; and in keeping with the godly, exalted, eminent relation that manifested in this glorious nation. When liberty ascends to its loftiest summit, when the soul is unhindered by the burdens or yokes of

---

are alive. Again, even though this level is not present for me at the moment, the very faith in its existence, the very yearning for it, transforms my life.

46. See *Expositions on Likkutei Moharan*, vol. 1, 269–71.

47. See *Tablets and Broken Tablets*, 194–95, 282.

any popular perceptions that do not derive from the source of Israel, then the ideas that progressively form in the light of this pure holiness are the very secrets of the Torah. Whether they are uttered in the same language and style employed by the kabbalists, or in another style or literary form, the abundance of the Holy Spirit runs from the spirit of Israel through them. And the nation of Israel was itself received (*kabbala*) by Moses at Mount Sinai.[48]

---

48. See Rabbi Kook, *Orot HaKodesh*, vol. 1, 135. The acclaimed Kabbala scholar Gershom Scholem agreed with Rabbi Kook on this point. See Scholem, *On the Possibility of Jewish Mysticism in Our Time* (Philadelphia: Jewish Publication Society, 1997), 13–17.

Chapter Three

Religious Life in the Modern Age

OBSOLETE SOLUTIONS

The esteemed organizers of this conference asked me to discuss religion's place in the modern world and the ensuing questions: Is the adoption of modern values by the national religious public, and their integration into our religious world, behind the rampant secularization in our communities? What sets us apart from Reform Jews, or at least Conservative Jews, who have also adopted these values? And finally, are we still capable of faith?

At the outset I would like to emphasize that the criticism I will level at Orthodoxy is uttered from within the movement. My intention is not, God forbid, to reject Orthodoxy, but rather to propose avenues

Based on a draft that was written in 5761 in preparation for a conference on Judaism and modernity. The lecture was not published during the author's lifetime and was edited after his death by Yishai Mevorach and Aviezer Cohen for publication in *To Illuminate the Openings*, 158–86. The essay was supplemented in editing with excerpts from other writings in order to add clarity in several passages. An opening dealing with Ḥanukka and surrounding culture was removed from the essay for publication in this volume.

of renewal and self-awareness – such that can facilitate change in the religious lives of the faithful.

We conceive of modernity as being in contradiction with faith. Modernity, as a movement that sees constant change as positive and necessary, stands opposed to Orthodoxy, for in our symbolic world, the religious realm – and certainly halakha – is associated with tradition and conservatism. Halakha expresses the eternal, constant, and unchanging. Furthermore, the state of flux is an essential characteristic of modernity, a value in itself, linked to other values and stemming from a distrust of tradition. Modernity saddles the individual with responsibility for himself and his world, so he can no longer rely on what is external to him. He must show initiative and create his own values and conceptions. Hence modern values – at least in their accepted sense – are secular values: They place the individual in the center, shifting God from His once preeminent position and even rendering Him irrelevant. Any effort at merging Orthodoxy and modernity, then, is an attempt to unify opposites. Is it even possible? Is the price – the superficiality and reduction of both religion and modernity – too high to enable such an amalgamation?

There have been several attempts at such a merger. The first was *Torah im derekh eretz* ("Torah with worldly involvement"), espoused by the school of Rabbi Samson Raphael Hirsch, which sought to make Jews citizens of two cultures – the Jewish and the modern. A number of attitudes emerged in response, and I will arrange them in roughly chronological order. The teachings of Rabbi Kook aspired to sanctify the material world, meaning modernity, thus harmonizing the two ostensibly opposite worlds. The antithesis of Rabbi Kook's stance was Yeshayahu Leibowitz's compartmentalization approach. Leibowitz formulated a religious outlook wherein the world of phenomena, or reality, is neutral, i.e., secular; and holiness, meaning the religious world, is relegated to the well-defined realm of man's religious service and rendered utterly irrelevant vis-à-vis concrete reality. Rabbi Joseph B. Soloveitchik posited a compromise between the approaches of Rabbi Kook and Leibowitz, presenting compartmentalization as the first stage in a dialectic. To his mind, the pain and suffering entailed by compartmentalization, and the schism between the holy and the secular, would facilitate the emergence of the next stage – harmony. I have discussed these proposed solutions elsewhere,[1] and it is my contention that not a single one of them is still relevant. The present-day problem is not the integration of modernity and Orthodoxy, but rather the fact that in our postmodern world, both have been rendered obsolete.

One can assert, from a certain perspective, that the contrast between Orthodoxy and modernity is fallacious, for Orthodoxy itself, like the Reform and Conservative movements, is a distinctly modern phenomenon; more precisely, a modern reaction to modernity.[2] I refer not only to the movement known as Modern Orthodoxy but to Orthodoxy in general, which can be perceived as a mirror image of modernity, hopelessly enmeshed in it. As we will establish below, Orthodoxy – in its rigid and binding literal sense of the right belief, or *doxa* – is foreign to Judaism. It is a modern phenomenon, a defense, in the spirit of the times, from the spirit of the times. That is why "both he that helps shall stumble, and he that is helped shall fall" (Is. 31:3): As modernity's allure waned,[3] Orthodoxy – doubly so Modern Orthodoxy, whose authenticity and credibility, like those of other syntheses, were in doubt from the outset – lost its relevance. While some modern values and causes became self-evident, obviating the fight either for or against them,[4] others became irrelevant – or at least lost their claim to exclusivity in our worldviews.[5] Thus, solutions that aimed to integrate Judaism and modernity were rendered obsolete. When modern ceases to be the modern thing to be, one is no longer compelled to come up with modern syntheses, which is why the grand narratives of both modernity and Orthodoxy have all lost their power.

I should add that in discussing Modern Orthodoxy I refer not only to the American scene. For decades, Modern Orthodoxy in the United States and national religious Judaism in Israel constituted two

---

1. See above, "Faith and Science: Two Different Worlds?" pp. 25; Rabbi Shagar, *On That Day*, 244–65.
2. See Jacob Katz, *Halakha in Straits: Obstacles to Orthodoxy at Its Inception* [Hebrew] (Jerusalem: Magnes Press, 1992).
3. And postmodernism commenced.
4. A trivial example of this is women's suffrage.
5. One example is the approach to the "truth" of science.

distinct movements. However, with the rise in the standard of living in Israel, and as the country is swept by Western cultural influences, I predict that the differences between the two groups will erode, along with the differences between the challenges they both face.

For example, when I study or teach the writings of Rabbi Kook, I often confront tough questions regarding the all-encompassing universality of his teachings: Does Rabbi Kook's universality – which at once embraces and dissolves the Other, by elevating and sanctifying him – offer a credible solution to today's questions of the Other and otherness? Can it answer the questions of the secular Other and the non-Jewish Other with which we are forced to grapple in the State of Israel? I ask this with no intention to detract from Rabbi Kook's obvious greatness and from the fact that he was, quite literally, a man of God.

The distance and discomfort – distrust, even – that many experience in studying Rabbi Kook (notably his essay *HaDor*, on the secular Other, and various passages of *Orot* relating to the non-Jewish Other) stem primarily from the fact that the solutions he proffers do not jibe with the contemporary zeitgeist of pluralism and multiculturalism. These days, to me, the question of the Other has ceased to be a matter of concern, and to the extent that it does occupy me, it is no longer the question asked in Rabbi Kook's time.[6] My point is that, in contrast with Rabbi Kook, and in light of the multiculturalism that characterizes the postmodern condition, I no longer feel the need to justify myself to the Other or, conversely, to recognize him in me – and this is true of both the Jewish Other and the non-Jewish one.[7] Thus, I have relinquished the effort, shared by many religious Jews, to turn the secular Jew into a religious one, modeled on my own image. Let him join us if he so wishes,

---

6. In the same vein, Rabbi Soloveitchik's conceptions of self-actualization, the pathos of choice, and the joy of creative Torah study all provide no answer for our wary and critical era. Ours is a far humbler, soberer world, one that is far more skeptical as to whether human autonomy is truly the key to creating a utopia.
7. As I have argued elsewhere, our approach to secular Jews should not be founded on embraces and appropriation, but rather on a multiculturalism that features both universal respect for all human beings and the cultivation of religious community. For more, see Rabbi Shagar, "*Tinok Shenishba*," in *This Is My Covenant: Conversion, Secularization, Civil Marriage*, 97–61.

or not. "Israel is eternal and shall not perish" (I Sam. 15:29).[8] I am not the guardian of its existence.

TRADITIONAL ROOTEDNESS

How, then, does one resolve the problem of the religious person moving through a modern world that is utterly in conflict with the realm of halakha and tradition? I put my hope in two things: traditionalism, even if it is not necessarily halakhic,[9] and its opposite – authentic *ḥaredi* Judaism (as opposed to present-day ultra-Orthodoxy).[10] I wish to focus first on traditionalism and later elaborate on authentic haredism as well.

Traditionalism clashes with both Modern Orthodoxy, which heeds the clarion call of modernity and is swept up in its spirit of unceasing change, and the stiff and dogmatic contemporary Orthodox streams, because traditionalism is, first and foremost, a rootedness. In the Jewish context, it is a rootedness germinated by a consciousness of chosenness, which among Jews is based on the self – not on a problematic sense of superiority over others. Our "You chose us from among all the nations" is not founded on a comparison between us and the Other. Rather, the "You chose" is the abundance of Jewish self-presence, fullness, and intensity. The emphases are placed on the "You" and the "chose." Jewish joy does not depend on the rest of the sentence, on the "from among all the nations," which anyway refers not to specific nations from among which we were chosen, but to nameless nations, to the void. "You chose us" from the void; we passed from nothingness into being in a state of chosenness, and to rejoice in that is to rejoice in one's very Jewishness. In

---

8. Its disappearance, God forbid, is as unthinkable to me as my own nonbeing.
9. Despite being a-halakhic, traditionalism has its supporters among religious and secular alike. [Ed. note: The original Hebrew term, *masortiyut*, connotes an affinity for tradition rather than strict adherence to halakha.] One secular thinker who recently raised the banner of traditionalism was the philosopher Meir Buzaglo. See his "The Traditional Jew," in *Multiculturalism in Israel*, ed. Ohad Nahtomi [Hebrew] (Jerusalem: Magnes Press, 2003), 153–62.
10. In the context of the national religious movement, "authentic *ḥaredi* Judaism" certainly cannot be identified with the *ḥardal*, or nationalist *ḥaredi*, community, which derives from a rootless Judaism. See Rabbi Shagar, *Tablets and Broken Tablets*, 188–90.

its authentic manifestations, that joy does not aspire to enlarge itself at the Other's expense, and thus has no need to justify itself to the Other. We do not pursue the larger things; we prefer the small garden, meager as it may be, and have no desire to beautify it in the other's eyes, just so that – as in the beautiful story of the Little Prince and the fox – it remains our own. [11]

The traditional Jew is rooted in his belonging. Because he both lives within tradition and is borne upon it, he feels no need to update it or justify it to the zeitgeist. His lack of awareness keeps his tradition from ossifying into orthodoxy, a cult of the right deed. Only someone aware of the relationship between changing times and his way of life and native context will attempt either to prevent the familiar from changing along with the times or to formulate synthetic adjustments. Thus, tradition is, first and foremost, belonging. Those who question tradition, who are compelled to justify, defend, or preserve it, no longer belong to it, for it is, by definition, a function of self-identity rather than reflexivity. [12]

I therefore have no intention of arguing that traditionalism can give rise to full commitment to halakha; rather, I maintain that a lifestyle of halakhic commitment bereft of the rootedness of traditionalism is soulless – and the soul, as we know, is the essence. Moreover, the source of halakha's conservatism is intimacy and rootedness in tradition. The moment it loses its intimacy and rootedness, halakha becomes a lifeless body, and conservatism morphs into religious fundamentalism. Indeed, Rabbi Yehuda Amital long claimed that youth who reject the religious lifestyle generally suffer from a deficiency of *kneidalach* (matza balls) and noodle kugel, [13] or perhaps of the Passover Seder's aromas and the melodies of the High Holy Days. The point is that they lack the

---

11. "To be sure, an ordinary passerby would believe that my very own rose looked just like you [the other roses], but she is far more important than all of you because she is the one I have watered. And it is she that I have placed under a glass dome. And it is she that I have sheltered behind a screen.... And it is she I have listened to complaining or boasting or sometimes remaining silent. Because she is my rose." Antoine de Saint-Exupéry, *The Little Prince* (Ware, England: Wordsworth, 1995), 82.
12. See Rabbi Shagar, *A Time of Freedom*, 122–30.
13. Clearly, Rabbi Amital referred to matza balls because he was of Hungarian descent; were he of Yemenite extraction, he would likely have cited a far spicier dish.

self-contained experience of the ancestral home, which breathes life into the religious existence.

I wish to emphasize that I am not advocating a saccharine nostalgia or blind veneration of the past. I will admit that what once kindled envy in me I have since learned to recognize as a rather unappealing superficiality: It is a commonplace for the modern man, having diverged from the ways of his fathers, to yearn for a return to the good old days.[14] Indeed, it is not in such an idealized homecoming that I see religious potential for us, but rather in empowering the intimacy with Jewish literature that is becoming prevalent among so many in our community. It is an intimacy that places the book in the world of my ancestors, the world in which I often encounter myself. My approach is not nostalgic, and it does not absolve the past of criticism; on the contrary, precisely through feelings of continuity and intimacy, through knowing it is my home, can I acknowledge its imperfections. It is as if my home were full of various objects, among them a gleaming state-of-the-art stereo system, but also an old tape recorder and a threadbare rag doll. Must one choose between them? The old, broken knickknacks are no less part of home than the gleaming high-tech gadgets. I am aware of the differences between old and new, but I choose to hold on to both.

It would not be an overstatement to say that one of the key arguments between halakhic Judaism, on the one hand, and the Reform and Conservative movements, on the other, concerns the place of the old in the home: What is the correct reaction to modern perceptions of progress, development, and change?

THE PROCESSION OF THE BLOOD

As we have established, our current challenge vis-à-vis the outside world is not modernity and the problems it poses for religion, but rather the question of religious life in *our* world, which is largely postmodern. To define this challenge and how it differs from that of modernity, I will move on to the third question posed to me: Are we still capable

---

14. Such is the case with the poet Hayim Nahman Bialik in his poem "Before the Bookcase," in S. Daniel Breslauer, *The Hebrew Poetry of Hayyim Nahman Bialik (1873–1934) and a Modern Jewish Theology* (Lewiston, NY: Edwin Mellen Press, 1991), 123.

of faith? This question will serve as a basis for portraying Orthodoxy's problems in facing modernity, and the differences between the various streams of Judaism.

Questions about faith often implicitly assume that religion- or faith-related arguments have a truth value. The problem is that this value is never defined, because there are a variety of kinds of truths: Metaphysical truth has its own truth value, as does historical truth. The same goes for social or halakhic truth.[15] We must also establish what it means to "believe." Is it to think something, or feel something, or perhaps to do something? Where does faith reside? A talk delivered by Rabbi Naḥman of Breslov on the eve of Ḥanukka 5569 (1808), titled "The Days of Ḥanukka Are Days of Thanksgiving," can help answer these questions. Rabbi Naḥman links the thanksgiving that lies at the heart of Ḥanukka, knowledge of God, and adherence to halakha:

> The days of Ḥanukka are days of thanksgiving, as it is written: "And they established these eight days of Ḥanukka in order to give thanks and praise"…and thanks, which is the delight of the World to Come, corresponds to halakhot…for when a new halakha is divined, the mind and knowledge are renewed, and knowledge is the foremost delight of the World to Come, as we have established…
>
> For thanks are given when one escapes from calamity, because when one is afflicted by calamity, God forbid, it affects the heart most of all, as the heart knows and feels the calamity most intensely…[for when there is calamity] all the blood gathers and rises to the heart… flooding the heart, and the heart is very anguished and congested…. That is why, when one experiences a calamity, God forbid, one's heart pounds violently…and then, when one escapes the calamity, the blood flow returns to its former order in the passages of the body.

---

15. This assertion was already propounded by Maimonides in his discussion of "necessary truths" that are not necessarily metaphysically true. See *Guide of the Perplexed* III:28.

That is why thanksgiving after one is delivered from calamity is called halakha [which derives from the same root as "walking" or "proceeding"] – after the blood flow that resumes its former order.[16]

We learn from Rabbi Naḥman that halakha, the Jewish way of life, constructs a world through which one can come to know God – faith becomes a concrete fact of one's life. Halakha's role in the life of the believer is elucidated through Rabbi Naḥman's comparing it to the flow of blood in the veins, an "orderly procession."[17] It is an order that elicits thanks – for the fact that it is halakha that provides the world with a framework of life, stability, and meaning – and, one might add, an acknowledgment of truth: of the existence of God and the religious way of life.

Wittgenstein's philosophy of language can serve to elucidate this point. To him, language, including religious language, does not express or represent, but rather utters. Its significance lies within itself, meaning that we do not use language for signification – it does not function as a collection of symbols that stand for something outside themselves. Rather, it is a skill or ability derived from the lifestyles of those who employ it, and from their lifestyles it derives its significance. As Wittgenstein said, "the *speaking* of language is part of an activity, or of a form of life."[18] The point is that a language's sense – including that of a religious language – does not depend on the existence of a signified essence or object, but is derived from practice, from moving through reality, from what Wittgenstein called "language games."[19]

Such is the case with Rabbi Naḥman's statements as well: The faith they evoke is not a feeling, experience, or thought, one that the believer must give thanks for or acknowledge when he says,

---

16. Rabbi Naḥman of Breslov, *Likkutei Moharan, Tinyana* 2:1–2.
17. See Ephraim E. Urbach's similar definition of halakha in *Encyclopaedia Hebraica* [Hebrew], vol. 14 (Jerusalem and Tel Aviv: Encyclopaedia Publishing Co., 1967), 498.
18. Ludwig Wittgenstein, *Philosophical Investigations* (Oxford: Basil Blackwell, 1958), 11.
19. For an in-depth discussion, see Rabbi Shagar, "Faith and Language According to Rabbi Shneur Zalman of Liadi," in *We Will Walk in Fervor*, 173–99.

"I believe."[20] When one leads a halakhic lifestyle, the faith derived from
the "procession of the blood" is neither feeling nor thought, but fact.
God is present even if one does not think of Him or sense Him or
even believe in Him, since God is in the very structure and contours
of one's life. I am fully aware, and freely admit, that this assertion is
far from self-evident, so I will attempt to explain it: A Jew who visits
the synagogue every day, who dons tefillin and recites the *Shema*, is a
partner to belief even if his mind is elsewhere while he prays, even if
he does not even notice that he is praying. This is so because faith, in
this context, is not a representation of the worshiper's belief – indeed,
it does not require any mindfulness on his part – but rather a fact, a
presence in the order and the flow of his blood. The existence of such
faith is a fact of life, just as the desk in front of me is a fact of life, and
the chair on which I sit and the people with whom I speak – even if I
am not always mindful of these truths.

As Wittgenstein explains, the believer's actions and utterances
emanate from a state of mind; they do not report upon a state of mind.[21]
Rather than being a feat of consciousness or spirituality, faith resides in
the situation, in a life of commitment to the various mitzvot and customs.
Indeed, I have often found, as someone immersed in the "blood flow"
of the Jewish lifestyle, that I cannot conceive of a world devoid of God.
This stance of mine is linked to the halakhic ruling to the effect that even
though mitzvot require intention, when one, for instance, dons tefillin
in the synagogue without awareness of his action, the very context – his
presence in the synagogue – is considered intention enough that he
is seen as having fulfilled the mitzva.[22] This is because intention, like
faith, is not so much a mental *action* as it is an action's *context*. When
one is fulfilling the mitzva of donning tefillin, one's practical position
lends meaning to the action, beginning with the words that one uses
to describe it. We are discussing a man who got up in the morning and

---

20. And yet it is impervious to mere behaviorist reductionism.
21. See Eliezer Malkiel, *Intention, Sensation, Emotion* [Hebrew] (Jerusalem: Magnes
Press, 2000), 160.
22. Based on the *Mishna Berura* on *Shulḥan Arukh, Oraḥ Ḥayim* 60:10 and the *Bei'ur
Halakha* there.

proceeded, without devoting conscious thought to it, to occupy himself with tefillin – and not with mere black boxes or cubes. By contrast, one who has not encountered a Jewish lifestyle, and is unaware of the function of tefillin, won't see tefillin – only a pair of boxes with strange straps dangling from them. Our very use of the word "tefillin" in relation to these objects constructs our world in a certain way. And the position in reality of someone who dons tefillin, meaning the relation of his action to other people and objects, is embedded in the use of the word.

Halakha lends order to reality, structuring and anchoring the world. This structuring relates to body language, movements, inflections, and manner of speaking, all of which provide a context that incorporates the transcendent. Thus, the performance of halakhic practices entails internalizing the starkness that is part of the "grammar" of the halakhic language.

Moreover, awareness of the fact that halakha manifests the divine absolute can also explain why Jewish law is always behind the times, and why it should not strive to be too up-to-date: In relation to halakha, the absolute appears as resistance and disruption. In other words, the fixations and neuroses that accompany the halakhic lifestyle are part and parcel of that lifestyle, and one must not be too quick to dispel them with some "religio-psychological" treatment or other. The desire to purge one's religious life of such aspects is tantamount to a psychiatric treatment that targets and eliminates the patient's symptoms. It may ease one's suffering, but it does so at the price of blunted emotions and a personality of diminished vitality. Instead, one should acknowledge that the symptoms are not a coincidence but rather an inherent aspect of one's personality. In a similar vein, one should see the symptoms of a language – in this case, the halakhic language – as being deeply embedded in its grammar. Thus, halakha should be revised only in its own language, with empathy toward its internal logic and symptoms, and not from an external vantage.

The test of halakha is not its truth, but its ability to maintain the integrity of its character as a linguistic and practical system. This character is the core of halakha, whose scale of values and beliefs – which neither proves nor justifies it – is merely a byproduct of the nature of the halakhic system. Thus, rather than justify or rationalize halakha, we must describe it phenomenologically. For instance, we should examine how the laws of family purity shape the relationship between husband and wife, instead of propounding justifications for them with facile pronouncements about how halakha "exalts women," or "acknowledges the body," or "values emotion," and so forth. Such apologetics emanate from a self-deceptive desire to beautify the halakhic world in the face of criticism from the world of Western cultural values. Instead, one should lay down the ethical and existential consequences of halakha: What sort of romance is shared by couples who lead such a lifestyle, how their passion manifests, and so on.

Torah and mitzvot instill our world with divine transcendence and absoluteness. Indeed, the divine absoluteness of halakha is expressed not through faith *in a* fact, but rather through faith *as a* fact. The Torah's transcendence is not some pure spiritual attainment, but a concrete, present fact. In that regard, halakha is not a metaphysical truth; it is a phenomenon with its own attributes and uniqueness. That it incorporates the transcendent and the absolute is not so much a metaphysical fact as it is a context or backdrop for a person's actions.[23] As Wittgenstein

---

23. Like every language, the halakhic language – or, more accurately, the halakhic language game – constructs a world with its own set of laws, establishing meanings and connotations that derive their power from the halakhic lifestyle. Yet when it comes to the halakhic language game, these meanings go beyond mere mundane human meanings, establishing a divine ideal – holiness – striven for by human action. The halakhic existence can be summed up as a series of acts that identify the human as a revelation of the divine, a thing of supernal provenance; thus, it aims to return humanity to its source on high. Here is an example:

I used to live close to the bakery in Jerusalem's Beit Yisrael neighborhood. On Fridays, I would buy halla there for Shabbat. I once witnessed a man exit the bakery with a halla, which he proceeded to tear apart and devour. I was shocked. The very same holy Shabbat halla that we would cover during Kiddush, to spare it the humiliation of knowing it was not the first to be blessed, was being raped! To me, the halla is not merely a loaf of bread; its context turns it into something entirely different – a Shabbat halla, one whose very flavor differs from that of commonplace, weekday bread. I consider this not a poetic issue, but a concrete fact.

This is the meaning of the kabbalists' statements about the words of the Torah raising up and sanctifying physical objects: Language structures the world, and the words of the language of the Torah – the halakhot, blessings, and prayers – sanctify objects, including halla.

aptly stated, "The way you use the word 'God' does not show whom you mean, but what you mean."[24]

THE DIFFICULT POINT

Now we can begin to discuss the second question we posed, about the difference between us, the Orthodox, and Reform and Conservative Jews. The argument between the various denominations is usually boiled down to the question of the divine origin of the Torah. Belief in divine origin would ostensibly entail an avowed opposition to any change in halakha, which is impervious to human criticism and transcends the vagaries of time. But the assumption is inaccurate, as some Conservatives, for example, also believe in the divine origin of the Torah – a belief that plays into their own attempts to modify halakha.[25] That is why we actually face the opposite problem: The question that divides the various denominations is not whether the Torah is of divine origin, but whether the Torah emanated from heaven only to remain there. In other words, does halakhic discourse conceive of the Torah as a specific revelation – be it historical, ethical, or logical – that forever remains somewhere in that specific realm, never descending into the ever-fluctuating human reality? A Torah constrained in heaven can lead to two reactions. In one, the *posekim* acknowledge historical, archaeological, or scientific truths – and with them, ethical truth – and are willing to judge and implement the halakhic text only in light of their implications. In the other, *posekim* sanctify a long-gone past, meaning that "anything new is forbidden by the Torah,"[26] and that they cannot progress one iota beyond what was stated by their predecessors. At most, they can reinforce that which has already been said.[27]

The critical question, then, is whether the Torah embodies some sort of "ongoing revelation," where its continuity lies in its development and interpretation at the hands of the Torah sages: "and everything a

---

24. Gilead Bar-Elli, "Religious Belief and Form of Life: Leibowitz and Wittgenstein" [Hebrew], *Iyyun* 42 (1993): 493–507.

25. This point is elucidated below, in the discussion of "ongoing revelation."

26. See the responsa of Rabbi Moshe Sofer (*Ḥatam Sofer*), pt. 1, chaps. 28, 181.

27. See *On That Day*, 267–84, 285–308.

veteran scholar is destined to innovate has already been revealed to Moses at Sinai."[28] Such an approach is apparent in the variety of hasidic expositions surrounding the miracles of Ḥanukka and the jar of oil, which are notably linked to the revelation of the Oral Torah. Here, for example, is Rabbi Tzaddok HaKohen of Lublin:

> And that is the meaning of the giving of the Torah as a gift, making it theirs, and through it they acquired the Oral Torah, which emanates from the fact that the Torah was given to them as a gift and is no longer in heaven…. Truly, the gist of the Written Torah accords with the interpretations of the sages of Israel in the Oral Torah…. And they found a jar sealed with the high priest's seal, and they used it to light [the Menora in] the Temple, meaning the manner in which we shine before Him, so to speak – and that is the power of the Oral Torah.[29]

It seems that conceiving of halakha as a language is the best way to encapsulate its revelatory aspect vis-à-vis halakhic rulings. The *posek* employs the halakhic language, and through it expresses the revelation. For, like other languages, the halakhic language is dynamic, adapting itself to time and place, and enabling a variety of expressions. Allow me to explain: The conception of halakha as a behavioral or linguistic system with self-contained meaning and significance requires that updates to that system can be effected only through its own language and inner logic – and not from an external vantage. Indeed, an examination of the "grammar" of the halakhic language reveals openings for updating it, one of which is, counterintuitively, the internalization of its transcendent aspect. This aspect depends as much on halakha's capacity to change as on its conservative, rigid character, for change manifests the fact that halakha is indeed a platform for revelation, that the divine is present in halakha in the present. Thus, in a certain sense, various approaches to halakhic rulings among some of the Orthodox *posekim* allow for greater

---

28. Y. Pe'ah 13a.
29. Rabbi Tzaddok HaKohen of Lublin, *Likkutei Ma'amarim*, section 15. See also Rabbi Yehuda Aryeh Leib Alter, *Sefat Emet*, vol. 1, Ḥanukka 5631.

freedom in relation to halakha and its adaptation to a given epoch. [30] In contrast to approaches that consign the Torah to heaven or to the historical past, the Orthodox *posek* has inexhaustible options for maneuverability in his interpretations – as the mishna states, "Turn it and turn it again, for everything is in it."[31] He can extract whatever he needs from the text through interacting with it, by way of an *ukimta* or other halakhic techniques. According to this conception, a *posek* who updates halakha is not subverting the truth, for the truth is manifest in the *posek's* very use of halakhic language.[32]

That being the case, one can offer the sweeping assertion that while Reform Judaism has entirely shrugged off halakhic discourse, Conservatives do not disown halakha, but in practice have not retained its characteristic inhibitions, thus preventing the "halakhic game" from progressing according to its own rules. In practice, they are unwilling to accept and play the halakhic language game as is, instead subjecting it to external criticism and an external values scale, in light of which they update it. Ultimately, they destroy the soul of halakha and, on a profound level, prevent it from evolving while retaining the rules of its game.[33]

It follows that the difference between the various approaches will relate to the difficult point: the compulsiveness and neurosis that, as noted, create the halakhic taboo and are internalized by halakha itself. Only by positing this difficult point can halakha impart belief in a Torah from heaven that does not remain in heaven, implying the absoluteness of halakha. That is the mystical aspect of it, one that has

---

30. See *This Is My Covenant*, 79–91. Obviously, in discussing the possibility of updating halakha in the Orthodox context, I do not mean that every Orthodox *posek* should do so.

31. Mishna Avot 5:25.

32. Contrast this conception with the academic perspective that informs much of the Conservative worldview, which is subordinate to the objective, ethical, and historical conditions that gave rise to halakha. This perspective tends to reduce the text to a set of literal readings that stand in the way of change.

33. Do we acknowledge the historicity of halakha? Indeed, we do. Yet for us, the history is performed rather than stated. It is not a parameter that emerges explicitly in our deliberations, but rather a stance that must remain implicit if it is to enable us to play the halakhic game. The Conservative Jew, in contrast, submits to the objective historical, archaeological, and scientific truths, just as he submits to the ethical truth.

been dulled by the Conservative movement. The difference therefore lies not necessarily in the basic assumptions about the method of study – about which the two sides may be in accord – but rather, as we have said, in the approach to retaining the language of halakha: in practice, in discourse; even in body language and facial expressions. The test is the totality of one's dedication.

One final note: This point goes against the ethical and intellectual dimension upon which both Conservatives and many Modern Orthodox attempt to base halakha. But it is precisely this approach that can retain the mystical core of halakha – which opposes the ethical intellectualization of the religion – without impairing its capacity for pragmatism, or even for tolerance. That is why only Orthodoxy – not Reform or Conservatism – can safeguard an authentic Jewish mysticism. I do not believe in any other kind of Jewish mysticism; the exotic flowers will blossom only in the Orthodox garden. Other soil will germinate greatness – brilliant scientists, authors, even righteous and religious people – but not people devoted to Jewish religiosity.

Someone may ask: Who are you to decide what Jewish religiosity looks like? Do Orthodox Jews have a monopoly over Jewish religious literature? Indeed, we have no monopoly over the definition of who, or what, is a Jew, and I wish many more would become acquainted with the corpus of Jewish religious literature. Neither do I mind if more shelves are added to that bookcase. Indeed, my claim is far more modest, if equally firm: Non-Orthodox denominations cannot produce Jewish religious leaders, Torah luminaries, who conform to the definition of Judaism to which my colleagues and I subscribe and in which we believe. To me, this definition is sufficient, and it is what I am fighting for. Is this definition rooted in one's decision, or faith, or lifestyle? That is the question we will discuss below.

A COLD KNIFE IN THE HEART OF FAITH

Now I wish to revisit various formulations of the question of faith. Modern man's question – "Am I capable of faith?" or "Do I believe?" or "Do I *truly* believe?" – is the kind of "calamity" described by Rabbi Naḥman above, something that impairs the "procession of the blood." Order is disrupted when membrane life is pierced by a foreign agent, and the procession of the blood loses its posture. A question that also turns inward – "Do I...?" – is such a calamity, as it introduces duality, dissolving the self-unity of one's faith.

Man's turn inward is like a cold knife in the heart of faith, because faith derives not from conscious reflection, but from an order that constructs a world. Questions about faith and its meaning prevent one from being oneself – as far as faith is concerned. In that sense, faith is as spontaneous as reason. This is not to say that it is equally rational, but to a believer anchored in a religious lifestyle, it is self-evident, like reason. Believers sense in it a limpidity and certainty – what Rabbi Naḥman often refers to as "innocence" – equal to the clarity and certainty that the philosopher senses vis-à-vis his reason. This is because they are not in a reflexive position of asking questions and feeling compelled to justify their faith, thereby divorcing themselves from it.

Indeed, were we to examine the questions of faith more carefully, we would find that they are really about the *consciousness* of faith, which is an entirely different matter. They deal with the believing subject, with the growing schism between him and his lifestyle, or between the various contexts of his lifestyle. There are contexts in which he leads a full Jewish lifestyle, with all that such a lifestyle entails – meaning, the frameworks of religious practice – and there are contexts utterly removed from the Jewish world; for instance, his place of work. Such a state by nature heightens one's awareness and the sense of dichotomy that arises from the attempt to reconcile contradictory contexts. Then come the questions of faith: its authenticity, its very possibility, its place, and so on. To my mind, this angst was precisely what Rabbi Yisrael of Ruzhyn and Rabbi Naḥman had in mind when they referred, respectively, to an era in which believing would be as hard as scaling a vertical wall, and one in which believers would be as much of a novelty as the Baal Shem Tov was in his generation.[34]

An awareness of the conflict between the halakhic, religious world and the outer, modern one can produce two compartmentalist reactions:

---

34. See Rabbi Yisrael of Ruzhyn, *Irin Kaddishin*, vol. 1 (Jerusalem: Siftei Tzaddikim, 5769), 82a; Rabbi Naḥman of Breslov, *Siḥot HaRan* (Beitar Illit: Mekhon Even HaShetiya, 2010), 36.

ultra-Orthodox seclusion, on the one hand, and Modern Orthodoxy's two-world approach, on the other. The conception of faith as a function of lifestyle facilitates the demarcations upon which these two schools of thought are founded. Among the ultra-Orthodox, or Haredim, the role of compartmentalization is to isolate the Jewish way of life, to prevent it from becoming adulterated through contact with other modes of existence and giving rise to a fundamentally tainted world. Meanwhile, for Modern Orthodoxy – as manifest in the Leibowitzian approach, for instance – compartmentalization splits the believer's life in two: an ethical part, governed by halakhic practice and the beliefs and ideas it entails, and a scientific part, which is secular. Similarly, Rabbi Soloveitchik posited halakha as an absolute value that is imbued with meaning solely by virtue of the divine imperative. Thus, halakha is impervious to criticism generated by the gap between the scientific or ethical worldview of a certain age and an incompatible religious outlook. The objective is to prevent the religious world from having to contend with the criticism of the scientific realm.

AUTHENTIC ḤAREDI JUDAISM

As noted, one cannot ignore the fact that *ḥaredi* compartmentalization in response to modernity has often been fanned by a fundamentalist and fanatic spirit. Compartmentalization is often accompanied by the delegitimization of all other modes of life – Jewish or otherwise – and presents ultra-Orthodoxy as the only possible truth. It seems as though this trend runs counter to the spirit of traditionalism, which does not require, when embraced as a lifestyle, a comparison to other ideas and traditions. Thus, we return to one aspect of religion's response to modernity: the *doxa* of ortho-*doxy*, the conception of religious truth as rigid and exclusive, formulated without room for change or flexibility. One can claim that such a response to modernity constitutes an internalization of modernity itself, for, in spirit, modernity believed in the existence of an absolute truth. This belief led to a demand for coherence and the resolution of all contradictions in a given language, be it historical, psychological, biological, or religious. Consequently, places where the resolution of contradictions proved impossible became increasingly rigid, even violent. That is the root of the rigidity of *ḥaredi* Judaism.

I yearn for a different haredism, an authentic haredism that maintains the compartmentalist approach – currently the movement's only possible approach, to my mind – but is not motivated by the rejection of other cultures or lifestyles or the attempt to identify them with haredism.[35] I pin my hopes on a haredism driven by an acceptance of multiculturalism that enables it to choose itself without rejecting or delegitimizing other cultures, and without becoming rigid. Such a haredism will excel at creating gaps between various frames of reference in a manner that retains the truth of each, and prevents the distortions that arise from attempted syntheses, while rigorously empowering and maintaining the boundaries of its own truth.

I must concede that if it is to have a future, the national religious movement must internalize such *haredi* outlooks or risk becoming either secular or *hardal* (fundamentalist *haredi* Zionism), for these days theology must be founded on alienation and absurdity, among other things. This means that, in the absence of an absolute truth or language, the fabric of reality is permeated by myriad contradictory and irreconcilable truths. Only a religious outlook that succeeds in positioning itself as a hard, unconditional truth, while remaining open – absurdly – to the existence of other truths that contradict it, will be able to persist without losing its soul to rigid dogmatism or self-deception.[36]

---

35. The national religious movement's attempt to resolve the tension between modernity and religious life through integrations and harmonizations has also yielded a dogmatic approach. Religious Zionism has undertaken to internalize modern secular values, but not by acknowledging their secularity. Instead, it seeks to encircle them in a harmonious yet suffocating embrace, identifying them with normative religious values. Furthermore, this approach was implemented without acknowledging that, oftentimes, the "sanctification of the secular" actually constituted a "secularization of the sacred." This critique of the national religious movement is often voiced in *haredi* circles.

36. The capacity to speak of various possibilities and perspectives, reconstructing the truth conditions of each, allows me to grasp them all simultaneously without having to choose between them. Thus, I can study the Talmud at once as an academic, a Litvak scholar, and even a kabbalist. But even such an approach, in which faith functions as part of a language game, cannot rule out other language games. Clearly, from such a point of view I can observe the truth conditions of the secular Jew, and through them vindicate him, but I will also be unable to escape my own truth conditions. Will this lead me to relativism or nihilism? Not necessarily. Generally

Furthermore, the adoption of haredism could provide a solution of sorts to the rampant secularization among the national religious. It is a secularization brought on by nothing other than the lack of an intensive Jewish lifestyle. Religion – as a palpable aspect of life, as a profundity that drives its currents – is dissipating, leaving in its wake only the social link, the sense of belonging to a group. That is insufficient in a highly secular era. In such an environment, social relationships are not enough to shore up a religious person. The alienation between the national religious individual and the Torah derives from our rabbis' failure to create a situation wherein the Torah, Judaism, sparks interest and constructs a rich and spiritually abundant world. Judaism holds no *interest* for such an individual. This trend is especially apparent among national religious youth, who, even when they do not renounce religious practice, are often relegated to a far worse situation: They become materialistic.[37]

Consequently, our response to the world around us should somehow correspond to the *ḥaredi* one. There must be a certain seclusion that aims to strengthen the religious community, in order to create a profound and meaningful religious world that can coexist with other worlds. Among members of our community, I often sense the emptiness of religious rituals. Is our Shabbat truly a "day of the soul," a time for renewing the covenant and working on our family relationships in order to attain spiritual uplift? I'm afraid not. I have similar feelings regarding the days of celebration and mourning, the funerals and weddings, which are so often superficial, shallow, and devoid of religious vitality. Such a state is but a hairsbreadth from the rigidity and fundamentalism arising out of fear of losing one's depleted religious world – or from the abandonment of religion altogether.

---

speaking, will I be forced to prioritize my faith in order to defend it, to formulate some hierarchy in which my outlook is better than others? I think the fact that it is my faith is sufficient, that it is my covenant with God, which I chose myself. This does not close the door on other language games, which can either appear alongside my faith on an entirely different plane, or enrich me, or – as we will see below – even merge with me.

37. Witness the disproportionate number of hesder yeshiva graduates studying business and law in Israeli universities.

BOUNDLESS ROOTEDNESS

The process of Haredization that I propose entails another stage, in which the compartmentalization and turning inward – embracing the Jewish lifestyle in order to bolster faith – are reversed, enabling an openness unimpeded by restriction or boundary. To elucidate this stage, where authentic haredism meets traditionalism, I shall briefly reiterate the Orthodox outlooks, both *haredi* and modern.

Despite ascribing much importance to the perception of faith as an amalgam of language and practice, I acknowledge that such a perception raises acute questions perhaps unasked in Rabbi Naḥman's day, before secularization and the exodus from the warm embrace of the Jewish household. Hasidism emphasizes that "the entire world is filled with His glory" (Is. 6:3) and that "no place is empty of Him,"[38] but how can the Divine Presence manifest without a religious lifestyle to bolster it outside the synagogue? Indeed, the problem of faith in the modern world was born of a situation in which the synagogue is filled with faith, but the entire world is not. Language is meaningful only within the framework of codes that are extant in a lifestyle, so that in the context of the modern world, which is secular in essence, religion retains meaning within the bounds of the religious lifestyle, but not beyond it. As we have shown, therein lies one of the critical shortcomings of Orthodoxy, both *haredi* and modern, which generates the angsts at the root of religious life in our time.

True, the Jewish lifestyle builds faith; however, such an assertion can be construed in various ways, including – and here I diverge from the picture painted thus far – to the effect that a religious lifestyle endows one not only with the *meaning* of Jewish faith, but also with Jewish *rootedness*. One's lifestyle is equivalent to a tree's fertile soil, and faith is the Jewish presence and fullness within life. This statement can be better understood in light of Franz Rosenzweig's excellent observation

---

38. *Tikkunei Zohar* 81b. See Rabbi Kalonymus Kalman Shapira of Piaseczno, *Mevo HaShe'arim* (Jerusalem: 5761), 214–15: "The foundation of the Torah of the Baal Shem Tov is enfolded in the literal reading that he discovered in the verse 'The entire world is filled with His glory.' … Not only does His divine essence permeate everything in the world … but both the corporeal and the earthly only appear material to us, while in truth everything is [composed of His] divine [essence]."

that Jewish wit and Jewish dishes are not Jewish for their content or for the practical frameworks in which they take part, but because the jokes are told and the foods cooked and consumed by Jews deeply rooted in the rich world of Judaism.[39] The actions of someone deeply rooted in the Jewish world and its ways are all informed by his Judaism – he is unbounded. Such an individual is precisely the kind of person who is immersed in the life of a community that follows the ways of Judaism, its rituals and customs.

The various shades of modernity and Orthodoxy have removed Jews from the more rooted Judaism. Orthodoxy's insistence on a Jewish lifestyle "by the book," as a *doxa*, in order to compartmentalize – inside and out, present and future – has eliminated the unbounded Jewish rootedness from that lifestyle and faith. Here, too, Rosenzweig is apt: "Where, in the Judaism of the West, the law still continues to be observed, it no longer constitutes the 'Jewishness' of life that was."[40] Rootedness is never "by the book"; rather, it is embedded in the current of life. The halakhic Jewish lifestyle is the flow of Jewish life – not the study of halakhic tomes. The fullness, which is the soul of the halakhic life, is engendered in this stream, establishing the tribal ethos that shores up our forefathers' customs and is thus rooted in them. Without this soul, our forefathers' customs, and the faith enfolded therein, would wither. To put this in the context of Rabbi Amital's statement above: What he means is that what many people miss in the religious world is not so much the smell of the food as the connection to that world, *the sense of belonging* generated by the customs, flavors, smells, and scenes that are all unique to the religious lifestyle. These things make one's lifestyle cozy and intimate, Shabbat-like, such that one cannot step outside it, just as one cannot truly leave home – one belongs to it, wherever he may be. Thus, what is lacking today is the taste and smell that are themselves the content.

---

39. Franz Rosenzweig, "The Builders," in *On Jewish Learning* (New York: Schocken, 1965), 82–83. See also Nahum N. Glatzer, *Franz Rosenzweig: His Life and Thought* (New York: Schocken, 1953), 64.

40. Franz Rosenzweig, "Open Letter to Eduard Strauss," in *Textual Reasonings: Jewish Philosophy and Text Study at the End of the Twentieth Century*, ed. Peter Ochs and Nancy Levene (London: SCM Press, 2002), 233.

The modern era alienated man from this content and severed him from his home, dealing a deathblow to intimacy. It was an era that gave rise to the Orthodoxy that lives by the book but is bereft of its Shabbat-like soul.[41]

ARE WE CAPABLE OF FAITH?

In conclusion, and in light of the connection we have established between traditionalism and haredism, I wish to rephrase the question of faith presented at the outset, and through it to sum up the discussion. The question I asked was "Are we still capable of faith?" not "Is faith real?" The question implies an interest in believing, and the problem is whether we are still capable of it. But why should this question matter to us? If we are incapable, that means we do not believe, so why would we even care about faith? The implication is that if we ask ourselves, "Are we capable of faith?" ostensibly we do not believe, and we're asking if we can bring ourselves to believe. Yet where does the urge to believe come from? What is its source? Is it an interest? If so, of what sort? Existential? Social? Perhaps reflecting a desire to retain one's lifestyle and a certain world order? Or does such a question merely betray some tautological self-reference (not a turn inward that creates duality), meaning an image of the believer, or group of believers, that we have created or that is etched in our selves? Again we ask: Whence our desire to perpetuate this image? Someone can claim it derives from a Spinozesque *conatus*[42] or a Freudian self-delusion. Perhaps so. I cannot discount these options, but to me they do not constitute a plausible explanation for an intrepid insistence on faith. I realize that all the answers I hold to the question of the motive for faith do not jibe with the actual appearance of faith; they do not provide a causal explanation for its appearance. In such a situation, the duality-entailing turn inward becomes a self-reference dependent on unity.

41. [Ed. note: See Haym Soloveitchik, "Rupture and Reconstruction: The Transformation of Contemporary Orthodoxy," *Tradition* 28, no. 4 (summer 1994).]

42. On Spinoza's theory of *conatus*, the "striving to persevere in being," see "Spinoza's Psychological Theory," in *Stanford Encyclopedia of Philosophy*, http://plato.stanford.edu/entries/spinoza-psychological/.

Yet it is clear to me that self-reference bears the promise of self-acceptance: I have no need to prove to others, or even to believe, that my faith is the truth or the Good; it is sufficient that it is I and the way I am. I cannot, and perhaps do not, wish to be otherwise. I choose myself and accept myself, and accepting myself means accepting my existence within God; that is to say, that God loves me. My existence inherently justifies itself.[43] That is because choice and acceptance are not meta-physical or psychological terms, but rather the will of God: "For the Lord hath chosen Jacob unto Himself, and Israel for His own treasure" (Ps. 135:4). It is the moment when man says, "I cannot be otherwise." This applies to both sides of the coin – the religious and the modern. That is the meaning of the rootedness discussed above.

The bottom line is that choice and acceptance are reality, facts of reality, and as such, they are self-contained and self-evident.[44] In such a state, the rituals of my religious lifestyle are imbued with uniqueness and sometimes even strangeness – they are what they are, devoid of rhyme or reason. When I accept myself, I cease to rely on some external framework that is necessary for my existence; I am I, myself. Anywhere I go, I will be, and the divine will be with me – "the entire world is filled with His glory." A consciousness moored in the intimacy of a certain existence needs no walls, definitions, or separations. As stated, traditionalism and authentic haredism are praiseworthy for their mooring in tradition and lifestyle, in intimacy. This mooring manifests an unpretentious existence, one that does not endeavor to prove itself or surpass itself, but rather is what it is, justified in itself, without carrying any banner.

---

43. Rabbi Tzaddok HaKohen wrote, "Just as one must believe in the Lord, blessed be He, so too must one then believe in oneself. Meaning that the Lord, blessed be He, has dealings with him, and that he is not merely an idle worker who 'perish[es] in a night' (Jonah 4:11), or like the beasts of the field, which are lost and gone after they die. One must believe that one's soul derives from the Source of Life, blessed be His name, and that the Lord, blessed be He, is delighted and derives pleasure when [the soul] does His will. That is the meaning of 'and they believed in the Lord, and in His servant Moses' (Ex. 14:31): The meaning is that Moses – in other words, the six hundred thousand souls of Israel in that generation – believed that the Lord, blessed be He, had chosen them and wanted, and was gladdened by, the goodness in them" (*Tzidkat HaTzaddik*, section 154).
44. Choice chooses itself as a choice, and acceptance accepts itself as acceptance.

I wish to return to the passage from Rabbi Naḥman with which we opened. Halakha, to his mind, is not merely the order that constructs the world, but rather "the delight of the World to Come": "And days of thanks correspond to the delight of the World to Come…and thanks, which is the delight of the World to Come, corresponds to halakhot." In many hasidic traditions, the term "delight" (*shaashua*) denotes selfhood. Just as the delights of love are the quintessential expression of the nonpurposefulness of the amorous bond between two persons, so too the delight of the World to Come emerges when one leads a nonpurposeful life, when one is fully true to oneself, and when one's selfhood needs no purpose to shore itself up. In this, delight is the most precise expression of faith.

Chapter Four

Freedom and Holiness

M any people, religious and secular alike, consider holiness and freedom mutually exclusive. Holiness is the realm of the religious; it represents transcendence, a manifestation of God before which man stands, awestruck and submissive, head bowed. Freedom, on the other hand, expresses human immanence, strength, and fullness; its markers are initiative, industriousness, and autonomy. It is part and parcel of a secular, devil-may-care attitude. The contrast between holiness and freedom is the contrast between ponderousness and ease, among other things.

According to the conception of freedom that is the basis of modern humanism, man inherited the classical attributes that Jewish

Based on a talk delivered at a Ḥanukka event at Yeshivat Siaḥ Yitzḥak in 5763, and edited by Odeya Tzurieli and published with the title "Freedom and Holiness" in Rabbi Shagar's *Broken Vessels* (5763), 46–66. The material was re-edited after the author's death by Dr. Zohar Maor and published in *Tablets and Broken Tablets*, 86–104. The material was expanded from a handwritten draft on the topic of freedom from 5740; two essays, written in Adar and Nisan 5762, which deal with freedom in the Maharal of Prague's writings and in the context of Passover; and an essay on Maimonides' ideas about choice and freedom, written between 5753 and 5755. For more on freedom, see Rabbi Shagar, *A Time of Freedom*, edited by Yishai Mevorach.

philosophers ascribed to God: aliveness, wisdom, capacity for action, will.[1] Man has attained the will and capacity for action, as well as God's wisdom and freedom. As we read in Ecclesiastes, man's word is law, "and none can say to him, 'What are you doing?'" (Eccl. 8:4). Indeed, these days, when the voice of God is inaudible, there is no one to tell man what to do. But as we will see, it is a rather unpleasant situation that demonstrates the intrinsically problematic nature of the term "freedom" (or "liberty"): the ease with which freedom slides into nihilism. I wish to discuss this problem, but also to examine whether holiness and freedom are indeed diametric opposites, or whether freedom can perhaps cleanse and exalt holiness.

CHOICE AND FREEDOM IN THE BIBLE

The Torah recognizes man's freedom to choose:

> See, I have set before you this day life and good, and death and evil, in that I command you this day to love the Lord your God, to walk in His ways, and to observe His commandments, statutes, and ordinances; then you shall live and multiply, and the Lord your God shall bless you in the land when you go in to possess it.... I call heaven and earth to witness against you this day, that I have set before you life and death, blessing and curse; therefore choose life, that you may live, you and your seed. (Deut. 30:15–16, 19)[2]

What is the freedom propounded by the Bible? It is easier to say what it is not: The Bible's freedom is not modern freedom; it is not the freedom of modern man – personal freedom, individuality, and individual autonomy. Man's capacity to be master of his own fate, to build his life and establish his truths, is not extant in the biblical idea

---

1. See, for example, *Guide of the Perplexed* I:53.
2. The statement "therefore choose life, that you may live" is a tautology, and freedom is indeed tautological in the sense that it would otherwise be subordinate to the reasons for its being what it is. However, being what it is, emanating only from itself, it is imbued with a divine attribute, for the significance of God's singularity – "there is nothing other than Him" (Deut. 4:35) – is that there is nothing outside (or within) Him that forces Him to be what He is. We will revisit these arguments later.

of freedom – there, it is beyond reach. One can choose between good and evil, but not what is good and what evil. The Western ethos of making oneself by oneself is far from the Torah's conception. It is a basic article of faith that a thing cannot make itself. The freedom of the Bible is not a capricious freedom to do as I please; nor is it the Nietzschean freedom to make myself by myself, or even the existential freedom to be what I already am.

Biblical freedom hinges on the sense of justice, and the hatred of slavery, that lies in the most ancient strata of Jewish faith. It plays a key role in the shaping of the history of a nation that rebelled against slavery and paid dearly for it (for example, in the wake of the Great Revolt against the Romans and during the Bar Kokhba Revolt). Suffice to mention the centrality of freedom in the context of the Exodus from Egypt, the house of bondage, which the Torah cites as a rationale for many mitzvot. It is a freedom from the authority of a capricious, exploitative regime, and an acceptance of the yoke of God's righteous law. In this regard, freedom is linked to equality: both equality before the law and economic equality, as expressed in mitzvot such as *Shemitta* and the Jubilee year.[3]

The Bible's hatred of slavery springs from the injustice inherent in one person's enslavement of another, who is made subject to him, who becomes his property. Freedom is a manifestation of equality among Jews, all of whom came out of Egypt and belong to God, and thus cannot be the property of another: "For they are My servants, whom I brought forth out of the land of Egypt; they shall not be sold as bondmen. You shall not rule over [your brother] with rigor; but shall fear your God" (Lev. 25:42–43). Yet the biblical freedom is a collective freedom; the individual as a free subject had yet to emerge, for the subjects of the Bible were the community, the tribe, and the family.

This freedom is also the story of the enslavement to the God of Israel. Is there no contradiction between the two? Did the Jewish people, fresh from bondage, readily accept servitude to God? Were there no conflicts? Indeed, our biblical forefathers were fully aware of this tension, and the thorny relationship between the Jewish people and its God-King was riddled with intense struggles. The history of sin in Israel is largely

---

3. For more, see Rabbi Shagar, *On That Day*, 209–16.

the story of repeated attempts to shrug off the burden of religion and escape from bondage to God. Idolatry, in this context, posed the promise of breaking the fetters of morality, culture, and religion, and attaining a unity free of limitations. The divine imperative was perceived as a yoke imposed from above, and the reaction was to embrace a pantheistic idolatry that tore down the barriers between man and god. The sin of the Golden Calf is one example of idolatrous anarchy – an outbreak of id and the forces of chaos. This abandon was expressed, among other things, in idolatrous celebration and promiscuity, itself an expression of freedom: "…that pant after the dust of the earth on the head of the poor, and turn aside the way of the humble; and a man and his father go unto the same maid, to profane My holy name" (Amos 2:7).

But God does not give up, as we see in the prophet Ezekiel's message to the nation that resisted servitude to Him:

> And that which comes into your mind shall not be at all; in that you say: We will be as the nations, as the families of the countries, serving wood and stone. As I live, says the Lord God, surely with a mighty hand and an outstretched arm, and with fury poured out, will I be king over you.… And I will cause you to pass under the rod, and I will bring you into the bond of the covenant. (Ezek. 20:32–33, 37)

Indeed, God does not give up, but the Bible's ideal is not to enslave man to God in the narrow sense of the word. The conflict between freedom and holiness emerges only with man's sin. Ideally, however, idolatry's quest for unity with nature is justified, as Job states, "For you shall be in league with the stones of the field, and the beasts of the field shall be at peace with you. And you shall know that your tent is in peace, and you shall visit your habitation and lack nothing. You shall also know that your seed shall be great, and your offspring as the grass of the earth. You shall come to your grave in a ripe age, as a shock of corn comes in in its season" (Job 5:23–26). But such unity with nature can come about only through adherence to the law, not by transgressing it. Like animals, man was created to be part of nature, which obeys the laws that God imprinted in it. The Bible maintains a profound connection between holiness and consistency, order – as opposed to idolatrous chaos. The Torah teaches us that to obey the law is to engender holiness, which in turn causes nature to abide by its own laws, with rain falling in its season and the earth yielding its fruit.[4] Freedom, in its ideal, rectified sense, is harmony, a return to nature and the divine law that gave rise to it.

The dichotomy between Creator and creature was generated by the sin of Adam, who sought to be like God and escape his creatureliness. Yet in the ideal, prelapsarian world of Eden, freedom and holiness were one and the same, as we see in the passage about Shabbat, the first mention of holiness in the Bible.[5] Shabbat is rest, a return to the fullness of nature that requires no action. An expression of this idea is found in Isaiah, who was well acquainted with the transcendent holiness that subdues man's pride: "And the loftiness of man shall be bowed down, and the haughtiness of men shall be brought low, and the Lord alone shall be exalted on that day" (2:17). It evokes the Torah's "holy and awesome" name of the Lord but also establishes a new idea of holiness, a holiness of fullness, the harmony of Shabbat: "If you turn away your foot, because of the Sabbath, from pursuing your business on My holy day, and call the Sabbath a delight, and the holy of the Lord honorable" (58:13). Holiness is delight.[6]

---

4. See Lev. 18:1–5, 24–30; 20:7–8, 22–26. And see Rabbi Shagar, *We Will Walk in Fervor*, 218–20.

5. Gen. 2:2–3. Holiness is thus the freedom to refrain from doing, but also the freedom to not feel compelled to do – unlike the modern conception of freedom, which is a freedom to act. It is not negative, idle rest; nor is it rest to gain strength for the next day. Rather, it is a rest that is fullness. Such fullness leads not to idleness but rather to rest: to faith in one's deeds, to the conviction that one's actions are pleasing to God. This sentiment is apparent in the following statement by Rabbi Naḥman: "At the start of Shabbat and festivals I hand over to the Lord, blessed be He, all the manners and customs and movements of that Shabbat or festival, so everything is in keeping with His blessed will. And then, no matter how one conducts oneself on that Shabbat or festival, one is not preoccupied or fretful over whether one did not fulfill one's obligation vis-à-vis the holy customs of that day, for one has already handed everything over to the Lord, blessed be He, and one trusts in Him alone" (*Siḥot HaRan* 2).

6. This idea also appears in the famous verses in Nehemiah regarding Rosh HaShana: "Then he said unto them, 'Go your way, eat the fat, and drink the sweet, and send

The Torah comes full circle in the Ten Commandments of Deuteronomy, where Shabbat and its holiness are tied in to the Exodus from Egypt:

> Observe the Sabbath day to sanctify it, as the Lord your God commanded you. Six days shall you labor and do all your work; but the seventh day is a Sabbath unto the Lord your God. You shall not do any manner of work – neither you nor your son or daughter, nor your manservant or maidservant, nor your ox, your ass, or any of your cattle, nor your stranger who is within your gates; that your manservant and maidservant may rest as well as you. And you shall remember that you were a servant in the land of Egypt, and the Lord your God brought you out thence by a mighty hand and an outstretched arm; therefore the Lord your God commanded you to observe the Sabbath day. (Deut. 5:12–15)

Shabbat is to provide rest first and foremost to the slave, not to the master.

The Bible thus presents two aspects to holiness: the struggle against slavery and bondage, and the return to a natural unity and harmony. The two dimensions are interlinked, as the demand for freedom from bondage is part of the very nature of man, who was created in God's image and is thus worthy of freedom.

MAIMONIDES AND THE PARADOX OF FREEDOM

The issue of freedom receives in-depth treatment in Maimonides' writings.[7] His views on the matter tie in to the paradoxical nature of the idea of freedom. On the one hand, if one does things for particular reasons, he is not acting out of freedom; on the other, must a free action necessarily be random or capricious? Intuitively, it is difficult to accept such a conclusion. For instance, why get out of bed in the morning? Were I to provide external reasons, that would seemingly establish that

---

portions unto him for whom nothing is prepared, for this day is holy unto our Lord; neither be you grieved, for the joy of the Lord is your strength'" (8:10).

7. See the discussion of Maimonides' conception of repentance in Rabbi Shagar, *The Human and the Infinite*, chaps. 2, 4.

I am not a free man. On the contrary, I must work to overcome these reasons. Yet the result of this process may be that I remain in bed. Must freedom necessarily entail anarchy or nihilism?

Spinoza's response to this question was that freedom means acting out of one's inherent nature (i.e., out of immanent rather than external reasons). Yet if one's nature is known and given, freedom gives way to determinism, as Spinoza himself acknowledged.

The paradox can also be explained using the Aristotelian terminology adopted by Maimonides and many who followed his example. Everything in the world exists in matter and sustains a duality of matter and form. Matter marks the pole of a thing's existence as an object, while form also belongs to the world of the subject.[8] There is no perfect harmony between form and matter, for were matter not a certain negation of its form, it could not manifest a new form. Hence the idea of privation and the Aristotelian "special privation" that characterizes matter.[9] This privation is the source of the gap between matter and form that eventually leads to a thing's disintegration and annihilation – including man's. Privation also means that the existence of everything in nature is merely possible, contingent; existence is not the quiddity of the thing. Man is not in actuality, for he cannot fulfill his essence as a thinking being every moment. Owing to his matter, he is forever in potential. Because the perfect connection between form and matter is unattainable, man's existence is incomplete.

Thus, man's nature is essentially dual: While his form and essence are intellect, his materiality is deeply opposed to that intellect. That is why he requires an external motivation for action – for his materiality, his existence as an object, perceives only the existence of the physical world, which is man's external motivator. From that point of view, he lives in the world of phenomena, of material causality.

---

8. Maimonides' statement (in *Guide of the Perplexed* I:68) regarding the unity of the intellect, the intellectual apprehender, and the intelligible is well known: Only the material stands between human consciousness and the world; or, as Maimonides writes, between man and God (ibid. III:8).

9. See *Guide of the Perplexed* I:17; Maimonides, *Treatise on Logic*, chaps. 5, 9.

As a result, although man may be able to influence external reality, he cannot construct something *ex nihilo*, cannot create – and therein is another expression of his lack of freedom. Freedom is for God alone; it is action motivated by oneness. But man is embedded in dualism, and his materiality keeps him from becoming fully actualized, so he cannot attain the freedom reserved for God, who exists unto and for Himself.

Yet Maimonides asserts:

> It is a fundamental principle of the Law of Moses our Master, peace be on him, and of all those who follow it, that man has an absolute ability to act; I mean to say that in virtue of his nature, his choice, and his will, he may do everything that it is within the capacity of man to do…. And [[God] has willed it so; I mean to say that it comes from His eternal volition in the eternity *a parte ante*…that man should have the ability to do whatever he wills or chooses among the things concerning which he has the ability to act.[10]

Man's choice derives from his godly image, which is his intellect. As Maimonides writes in *Eight Chapters*, his commentary on Mishna Avot:

> "Behold, the man is become as one of us, to know good and evil" (Gen. 3:22). The Targum, in paraphrasing this passage, explains the meaning of the words *mimmenu ladaat tov vera*. Man has become the only being in the world who possesses a characteristic which no other being has in common with him…. It is that by and of himself man can distinguish between good and evil, and do that which he pleases.[11]

Choice arises from acknowledgment, understanding, and awareness of one's action. Because one knows what one is doing, one can

10. *Guide of the Perplexed* III:17.
11. Maimonides, *The Eight Chapters of Maimonides on Ethics*, trans. Joseph I. Gorfinkle (New York: Columbia University Press, 1912), 92.

choose to act otherwise. This knowledge is self-knowledge: I act thus. This "I" is not something that stands apart from me and that I am forced to contend with, to move in order to enforce my will; it is myself, and the source of my control over my actions. Choice and freedom lie in self-awareness, which is why freedom is a function of consciousness: The more aware we are of ourselves and our actions, the freer we are. As we know, Maimonides considered this awareness to be man's very purpose. When man becomes fully intellectual, he transcends his haphazard, possible, contingent life and merges with divine necessity.

For Maimonides, however, man's freedom is limited. On the one hand, he writes, humans manufacture their eternity, their World to Come, which is identical to truth; they weave it out of the world. It is not vouchsafed them, but rather must be constructed. Yet this is not to say that we mortals establish the truth. According to Maimonides, truth is a given, independent of us. The world is primed to enable the extraction of eternity and truth, which are associated with God, blessed be He. Otherwise, man would be unable to extract them. This eternity precedes man's manufacturing of it, but man is created with the ability to become a part of it.

But herein is an expression of the paradox we discussed above. For intellect cannot be irrational. According to Maimonides, one who comes to clearly grasp the effect of fire on his body will not put his hand in the flames. Choice is thus not an option, but rather a compulsion to do the right thing. Choice, in the sense of a capacity to do the wrong thing, arises from an incomplete worldview, when consciousness – due to its submersion in materiality – is not identical with reality. It follows that one who is fully enlightened has neither choice nor freedom.[12]

This paradox leads us to sharpen our conception of Maimonides' freedom. One can resolve the paradox by separating internal from external impetuses for action. It is apparent in the quotation above, from his introduction to Mishna Avot, that choice implies an absence of external compulsion; rather, it is internal identification, i.e., choice in the

---

12. This is the import of the Tree of Knowledge in Maimonides' famous explanation in *Guide of the Perplexed* I:2, namely, man's fall from the world of "intelligible matters" to the subjective world of "matters of convention."

sense espoused by Spinoza. Hence Maimonides' astonishing reading of Ḥazal's statement that "everything is in the hand of heaven except fear of heaven."[13] Maimonides argues that "all of man's actions, which are subject to his free will, undoubtedly either comply with, or transgress, God's commands.... Moreover, to this faculty of the soul (i.e., the freedom of the will) 'the fear of God' is subservient, and is, in consequence, not predestined by God, but, as we have explained, is entirely in the power of the human free will. By the word 'all,' the rabbis meant to designate only natural phenomena which are not influenced by the will of man."[14]

Everything is in the hand of heaven – the entire world is subject to an immanent set of rules, natural laws that express the divine wisdom – other than the fear of heaven: The element of chance, the material, transcends nature and enables choice. Yet the object of choice, which Maimonides identifies with fear of heaven, is to restore the realm of chance to heaven, that is, to the wisdom and order of providence. Choice pertains not only to mitzvot, but to all of man's actions; as Maimonides emphasizes at the end of *Guide of the Perplexed*, the patriarchs also applied themselves to the realm of the mundane, and in acting there, too, for the sake of heaven, made it an area of divine knowledge. Man's purpose is to actualize form in matter, to bring order and lawfulness to randomness and individuality.[15]

It would appear, then, that the purpose of man's freedom is to be freely relinquished by man. Could it be, thus, that Sartre's critique of Spinoza – "And since this order could not be eluded, Spinoza preferred to sacrifice human subjectivity to it"[16] – holds true for Maimonides as well?

I believe the answer is no – which brings us to a different solution to the paradox, and to an alternative reading of Maimonides' idea of choice. Maimonides, in contrast to Spinoza, conceives of God not merely as intellect, but also as will (hence, for example, his rejection of the eternity of the

13. Berakhot 33b.
14. Gorfinkle, *Eight Chapters*, 89.
15. See *Guide of the Perplexed* III:54. Regarding the term "for the sake of heaven," see Gorfinkle, *Eight Chapters*, 73–74.
16. Jean-Paul Sartre, "Cartesian Freedom," in *Literary and Philosophical Essays*, trans. Annette Michelson (New York: Collier, 1962), 81.

world). It is clear to him that in God, will and intellect are one and the same. Yet a human perspective does not see it that way, for man, who is embedded in matter, cannot fully apprehend God.[17] If intellect expresses the pole of order and law, then will is an expression of divine freedom, which gives rise, in turn, to human freedom.[18] Human freedom is a function not only of man's state of being in potential, of the turbidity of consciousness, but also of the human autonomy engendered – as Maimonides states in *Guide of the Perplexed* – by the divine will. Human freedom emanates from the absolute divine will, and as such is equal to it. It emerges that, according to Maimonides, one can distinguish between two types of freedom: a lower freedom that derives from man's materiality, and a higher freedom vouchsafed one who cleaves to God and His freedom.

Maimonides derives his religious fervor from the fact that there is an absolute truth identified with God, the "Possessor of truth,"[19] but is no less enthusiastic regarding man's freedom to convert himself to that truth. Freedom is a prerequisite for the infiniteness of truth; without it, truth ossifies and becomes dictated and alienating, i.e., material. Freedom is thus the infiniteness of holiness. Freedom connects man to the divine will that is beyond order, generating boundless love and fervor.[20]

---

17. Still, the idea of will as an aspect of the Godhead is not merely an embodiment of man's limited point of view; it expresses a characteristic of God that is no less inherent to His nature than intellect, which Maimonides sees as an essential attribute. Man's limitation is apparent in Maimonides' sharp distinction between an intellectual aspect, which is expressed through nature and order, and a will, which is expressed by breaking the laws of nature. This duality permeates Maimonides' thought, including in his contrast of the wise and the pious. See Rabbi Shagar, *In the Shadow of Faith*, 198–203.

18. This duality is analogous to the conflict between Maimonides' assertion that God is to be apprehended through negative theology, and his conception of God as intellect, i.e., a positive attribute. His will is associated with His attributes of negation, and both emanate from the divine infinitude.

19. "This is implied by the prophet's statement 'And God your Lord is true' (Jer. 10:10), i.e., He alone is true, and no other entity possesses truth that compares to His truth. This is what [is meant by] the Torah's statement 'There is nothing else aside from Him' (Deut. 4:35), i.e., aside from Him, there is no true existence like His" (*Mishneh Torah*, Laws of the Foundations of the Torah 1:4).

20. Hence Maimonides' famous description of love of God, which employs the metaphors of illness and insanity (ibid., Laws of Repentance 10:3).

MODERN FREEDOM

If for Maimonides freedom is the liberty to choose a given truth (thus, as we have explained, enabling the manifestation of that truth in the human world), in the modern world freedom is one's liberty to establish one's own truth and values. Such a conception of freedom lends itself to two interpretations. The first perceives truth as authenticity. The second sees it as something created.

For Maimonides, truth emanates from an "I," but here that self is not identified with an objective intellect. Freedom is an action spurred by one's "existential truth," by what one is, an existence that is not necessarily logical. Freedom is therefore the liberty to choose oneself and authenticity, or to reject oneself; while, like the truth of the intellect, the truth of the self is also predetermined.

The conception of freedom as authenticity can be found in the works of the Maharal of Prague, who links freedom to *peshitut* (plainness), which is immanent selfhood, stripped of all external properties:

> For the unalloyed stands apart and is not joined to another thing, like the redeemed man, who stands apart and cannot be linked or joined to his master. In contrast, the enslaved man is not unalloyed, for he is joined to his enslaver... and furthermore, anything that is not unalloyed but rather compounded is clearly characterized by enslavement, for all the constituent parts of a compounded thing enslave one another to the extent that they cannot be free. Therein is another of the rationales for matza – that matza is unalloyed, unlike *ḥametz*, which is compounded.[21]

Matza is the bread of *oni*, implying either affliction or meagerness, which on the face of it symbolizes bondage. For the Maharal, however, meagerness paradoxically becomes a symbol of freedom, as it bespeaks an individual's loyalty to himself.

In the modern world, this idea has been expressed in various ways, the gist of which is that freedom means being true to oneself and rejecting all external coercion. In the modern system of signification,

---

21. Maharal, *Gevurot HaShem*, chap. 26.

freedom is the subject's subjectivity. Rabbi Kook elevated these ideas to
the realm of the holy by differentiating between holiness and freedom in
its modern sense. In one of the better-known passages in his works, he
describes self-betrayal as the original sin of mankind and all of creation:

> Adam's sin was that he became alienated from himself, that he
> turned to the serpent's knowledge and lost himself, and did not
> have a clear answer to the question "Where are you?" for he did
> not know his soul, for his true I-ness was gone from him with the
> sin of bowing to a strange god. The sin of Israel was that it went
> astray after foreign gods, forsaking its own I-ness.[22]

Unlike Maimonides, Rabbi Kook associates man's godly image
with freedom, which he identifies with the self, as he writes in one of
his seminal letters:

> It is of no consequence to us whether the enhancement of being
> to the point of selfhood depends upon its inner essence or upon
> some means that we refer to as "free choice," whose ability is to
> highlight and reveal being in the depth of its selfness. Naturally,
> we tend toward unity in these matters and have no need to ascribe
> essential qualities to anything but free will.

Further along, Rabbi Kook emphasizes, "Therefore, the nature
of the will, as manifested in an observable, practical choice, is a mere
shadow and impression of the absolute selfness of the depth of the will
in its concealed source, upon which depends the essence of choice and
freedom."[23] Freedom is authenticity, fealty to one's inner self, and it is
only through this loyalty that one can find God.

Yet Sartre, who ridicules Spinoza's idea of freedom, also objects
to the conception of freedom as authenticity. To him, freedom is not
the liberty to choose a pre-dictated truth – of any kind, be it intellectual
or even existential – but rather to establish and create truth. Nothing

22. Rabbi Kook, *Orot HaKodesh*, vol. 3, 140.
23. Rabbi Kook, *Iggerot HaRe'iya* (Jerusalem: Mossad HaRav Kook, 5745), vol. 2, 41–42.

precedes my freedom, which is neither a choice between possibilities nor the uncovering of latent options.

Sartre's conception relies on a human duality similar to that which emerges from Maimonides' ideas. People are, on the one hand, in a state of being-in-itself, objects in a world of objects subject to the laws of nature; but people are also in a state of being-for-itself, meaning a reflexive reality that can give the world meaning. In this regard, man enjoys total freedom.

In one of his novels, Sartre powerfully conveys this point:

> He was no more than a sack upon other sacks, at the bottom of a truck. "Well, that would finish it, I would tell her this evening that I would marry her." The bus, huge, infantile machine, had carried him off; it swung him to the right and left, shook him, bumped him – events bumped him against the back of the seat and up against the window, the speed of his life had dimmed his senses, and he thought, "My life is no longer mine, my life is just a destiny".... Marry or not marry – "It doesn't concern me now, it's heads or tails.".... he was free, free in every way, free to behave like a fool or a machine, free to accept, free to refuse, free to equivocate; to marry, to give up the game.... He could do what he liked...there would be no Good nor Evil unless he brought them into being.[24]

Freedom is release from fixed values, but also from authenticity. The age-old contrast between freedom and holiness is further sharpened in this context. It is no longer merely a contrast between divine transcendence and human autonomy, but between the holiness that imbues existence with meaning and being, on the one hand, and a weightless, confetti-like, meaningless world, on the other.

The classic conception of freedom sees it as mere possibility and teaches us that one is not born free, and that to attain freedom, one must wage a grueling struggle against one's conditionings and

---

24. Jean-Paul Sartre, *The Age of Reason* (New York: Bantam Books, 1959), 275. See the parallel debate in Rabbi Shagar, "Graven upon the Tablets: From Purim to Passover," in *A Time of Freedom*, 163–68.

dependencies – physical, psychological, social, and otherwise. Sartre's freedom, in contrast, being nothing at all, becomes fate; man is "condemned to be free," as he put it.[25] His recurring attempts to move from a state of being-for-itself to being-in-itself are doomed to failure, for at the end of the day, even the deferral of choice is itself a choice. Let us revisit the question of getting out of bed in the morning. One may ask himself that question and then realize that every external impetus he comes up with is valueless. Such a person could collapse under the weight of the thought that there is no one to tell him what to do, that he is lying face-to-face with the abyss. Freedom becomes anarchy. Hence the "escape from freedom," as Erich Fromm titled his famous book: The secret attraction of many fascist movements (and nowadays, with fascism no longer *en vogue*, the draw exerted by assorted gurus and cults) is the release they offer from the burden of freedom. It is conceivable that much of a person's life is composed of various attempts to shirk that burden.

Man's redemption, Sartre would say, occurs at the moment freedom ceases to be a meaningless quest for a reason to get out of bed, and becomes the release from that question. Freedom is absolute choice, not choice that emanates from societal values or habit, or from a rigid, bounded conception of self. Freedom is man's conscious surrendering of all of life's moorings.

POSTMODERN FREEDOM: LIBERTY AS NOTHINGNESS

Sartre's conception of freedom was radicalized in postmodernist thought. Here, not only does man aspire to create truth, he considers any truth a human-social construct (including, of course, religious truths). Here, to be free is to sink into absolute nothingness, with nary a reference point.

We can better grasp the postmodern crisis, and its profound religious potential, by revisiting Maimonides' reading of Adam and Eve's sin. According to him, the eating of the fruit of the Tree of Knowledge represents the duality latent in mankind, the schism between the realms of the objective (intelligible matters, truth and falsehood) and the subjective (matters of convention, of good and bad). In the modern world,

---

25. See Jean-Paul Sartre, *Existentialism Is a Humanism* (New Haven: Yale University Press, 2007).

freedom was associated, as noted, with this duality: It focused on the subject and his struggle to break free of the influence of the world of objects, to which he was subjected.[26] Similarly, as Maimonides wrote, the act chosen by Adam, the act of freedom, is itself the sin. Sin is inherent in the very duality of object and subject, which renders choice a sin. The rectification of the sin can come only with the abolition of duality, something that, to Maimonides' mind, only a select few can accomplish. This will come to pass only on a broader scale on "that day," when "the Lord shall be One, and His name One" (Zech. 14:9).

Such a rectification, in fact, rests upon mystical freedom, when the aspiration to "be as God" (Gen. 3:5) ceases to be a sin and becomes a legitimate objective. Man's ambition to be like God sprang from a desire to be free as Him, but it achieved the opposite effect, ripping him from nature and flinging him into a world of duality that precludes freedom. On the contrary, the path to freedom passes through surrender to God, skirting the sin of hubris. Thus, man earns the Creator's freedom, the liberty to establish reality – "If the righteous desired it, they could be creators."[27] As we have seen, the postmodern world, which challenges the boundaries of reason and reality, enables new horizons of freedom, making it possible to establish worlds and form new permutations.

But can man be as God, as the postmodernists say, and create truth? Moreover, can he create holiness? If not, the contradiction between freedom and holiness is irreconcilable, even in its postmodern context.

It appears that, in spite of everything, something will always remain beyond the grasp of human freedom, a residue that cannot be manufactured by humans. This gap is filled by the inspiration of faith. The difference between a holy freedom and one that opposes holiness

---

26. The problem of modern slavery differs from that of the above-mentioned biblical slavery. Hegel defined it aptly in his master-slave dialectic. Freedom's subject hates slavery because it limits him, but, dialectically, is dependent upon it, for without it his subjectivity will crumble. Such is precisely the crumbling of the postmodern subject – when the world of objects is perceived as a collection of constructs. See G. W. F. Hegel, *Phenomenology of Spirit*, trans. A. V. Miller, foreword by J. N. Findlay (Oxford, England: Clarendon Press, 1977), 111; Yitzhak Klein, *The Dialectic of Master and Slave* [Hebrew] (Tel Aviv: Am Oved, 1978).

27. Sanhedrin 65b.

is also the difference between an inspired freedom and one lacking in inspiration, and the difference between faithful and faithless freedom. Faith in what? Neither in a truth external to man, nor in a given, clearly delineated "I," but in freedom's capacity to create in actuality. This holy freedom occurs in the place of unity, where God and man are joined. Hasidism interpreted the verse "For the portion of the Lord is His people" (Deut. 32:9) to mean that His people – the Jews – are a portion of God, literally a piece of divinity. That is mystical freedom. The postmodern freedom is man's capacity to create *ex nihilo*, but only inspiration can lend such a creation the actuality and absoluteness of God's creation. The prerequisite for inspiration is to choose choice, to believe in belief, and to pass from a posture of duality into one of covenant, into a space where one ceases to choose a thing because of other things (this is impossible under the rules of the postmodern game), but rather arrives where only that thing resides.

Only such a stance has the chance to allay the angst generated by postmodernist freedom, the meaninglessness of a world made up solely of constructs. Divine inspiration is what lends human constructs absoluteness identical to that of God's constructs.

The postmodern freedom facilitates a fresh approach to the holiness inherent in Maimonides' idea of freedom. Postmodern freedom has a purifying effect, similar to that of the negative theology through which Maimonides stripped God of His corporeality. Freedom signifies the divine infinitude, and postmodern deconstruction can further distill our conception of God. Holiness is freedom because any dictation entails externalization and alienation, which is why infinity can be realized only as freedom. Only freedom can build and be concretized without becoming ugly.[28]

We noted above that while Maimonides associates man's divine image with intellect, Rabbi Kook identifies it with freedom. Both are correct. Maimonides conducted himself in an age when reason reigned supreme (I claim that it is still relevant today, with requisite adjustments), when faith was attained through intellect, and the mind was a tool for grasping the absolute. In his era, freedom, too, was conceived

---

28. In all fairness, postmodern freedom also constitutes liberation from the rigidity of the rules of logic, something to which Maimonides was firmly opposed.

of in intellectual terms. Contemporary man, however, has apparently been endowed with a loftier divine image, from the world of *ayin*, an image of postmodern freedom and divine infinitude, "and you shall be as God."[29] It is mystical freedom, a liberation from positivism, from the absolute supremacy of the laws of nature, including the rules of logic, a freedom from reality that enables man to construct reality. Some have argued that postmodernism's defining literary genre is science fiction, through which one can establish an alternative reality, with rules altogether different from the ones governing our own.[30] It is a freedom emanating from infinity itself, which is so lofty as to not even be the source of worlds. It is not even present as absence; in fact, God's infinity represents only the negation of limitations and, through that process, the endowment of freedom.

Still, the test of freedom is not only our ability to break free. We are also tested in the extent to which we enable the other's freedom. The condition for a covenant with the Other is my belief in his freedom: that it will not impinge on mine and will truly lead to what is good. Only thus can I recognize the Other as a subject, without objectifying him. That is the deep meaning of recognizing the other's divine image. It requires seeing to the root of the other's soul on high, at the level of consciousness known as *yeḥida*, above all physical and spiritual garments.

In summation: Postmodern freedom can lead to holiness when it maintains an aspect of inspiration. It can express the infinite in man and in reality, the miracle that lies beyond natural law. It can also protect the holy from that which would ossify or limit it.

---

29. In kabbalistic terms, one can distinguish between a postmodern freedom linked to the *sefira* of *bina*, also known as the world of freedom, which is man's higher self; and the freedom linked to the *sefira* of *keter*, which is *ayin*, or nothingness, the divine will that precedes all emanation. See Rabbi Hillel Malisov of Paritch, *Pelaḥ HaRimon* on Song of Songs [Hebrew] (New York: Otzar HaHasidim, 1967).
30. See below, chapter 7.

Chapter Five

Living with Nothingness

THE POSTMODERN CONDITION

Postmodernism, as the word implies, is an intellectual, social, and cultural movement that emerged in the wake of modernity. It was engendered by a twofold process, social-cultural and philosophical, which are two sides of the same coin.

As several postmodernist thinkers have emphasized, postmodernism is, at bottom, not so much a philosophical theory as a mode of life and a state of consciousness – a cultural situation, some would even say. At its root is a loss of faith in grand narratives, in metaphysical goals, and in comprehensive theories.[1] One can cite many causes for this shift,[2]

This essay originally appeared in Rabbi Shagar's *Tablets and Broken Tablets*, 31–52. It was compiled from various drafts about postmodernism that remained unpublished during the author's lifetime. Edited by Dr. Itamar Brenner and Dr. Zohar Maor.

1. A similar description of postmodernism can be found in the preface to Jean-François Lyotard's seminal treatise *The Postmodern Condition* (Minneapolis: University of Minnesota Press, 1984).
2. For more on the difficulty of pinpointing a single cause for the emergence of postmodernism, as well as a specific event or point in time that signifies its onset, see David Gurevitz, *Postmodernism, Culture, and Literature in the Late Twentieth Century* [Hebrew] (Tel Aviv: Dvir, 1997), chap. 2. Gurevitz nevertheless proposes several origins for the emergence of postmodernism.

but what stands out among them is a profound sense that a significant portion of the twentieth century's horrors were the distinct products of an overzealous submission to overarching ideologies. Nazism, fascism, communism, and Maoism are the "usual suspects," and they are certainly guilty in this regard, but at the end of the day, capitalism is also an ideology in many respects, and it too is responsible for a great many injustices – some of them unbearable – that are a product (albeit sometimes unintended) of submission to the values it represents. Thus, the most egregious injustices in human history were committed in the name of one or another sweepingly applied "just" ideal, and were initiated at a time when great ideals were given significant expression by the powerful countries and major revolutionary movements that adopted them. Due to the ensuing disillusionment and other causes,[3] people lost faith in the idea of a cohesive world with a single, comprehensive meaning, a world governed by a clear and consistent set of principles. They also lost faith in the grand narratives, meaning the historical accounts constructed largely to justify one side or another, and with this their belief in an exhaustive moral and intellectual harmony upon which one could base one's life.

Under postmodernism, it was not only faith in the world that crumbled, but also faith in man. What emerged was a sense that the subject had been dismantled, along with the distinct, unambiguous identities of the modern past (which had supplanted the even more distinct identities of the premodern era). Postmodernism reflects a pervasive sense of having lost faith in man as an entity with a defined, cohesive identity. The process that began with the denial of God – which had its roots in the Protestant revolt against Catholicism and in Europe's ensuing Age of Enlightenment – culminated in the deconstruction of the individual. The defining moment of humankind's modern revolt against religion was Friedrich Nietzsche's famous assertion regarding the death of God. In the postmodern era, the revolt shifted to encompass man as well, as is evident in the inverse assertion, declared by God: "Nietzsche

---

3. For instance, Lyotard (op. cit., chap. 1) draws attention to the information explosion in post-industrial societies.

[i.e., the man who dared to ascend God's throne] is dead." Only this time the declaration remains unsigned.

As noted, postmodernism is a process of society and consciousness that also has philosophical facets. The roots of these philosophical aspects can be outlined briefly by way of the history of philosophy in the modern age. It begins, it seems, with Immanuel Kant's *Critique of Pure Reason*,[4] the gist of which – setting aside the complexity and diversity of its expression – is a perspective on reason, *from within* the subject, that sees reason as a form of subjectivity. What are the conditions and justifications for reason? What is Kant's critique of reason based on, and how does he establish the veracity of his claims? Therein, of course, lies the novelty of Kant's Copernican argument, which establishes truth by means of the subject: The thing-in-itself may be unknowable, but the subject perceives the truth of phenomena, and can corroborate it by examining it through the prism of his subjective faculties. It is the very subjectivity of the subject's perception of reality that lends it validity – the subject's manner of grasping what is impenetrable in itself. The subjectivity that Kant speaks of is not the subjectivity of a certain individual, but rather a universal human subjectivity.

Still, Kant opined, one can salvage truth and ethics – God, even – and establish them on the basis of subjective perception. But Kant's Copernican revolution led to thought systems that thoroughly decimated the idea of truth. For Nietzsche, for example, "truth" became subservient to the will, which precedes it. The subject's will – in fact, his desire for power, masquerading as a quest for truth – is what lends it justification. Later thinkers also dismantled the Nietzschean idea of will and the power-seeking self at its core. To them, will and self were feeble expressions of environmental conditions and circumstances. Freud's psychological theories and Marx's sociological ideas, Émile Durkheim and Max Weber – all refined these ideas, linking subjective truth and the subject itself to the conditioning arising from one's social and familial environments.

---

4. Although Kant was preceded by other thinkers, and the roots of modern philosophy are generally traced back to René Descartes, for the purposes of our discussion it would be best to treat the Kantian critique – and the new focus on the subject – as the onset of postmodernism.

In postmodern thought, as expressed in the writings of Michel
Foucault and other thinkers, truth and the presumption of truth are
mere expressions of power. But it is no longer a Nietzschean power,
from which one can piece together an anti-metaphysical metaphysics
and extrapolate a hierarchy. Foucauldian power also diverges from
Arthur Schopenhauer's idea of a blind will, a metaphysical, cosmic
being.[5] The power about which postmodern philosophers speak is
not a metaphysical, unitary, vast, and dominant thing, but rather a
network of myriad blind forces devoid of any point of origin or reference. This network is woven of modes of discourse/power – discourse
is nothing but power – that have no justification. Man is imprisoned
in this network of discourse/power, which dictates all his actions.
"Power circulates in all directions," as Foucault pointed out:[6] It does
not descend from above in a system of class relations (as Marx posited, for example) or some other hierarchy. It thus possesses no logic
and aspires to no order. According to the postmodern point of view,
every discursive action takes place in a web of random interpersonal
power relations and is thus the result of random conditioning. Every
human action is political (while politics is defined as power relations).
Human beings are not points of origin for autonomy and individuality: They influence one another as tremors in the network of power
relations. This arbitrary web of discourse/power is perceived as a
purely human construct, devoid of any metaphysical point of origin
or mooring outside itself.

Alongside the process of eradicating all traces of the metaphysical from the human world, we are witnessing, beginning in the
mid-twentieth century, important developments in the realm of language,
philosophy, and other subjects in the humanities. One of the major
aspects of this phenomenon is the loss of faith in language as a reliable
means of representing reality. Wittgenstein, whose later ideas played a

5. Arthur Schopenhauer, *Parerga and Paralipomena* (Oxford: Oxford University Press,
    1974).
6. Lois Tyson, *Critical Theory Today: A User-Friendly Guide* (London: Routledge,
    2014), 270. And see Michel Foucault, *The History of Sexuality*, vol. 1, *An Introduction*
    (New York: Vintage Books, 1980), 84.

major role in the emergence of this philosophical development, rejected the existence of a single idea "representing reality," and a single, all-encompassing significance to the "reality" represented by language. A large variety of language games describe reality, and they have many and varied connotations. However, the notion that language does not represent reality didn't shake Wittgenstein's conviction that things can be described. Communication means a group of speakers participating in a game. Within this context, their statements are subject to a distinction between "true" and "false."[7] Postmodern thinkers such as Jacques Derrida and Gilles Deleuze radicalized the deconstruction of the monolithic perception of representation to the point where they deconstructed the very idea of representation. They lost faith in the ability of language to represent reality and convey truth; instead of perceiving language as a method of representation, many postmodernists see it as a tool wielded by interested parties. Through discourse, people in society are subjected to a repressive power, the same arbitrary multi-directional force discussed above.

The shift from a modern to a postmodern consciousness and worldview entailed potent social, cultural, economic, and technological changes. First, the materialism of the postmodern era differs from that of the old modern era. Modern capitalism can be characterized, drawing from one of Rabbi Naḥman of Breslov's better-known stories, as a "land of wealth,"[8] a place where money is the only yardstick for measuring the worth, importance, and status of a person. In contrast, the materialism of the postmodern age is characterized by wastefulness. It is not ownership that matters but rather the act of laying claim; not what I have after making a purchase but rather the very act of purchasing. Shopping and consumerism have become ends in themselves, which makes them boundless: After consuming one product I can always consume another. The staggering variety of options creates a horizon that one never reaches, a yearning never fulfilled. The change

---

7. The famous "rule-following paradox," in §§138–202 of Wittgenstein's *Philosophical Investigations*, deals with this issue.
8. "The Master of Prayer," in Aryeh Kaplan, trans., *Rabbi Nachman's Stories* (New York: Breslov Research Institute, 1983), 278.

of emphasis also marks the relationship between manufacturing and consuming: In the postmodern consumerist society, a commodity is not manufactured because it is then consumed, but consumed because it is manufactured.

This process has led to a technology of consumerism. In the past, the act of consuming required concrete action, including contact with the real world. But the act of going to the market has been supplanted by the act of filling a cart in the supermarket, where no real human interaction is required. The market stall vendors and grocers of our youth have been replaced by faceless, interchangeable cashiers. Even food itself has been sealed away in cans and bags, to the point where one can barely touch, smell, or taste it. This technocratization and alienation has been completed with the increasing pervasiveness of online shopping.

In modern capitalism, objects were perceived as candidates for acquisition and ownership, with the objective of self-aggrandizement. In the postmodern era, on the other hand, where purchasing – not ownership – is the main thing, objects become commodities, "opportunities" for the fulfillment of consumerism's goal: the act of consuming and the race to consume. The postmodern act of buying is not about acquisition but about that race. In premodern ownership relations, where the act of purchasing was driven by deficiency, and in modern capitalism, whose overarching motivation was the desire to own more and more property – thus amassing power and social standing – buying had a purpose, an end: the fulfillment of needs and wants, which can engender a state of repose. In the postmodern era, the consumerist drive can never end, as it is an objective in itself.

Another expression of this shift is the growing inundation of media, buoyed by new mass-media technologies: radio, television, and, in more recent years, the Internet. This overload prevents one from pausing or standing still. Its main failing is not its contents – their vulgarity or materialism – but rather the nothingness at its core. The urge to grasp something, physical or spiritual, is of course ancient; the novelty of postmodernism is the absence of the urge, the inability to be inside a thing or to grasp it over time. The media inundation resembles the manufacturing-consuming excess described above: With its swarming superabundance and frenetic variegation, it erodes one's ability to stand still within the flow of information, to process and digest it.[9]

This phenomenon also ties in to changes in the interpersonal realm. Recall the faceless cashier who has taken the place of the neighborhood grocer, exchanging an ongoing personal relationship for a series of utilitarian, random meetings. It is the tip of the iceberg of a deep process in which social relations, too, are turning into consumer relations, a profusion of superficial, fleeting exchanges that cannot develop into a real relationship. Like other areas of life, the social realm has grown subservient to a need for constant stimuli that cannot, by its very nature, be gratified. This trend is especially apparent among couples, whose sex lives often become transient, devoid of depth and real love.[10]

Even the individual has become a commodity and, in a world of "human commodities," has begun to see himself as such. The resulting culture of extroversion engenders split personalities who constantly seek to market themselves to others, even at the price of their own identities. Consciousness becomes fragmented, disjointed.

As noted, these processes are accompanied by powerful technological changes. The virtual world generated by computers and the Internet is emblematic of postmodernism. The pleasure derived from computer gaming may be akin to that of outdoor games, but it cannot develop the social and other skills that they entail, which are acquired only by leaving one's house and being with others. The computer culture nourishes other abilities and proficiencies, represents another kind of friendship and connection, but the change inherent in it goes deeper than the level of know-how and social patterns. The experience of playing in the park with friends facilitates contact with reality. But what kind of reality can we encounter by playing computer games or chatting on the Internet? The computer represents a virtual reality, infinitely manipulative; such play is not rooted in real life, but is fed by the tension of the game itself. The computer screen lacks depth – it displays only the

---

9. In such a context, faith as depth, as pleasure and rootedness, as coziness, becomes impossible. For more, see *Tablets and Broken Tablets*, 226.
10. See Nir Menussi, "The Morning After" [Hebrew], *Eretz Aḥeret* 4 (5761): 40–46.

illusion of depth – and as such is a powerful representation of a flat psychological reality that never encounters anything real: The realness of a thing is replaced by its simulacra.

POSTMODERN NOTHINGNESS

What is the Archimedean point from which one can tie together all these descriptions of the postmodern era? What deep, basic insight does postmodernism voice? The answer is clear: The common thread of the phenomena we have listed is the discovery that there is no common thread, nothing behind them all. In kabbalistic and hasidic terms, postmodernism reveals the *ayin*, or nothingness: Truth has no metaphysical mooring in heaven above, no bedrock to bear it upon the earth below. Faith in the grand ideologies, in man, and in truth is lost; this is the source of the fantastic dimension of postmodern life.

As to the question of "why?" a postmodernist would reply, "Because." There is no justification, no basis. This nothingness is not of the formidable Heideggerian variety; nor is it the mystical, holy, and pleasurable Buddhist nothingness that purges one's awareness of all thought en route to nirvana. It is an unpretentious nothingness, one that has been termed a "dispirited rebellion."[11] It has already been stated that both the mystic and the heretic use the word "nothing"; the difference is that the mystic capitalizes it. The dispiritedness of the postmodernist has a humble quality to it, rendering his nothingness superior to the powerful nothingnesses that preceded it. Yet some describe the postmodern condition as "ecstatic" or "phantasmatic,"[12] highlighting the similar roles played by the nothingnesses that underlie postmodernism and mysticism. In both cases, nothingness is a source of ecstasy and fantasy.

To demonstrate this point, I wish to compare the postmodern nothingness to two other instances of nothingness – in twentieth-century existentialism and in the ideas of Rabbenu Baḥya ibn Pekuda,

---

11. Gadi Taub, *A Dispirited Rebellion: Essays on Contemporary Israeli Culture* [Hebrew] (Tel Aviv: HaKibbutz HaMe'uḥad, 1997).

12. Jean Baudrillard, *The Transparency of Evil* (London: Verso, 1993), 3; Judith Butler, *Bodies That Matter: On the Discursive Limits of Sex* (London: Routledge, 1993), 99.

active in Spain in the early eleventh century and author of the popular *Duties of the Heart* – a seminal text of the *Musar* movement.[13]

One of existentialism's most significant points relates to the question of the purpose of existence: namely, that there is none. Thinkers who arrived at this conclusion were not afraid to rigorously pursue the question of whether one should simply commit suicide.[14] At the root of the question is the excruciating realization that the world is a prison with no justification for existence. Like the existentialists, Rabbenu Baḥya felt trapped, or buried, in the world; he, too, asked himself why he should persist in existence rather than annihilate himself. Unlike them, however, he did not contemplate suicide; the temptation he faced in light of the meaninglessness of his earthly existence was that of renouncing the world, of annihilating his soul through rapturous cleaving to God.[15]

Camus phrased the challenge posed by the torment of meaninglessness as a question – "whether or not one can live *without appeal*"[16] – whose answer is: "Living an experience, a particular fate, is accepting it fully."[17] To cope with a life devoid of meaning, one must not seek out meaning, but rather affirm life as it is; not attempt to refute the disquieting conclusion that life is meaningless, but succeed in leading a meaningless life without becoming unsettled; defusing the potentially paralyzing discovery that there is no answer to the question of life.

For Rabbenu Baḥya, the pious man's response to the same challenge is complete trust in the Lord: He believes that everything befalling him expresses God's mercy and absolute goodness. Like the existentialist, he avoids disquietude by fully accepting his life, but unlike him, his affirmation passes through the religious belief that his life, with all its

13. For more on this comparison, see Rabbi Shagar, *In the Shadow of Faith*, 37–47.
14. For Camus, for example, the question took a very literal turn: To him, it was the only philosophical question. See Albert Camus, *The Myth of Sisyphus and Other Essays* (New York: Vintage Books, 1955).
15. See Baḥya ibn Pekuda, *Duties of the Heart* (Jerusalem: Boys Town, 1962), vol. 1, "Gate of Trust in God," chap. 7, 381. It is interesting to note that even Rabbi Judah Halevi, the most optimistic of the medieval Jewish philosophers, portrays the pious man, in the third part of the *Kuzari*, as one who wishes to die, who is burdened by life.
16. Camus, *Myth of Sisyphus*, 45.
17. Ibid., 40.

trials and tribulations, is a gift from God. Hence the psychological conclusion expressed in this delightful sentence: "I never resolved to do a
thing and longed [to do] something else."[18]

Such acceptance of reality is synonymous with the equanimity
(*hishtavut*) so often praised by the *Rishonim*. This approach eliminates
the conflict between the individual and his life; the duality is dispelled,
making way for an influx of grace. The two poles meet: The existentialist,
who affirms his life by denying outright the existence of a higher stratum of meaning – by rebelling against God – becomes analogous to the
pious man, who regains his life through utter dedication to God. But
the similarity does not efface the difference: To Rabbenu Baḥya, self-
acceptance brings redemption in the light of God's countenance and a
basking in His grace. In his dedication to God, the pious man attains
not only his sought-after tranquility, but also ecstatic love and devotion.
The existentialist, on the other hand, doggedly denies any glimmer of
redemption. His self-acceptance, his return to unity, brooks no deviation. The quiet that follows is not euphoric but gloomy. Even when the
bells of redemption peal – and one can occasionally pick up their faint
echoes reverberating through the foundations of existentialism – the
existentialist denies them outright. It is an essential aspect of his effort
to let go and accept himself.

So why the comparison? Doesn't such a deep disparity render
any similarities imaginary and superficial? Rabbenu Baḥya sets aside his
questions but gains a handsome reward, God's grace, and lives assured
that his is the best of all worlds. The existentialist's world, meanwhile, is
bleak and meaningless. Moreover, the existentialist sees the pious man's
faith as the primary impediment to self-acceptance. The pious man's very
expectation and yearning for something that transcends the human is
a deviation from the self, and as such inherently contradicts the effort
to attain self-acceptance.

But the picture is more nuanced than that, and to portray the
pious man as someone who has gained a prize is to overlook the deeper
meaning of his faith and trust in God. The source of his trust is not the
divine promise of happiness or redemption. It comes from surrendering

---

18. *Duties of the Heart*, loc. cit.

his very need for security, and from a willingness to accept the divine will, whatever it may be, and identify it as good. The pious man's trust is paradoxical, an insecure security, and it entails an excruciating, inhuman concession. His security does not include a material dimension – only thus can it lead to redemption. His world is the best of all worlds, because the meaning of *best* has been fundamentally altered – it is a meaning-less meaning. His world is full of nothingness, so his nothingness is full.[19] What we have here are two parallel psychological processes: The pious man relinquishes security; the existentialist, meaning. Both stand face-to-face with nothingness, which takes on a therapeutic role, annihilating the narrow straits of reality and breaking the individual out of his prison through a process of surrender. Postmodernism takes the existentialist idea further and relinquishes truth along with the very need for it, yet it would seem that the inner process advocated by Camus and Rabbenu Baḥya can be adopted there as well. The proposed surrender would be of a twofold nature: To relinquish truth is to let go of the need for truth, and the result is invariably self-acceptance.

What happens when we surrender and accept ourselves as we are? As noted, it is a dual relinquishment – of absoluteness and, at the same time, of the need for it. The second surrender, which minimizes the significance of the first, marks the release from angst and the onset of ecstasy. It is not the ecstasy of truth but that of life itself, which opens a window onto the vital, infinite joy of all of life. What enables it is the renunciation of the need to grasp, justify, and invoke infinitude. Thus truth ceases to be a condition for life and becomes a product of life, a feature of its vitality.

The comparison between equanimity and postmodern nothing-ness can also be phrased by way of the hasidic distinction between two aspects of God's existence in relation to the cosmos: *sovev kol almin*, "surrounding all worlds," the divine light that encloses the cosmos and is external to it, and *memalei kol almin*, "filling all worlds," the divine light that interpenetrates our reality and dwells within it. The *sovev*, denoted by a circle, is nonhierarchical, and has neither up and down nor good and bad. In terms of the divine infinitude, we cannot speak

---

19. See Rabbi Shagar, *We Will Walk in Fervor*, 147–72.

of absolutes; only the Holy One, blessed be He, is absolute. The rest is a consequence of His will.

Postmodernism's denial of absolutes comes from encountering the perspective of *sovev kol almin*, where nothing is absolute in itself, and there is no up or down. But man cannot live by *sovev* alone. As both Hasidim and *mitnagdim* agree, man exists in the aspect of *memalei kol almin*.[20] In fact, a life founded on the perspective of *sovev* generally leads to nihilism and moral decay. Yet such an outlook can also be positive. It creates a terrific opportunity, because it places one in a world where the divine – or the ethical, which springs from the divine – seems absent, allowing one to make an independent decision to accept the yoke of heaven. This inner process of choice is identical to the one we saw with Rabbenu Baḥya's pious man, who chooses God and, with Him, himself.

Postmodernism's relativist approach parallels aspects of the equanimity of the *Rishonim*, which, as noted, is synonymous with the kabbalists' *sovev kol almin*. From God's point of view, "the darkness is even as the light" (Ps. 139:12), and there is no difference between good and evil; "For I the Lord change not" (Mal. 3:6), which is why creation was never created.[21] Stacked up against the divine infinitude, everything is absolutely equal – not equally valuable, but equally paltry. The innovation of postmodernism lies in its turning this godly perspective into a human one. But that is not the only difference between the manifestations of this idea in Kabbala and Ḥasidut, on the one hand, and in postmodernist thought, on the other. There are two further differences that we must elucidate. First, in the hasidic world, *ayin*, or nothingness, paradoxically affirms *yesh*, existence and being. If not for *ayin*, Rabbi

---

20. Compare Rabbi Shneur Zalman of Liadi, *Tanya*, "Gateway of Unity and Belief," to Rabbi Ḥayim of Volozhin, *Nefesh HaḤayim*, gateway 3, chaps. 4–6.
21. The *Tanya* is a good example of this notion: "But as for His blessed Being and Essence, it is written: 'I the Lord change not'; neither in terms of changes in the development from the uppermost of levels to the nethermost [for just as He, blessed be He, is found in the upper worlds, so He is in precisely that measure in the nether worlds ...], nor in terms of temporal changes [for just as He was alone, one and unique, before the six days of Creation, so He is now after the Creation]. This is so because everything is absolutely as nothing and naught in relation to His being and essence" (*Tanya, Iggeret HaKodesh*, epistle 6).

Shneur Zalman of Liadi taught, everything would return to its source. The *ayin* sustains the *yesh*, for a simple reason: Being is fleeting, relative, and limited, and therefore nonexistent in relation to the light of the divine. Thus, its existence and affirmation must come from without, from a higher level – nothingness.[22] Postmodernism, on the other hand, does not attempt to justify and resurrect the *yesh* through the *ayin*; it leaves the *ayin* as is, seeing it and even trying to subsist in its shadow, so as to derive ethical, social, and political conclusions from it. This difference stems from another: The hasidic and kabbalistic *ayin* is divine, signifying a more sublime, unfathomable reality. In postmodernism, *ayin* is identical to the *ḥalal hapanui*, the void.[23]

HARD AND SOFT POSTMODERNISM

As noted, postmodernism acknowledges that there are no foundations and precepts, all ideals and truths are void, and everything is random and pointless. These aspects are intertwined: Many postmodern thinkers forbid experiencing absence as pleasure or horror, and instead preserve its pointless and random quality. Indeed, that is the criticism lodged by various postmodernist thinkers against the existentialist philosophy of Camus and his colleagues, who wished to celebrate nothingness. The postmodernist, rather, will aim to retain the pointlessness of nothingness. Furthermore, instead of attempting to escape nothingness, he will, on the contrary, try to derive consequences from it and live with it.

But can one truly live with nothingness? The question posed by *Ḥazal* – "Is it possible for a human being to walk after the *Shekhina*?"[24] – is

---

22. The spiritualization of the *yesh*, and the ability to make it infinite, is achieved by turning it into nothingness while maintaining its somethingness, thus rendering it at once finite and infinite. That is the paradoxical secret of *tzimtzum*, which is both "yes" and "no." See Rabbi Dov Ber of Mezeritch, *Maggid Devarav LeYaakov*, ed. Rivka Schatz-Uffenheimer (Jerusalem: Magnes Press, 1976), 24, 74. For more on the relationship between *yesh* and *ayin* in the thought of Rabbi Shneur Zalman of Liadi, see *Torah Or*, 21c and 36b.

23. That is why postmodernism is at risk of falling to the *kelipa* (husk), or evil spiritual force of Amalek, as we will establish below.

24. "R. Ḥama b. R. Ḥanina further said: What is the meaning of the text 'You shall walk after the Lord your God' (Deut. 13:5)? Is it possible for a human being to walk after the *Shekhina*? For has it not been said, 'For the Lord your God is a devouring fire'

---

as relevant to the postmodern nothingness as it was to the holy *ayin* of Ḥazal, the *Rishonim*, and the kabbalists. For nothingness is absence, and therefore it cannot serve as a guide. But beyond this, the crucial point is that one cannot become empowered through the experience of avoidance, deficiency, and disappointment. That is precisely postmodernism's criticism of the modernists, who sought to celebrate nothingness through its absence, to skirt the despair of experiencing nothingness with a process of self-acceptance. That celebration, postmodernism argues, is but another desperate attempt to adopt a posture of metaphysical ability.

And therein is the critical question: Must postmodernism persist as an absence, relegated to nothingness? Does randomness necessarily lead to pointlessness? Here the path forks into what several thinkers and experts have referred to as "hard" and "soft" postmodernism.[25] Hard postmodernism barricades itself behind absence and negation, consequently sliding into meaninglessness and nihilism, truthlessness and extreme relativism. It flattens and fragments reality. It moves to deconstruct the subject, ruling out entirely the subject's unity, and sees the subject as a mere junction in a game of discourse/power that is itself centerless, as it represents a disinterested interest. Soft postmodernism, meanwhile – if we take the question of ethical intervention as an example – translates nothingness into equality, freedom, and even merit. Its proponents argue that in the current climate, not only does postmodernist thought not necessarily lead to nihilism, but on the contrary, it alone can establish an ethical self that is not a self-deception. Only postmodernism can produce an individual who acts ethically without invoking assorted grand ideologies – which are doomed by their very absoluteness – to justify his ethicality. Indeed, one can find many patently postmodernist thinkers at the vanguard of the struggle

---

(ibid. 4:24)? But [the meaning is] to walk after [i.e., emulate] the attributes of the Holy One, blessed be He" (Sota 14a; cf. Leviticus Rabba 25:3).

25. For more on hard and soft postmodernism, see Ilan Gur-Ze'ev, *Toward Diasporic Education* [Hebrew] (Tel Aviv: Resling, 2006), 13–24. [Ed. note: This terminology was coined by Millard J. Erickson in his *The Postmodern World: Discerning the Times and the Spirit of Our Age* (Wheaton, IL: Crossway Books, 2002), 97, and popularized in D. A. Carson, *Becoming Conversant with the Emerging Church: Understanding a Movement and Its Implications* (Grand Rapids, MI: Zondervan, 2005).]

for social justice, proving that postmodernism does not invariably lead to moral decay and nihilism.[26]

Still, soft postmodernism does not deny the absolute absence to which hard postmodernism points. Moreover, in the ethical realm it seems that many postmodernist thinkers are not motivated by moral truth, for they rule out the possibility of shoring up such a truth: For them, the need for equality does not spring from a conception of all humans being equal and possessing value, since there are no values – no truth value and no value to truth. No, their hope for equality is founded on nothingness itself: Everyone is correct because everyone is incorrect, and all are thus equally entitled to injustice.[27]

How does soft postmodernism embark on this or that social struggle? Indeed, if there is no principle at its core, no truth value to which to aspire, how can one even struggle and debate? Is it inconsistent of postmodernism to become involved in ethical questions? What can it defend, and for what purpose? Clearly, the contradiction exists, but equanimity can overcome language at the level of such inconsistencies. Such is the restrained silence of Rabbi Naḥman, with which he vaults over the paradoxical conundrums of the *ḥalal hapanui* without obscuring or running from them.[28] The postmodernist remains vigilant, lest he turn that restraint into an exclamation of triumph, an expression of ability – not even a power to establish values – for doing so would betray the insight of nothingness. His silence is no more than a shrug, not even an elaborate gesture of despair. He remains humble; not with a humility that is too great or sees value in itself, but with a humility that grows out of an earnest acceptance of valuelessness.

THE HUSK OF AMALEK VERSUS SELF-ACCEPTANCE

Clearly, some postmodernists suffer from an internal contradiction. The paradox is well known: If everything is to be doubted – even the assertion that nothing has value and everything is based on conditioning – then

---

26. See below, chapter 6.
27. Hence the profound difference between modern and postmodern democracy. See *Tablets and Broken Tablets*, 275–82.
28. Rabbi Naḥman, *Likkutei Moharan, Kamma* 64; *Tablets and Broken Tablets*, 395–96.

the same can be said of their ideas, and even the preceding statement is not binding.[29] This is the case not only with soft postmodernism, but also with the hard variety, which ostensibly forswears all absolutes. The realization that the yardstick is part of what is being measured – "like the grasshopper, whose clothing is part of itself"[30] – that anyone applying a yardstick is already the product of the very same yardstick, leads to absolute immanence, the denial of any metaphysical or transcendent dimension. Consequently, one is once again left without an external perspective from which to gauge and justify things. But if so, the same can be said of the assertion itself: It too is a product of unprovable preconceptions. We thus arrive at the famous Wittgensteinian idea of "nonsense": the paradoxical questions that can be greeted with nothing but a silent shrug.[31]

In the final analysis, hard postmodernism too makes a positive statement. In asserting that all is a product of conditioning, or that all is random and pointless, it expresses an outlook, thus diverging from the silence it otherwise seems to apply to everything. Furthermore, its technique for subsuming things in nothingness is the opposite of the one practiced by the kabbalists: Instead of spiritualizing reality by bringing it into *ayin*, nothingness, it nullifies everything that lies beyond reality, stripping reality bare. In kabbalistic terminology, it constitutes the husk of Amalek, defending a conception of being that rules out all metaphysics and designates reality as – to quote Ecclesiastes – "under the sun."[32]

---

29. For a precise formulation of the paradox, see Gur-Ze'ev, *Toward Diasporic Education*, 22–23.

30. See Genesis Rabba 21:5; *Pesikta Zutra* on Gen. 3:22.

31. Wittgensteinian nonsense is not merely another of nothingness' gestures. In contrast to the postmodern stance, for Wittgenstein the solution is a silence that defends the mystical. See Wittgenstein, *Tractatus Logico-Philosophicus*, secs. 6.522 and 7, pp. 73–74; *Tablets and Broken Tablets*, 233–35.

32. At first glance (and perhaps this is the principal way of looking at it, the one that is most often relevant), hard postmodernism is the husk of Amalek, which, the Torah teaches us, cannot be raised up, only eradicated. Its purpose is to be struggled against, a struggle that may be fruitful but eventually must lead to the overcoming of the Amalekite outlook. Yet there is a higher level at which it *can* be raised up and rectified. I refer to Derrida's prayer or Gilles Deleuze's "non-spatio-temporal" view of reality, both of which eventually become mystical (see *Tablets and Broken Tablets*,

The hard postmodernist must recognize the nothingness of his stance, which comes up against an internal contradiction between its rejection of all external justifications and the fact that, like all stances, it itself requires such justification. This nothingness is identical to the nothingness of all *yesh*, or existence. The husk of Amalek, the conception of a pure *yesh*, cannot justify itself – it too must either concede the existence of external underpinnings or acknowledge its inherent contradiction.

But soft postmodernism, though often perceived as diluted and inconsistent, offers a more nuanced, sublime stance. Through it, one can take postmodernism's nothingness and randomness in another direction and say that in the absence of an absolute truth, truth becomes specific and relative. It is a truth whose unpretentiousness and humility are apparent in its very reluctance to refer to itself as truth. In fact, it represents the act of letting go, of accepting oneself as flawed. In this movement toward self-acceptance, an individual experiences once more the oneness of the *yesh* and the wholeness of reality, even if the wholeness is specific and consequently imperfect, even when he is aware that its justification is local and thus devoid of all-encompassing absoluteness. Despite the limitations of such self-acceptance, through it an individual can experience ecstasy and even mystical rapture.[33]

RANDOMNESS, POINTLESSNESS, AND ECSTASY

The difference between the two forms of postmodernism may lie in deconstructing the association of randomness with meaninglessness. According to hard postmodernism, randomness necessarily entails pointlessness, while soft postmodernism sees the second as independent of the first. That is the import of the willingness to let go of *the* truth and

---

235–40). These ideas are reminiscent of Rabbi Naḥman's approach to "conundrums from the *ḥalal hapanui*" (see Rabbi Naḥman, *Likkutei Moharan*, loc. cit), which at first glance cannot be raised up and must be vaulted over, but which the *tzaddik*, on second glance, can find ways to sublimate and rectify.

33. This is the meaning of the ecstasy, irony, fantasy, and similar experiences described by postmodernist thinkers as characteristics of the postmodern age. See Gur-Ze'ev, *Toward Diasporic Education*, 17–18, 27. Hence the carnivalesque, even pagan quality of this era, which is linked to the New Age movement. See below, chapter 9.

settle for a specific truth: The specific truth may be random, a product of the random circumstances and conditioning that have caused a person to live in a certain era and place, and yet it is not pointless – it has meaning for the individual who takes it upon himself.

How does soft postmodernism overcome the pointlessness that emerges from hard postmodernism's critique? Once one has fully apprehended the stark, all-encompassing randomness described by hard postmodernism, can one back away from it and affirm a random, specific truth, accepting it wholeheartedly and honestly as such? I believe such a development is possible, even if it necessitates painful compromises. Indeed, the ability to do so is linked to the two points discussed above. First is the dual relinquishment of both absolute truth and the need for it, a process we termed "self-acceptance." Second is the paradoxicality of hard postmodernism. The awareness that one cannot say anything absolute – which applies even to the very statement that one cannot say anything absolute – enables one to break free of all-encompassing randomness. That randomness, it turns out, also includes assertions that cannot be substantiated. It emerges that in the dual relinquishment lies the possibility of a life of greater exactitude.

But where does the ecstasy come from? Beyond the above suggestion that it is generated by the individual's acceptance of his flawed self, ecstasy arises in the soft postmodernist due to the release from the need for absolute truth – as a postmodernist, one is of course painfully aware of one's inability to shore up such a truth – and the acceptance of a specific truth as his life's truth. Such a person encounters the *ayin* and knows it; in effect, he conducts himself without pretense. The ecstasy, thus, emerges not from the specific truth itself, but rather from life with nothingness, which, as soon as one accepts it, is revitalized, becoming a full life, imbued with calm and inner suppleness. This acceptance, which can be described in hasidic terms as *bitul*, or self-nullification, is a relinquishment of truth and an expression of willingness to "celebrate" nothingness. To my mind, not only does this stance not contradict faith, it refines it. By denying the idea of truth and the modern ideological system, postmodernism frees faith from the clutches of modernity and the limitations (rationalism, positivism, historicism, psychology) that it imposed on the believer.[34] The postmodernist relinquishment of truth makes faith possible, rendering it more humble and playful, and consequently more spiritual.[35]

Ultimately, both hard and soft postmodernism derives from the most profound, basic will, in the Nietzschean sense of the word. In kabbalistic terms, the will is the inner aspect of the *sefira* of *keter*, the Crown, which precedes *ḥokhma*, Wisdom. Thus, the choice between (1) accepting ourselves, establishing a specific rather than general truth, and drawing the basic insight of postmodern *ayin* into our lives, and (2) leading a life fractured by nothingness, randomness, and pointlessness, is not a rational decision based on some insight or wisdom, but rather a stance emanating from the will. Indeed, will, too, cannot be established as anything other than the result of conditioning, but there is no need to establish it as such, since accepting it on a specific level also means accepting the conditionings of that specificity. To take such a stand is to live with nothingness humbly, but with the ecstasy of one whose humility has freed him of the painful burden of imaginary absoluteness.

---

34. This description echoes the way Rabbi Kook conceived of atheism: a historical process that sublimates faith, a repentance of sorts for religiosity. Modern atheism, he claimed, purges religion of the idolatrous traces in the attempt to define the divine. See, for example, Rabbi Abraham Isaac Kook, *Orot* (Jerusalem: Mossad HaRav Kook, 5755), 124–29.

35. This spirit of whimsy is expressed through the injection of faith with a humorous dimension. As Rabbi Naḥman wrote, the power of humor lies in its capacity to illuminate the limitations of our world in relation to the divine infinitude. See more in his story "The Humble King," in Kaplan, *Rabbi Nachman's Stories*, 128.

Chapter Six

Justice and Ethics in a Postmodern World

INTRODUCTION

In recent years many moral questions have arisen from the legitimization of ethical and moral pluralism and multiculturalism. Does the democratic West have the right to preach its own ethics to peoples who, for reasons of religion or tradition, oppose it? Is it incumbent upon the West to rail against such customs as widow burning and female genital mutilation, or is railing against these practices a vestige of patronizing Western colonialism?

Of course, questions relating to pluralism and moral relativism do not begin with postmodernism; they were part and parcel of the modern world and perhaps even preceded it. Yet there is no doubt that

---

This essay is based on a draft written in 5762 and was edited for *Broken Vessels* by Odeya Tzurieli under the title "Values and Faith in a Postmodern Age," 13–28; the essay included the discussion on postmodernism and mysticism. The sections regarding the question of morality in a postmodern world were re-edited after the author's death by Dr. Itamar Brenner and Dr. Zohar Maor for publication in *Tablets and Broken Tablets*, 68–84, and supplemented with other drafts to add clarity, especially regarding Rabbi Naḥman of Breslov, several aspects of whose outlook Rabbi Shagar deals with here.

in the postmodern framework – which cannot discuss absolute values because it does not acknowledge the existence of such values – the questions grow more acute.[1] Even the sanctity of human life and the attendant prohibition of murder are not absolute, overarching values or imperatives. There is no truth, certainly not with a capital T. In such a world, truth is a cultural product or artifact. Every truth hinges on specific cultural and social contexts and is perceived as something that benefits specific interests. That is the "politics of truth," or, as Nietzsche phrased it, "Values and their changes are related to increases in the power of those positing the values."[2]

Hence the paradox as to the proper response to acts of violence that are moored in certain cultures: On the one hand, our own values require us to uproot such atrocities and prevent them from occurring; on the other, we are aware, on a philosophical and anthropological level, that every society has its own culture and values, and that, from the point of view of some societies, violent acts such as honor killings protect the community and its values; it is even seen as immoral to refrain from such behaviors. From this vantage, one can argue that not only must we avoid preventing others from engaging in actions that we consider immoral, but that we should enable such actions, perhaps even fund them if necessary. Indeed, the Israeli anthropologist Dan Rabinowitz reports on such a trend:

> In some cities in England that feature sizable populations of African immigrants, and especially from places where it was customary to mutilate the genitals of female babies and children, city council members faced a difficult dilemma. The immigrant citizens, who constituted a significant electoral power, demanded

---

1. For a discussion of the problem of pluralism in this context, see, for example, J. J. Ross, "The Common Moral and the Public Moral and the Dilemma of Education," in Yuval Lurie and Haim Marantz, eds., *In the Labyrinth of Democracy: Philosophical Essays on Democratic Themes* [Hebrew] (Beersheba: Ben-Gurion University Press, 1990), 137–55.
2. Friedrich Nietzsche, *The Will to Power* (New York: Vintage Books, 1968), 14.

that the practices be included in the list of elective surgeries covered by National Health insurance.[3]

These citizens, who lead a Muslim lifestyle, demanded that the municipality not only allow them to circumcise their daughters, but finance the procedure.

> Thus they will save a lot of money, spare their daughters the risk inherent in carrying out the mutilation without medical supervision and basic hygienic conditions, and, most important, have the opportunity to preserve their culture proudly and publicly. There was at least one city in which the procedure was added to the list of treatments covered by public funds.[4]

On a theoretical level, such dilemmas pose interesting intellectual puzzles, but how, in our postmodern world, should we conduct ourselves in practice? Can I, as an ethical person, ignore the point of view of a member of another culture? Can I ignore a perspective capable of justifying the world of values that gives rise to such action, which according to my values is a despicable crime? Furthermore, in accepting the critical outlook that opposes the imposition of white, European values on a world that, to white Europeans, may appear primitive, can we avoid cherishing the other's point of view?

A QUESTION OF BOUNDARIES

Similarly, what is our position regarding *sati*, widow burning, which is still practiced by some in India? From our perspective, this custom is extremely immoral, yet some women believe that burning themselves alongside their husband's bodies is the best thing for the souls of all concerned. The perplexed postmodernist will have "double vision": While

---

3. Dan Rabinowitz, "The Twisting Journey for the Rescue of Brown Women" [Hebrew], *Theory and Criticism (Teoria U'vikoret)* 7 (1995): 14–15.
4. Ibid., 15.

railing against the practice, he will also be able to see the issue from the point of view of those who practice *sati*.

Such examples reflect, more than anything, the fact that our discussion revolves around a question of boundaries. Apparently there are issues about which even the staunchest relativist will put his foot down and say, "Enough!" Rabinowitz cites the anthropologist Melvin Konner, who states that the genital mutilation of women is "one place where we ought to draw the line." This means, Rabinowitz adds, that it is "a place where we must suspend relativism and stop what we perceive as evil." Yet he ultimately rejects Konner's assertion, arguing that any attempt to impose our own ethics on another culture that is, in one way or another, under our control is untenable. The best we can do, he says, is to discourage such actions, using rationales drawn from that culture.[5] Still, even Rabinowitz appears to have boundaries; he too finds some actions unacceptable, even when those who commit them consider them ethical. One example of such extreme action is genocide: While the genocidal culture may view the specific mass murder as an ethical act that rectifies society and the world, we cannot abide such action. We will rail against it and work to end it.

To prevent postmodernism from sliding into absurdity, we must set boundaries. Where is the line at which the postmodernist will refuse to accept the other's values? What criteria and methods should be used for setting such boundaries? And can one propose other ways of coping with the paradox of pluralism, which is amplified in the postmodern era?

SOFT JUSTICE

The question with which we are dealing is, at bottom, about possible manifestations of justice in a relativistic framework. In his discussion of justice in the postmodern world, the culture scholar David Gurevitz coined an apt term: "soft justice," or "weak justice."

> The question of justice is no longer a question of knowledge, no longer an epistemological question. It is a question of opinions, ones that are not shored up by conclusive reasoning and informed

---

5. Ibid., 12, 15.

by overarching metanarratives that posit ultimate codes for the interpretation of reality.... It is thus a "weak justice," deriving from a pluralistic reality that accommodates competing, irreconcilable models of justice.[6]

We no longer expect a grand, ultimate justice. Such a justice is unjustifiable and nowhere to be found. The best we can hope for is a specific, weak justice. That justice is generated not by a series of metaphysical arguments, but by human discourse and compromise. As Gurevitz emphasizes, by letting go of the need for hard justice, two rival sides can begin to communicate and resolve profound conflicts pragmatically, ultimately facilitating a reality far more just than the one engendered by the constant struggle between conflicting conceptions of supreme justice. There are several possible models of soft justice, all relinquishing the presumption of absoluteness. Yet, he notes, soft justice has its own limits, and at bottom relies on nonrelativistic assumptions, such as the belief in human rationality, whose absence would preclude fertile discourse and accord.

Phrasing the ideals of soft justice requires terminology that diverges from the language used to define hard justice. For instance, Richard Rorty claimed we should set aside the metaphorical notion of finding truth in favor of the idea that truth is made and shaped.[7] The discovery metaphor causes people to feel they have found *the* truth, which leaves no room for other truths. The idea that truth is created, on the other hand, encourages one to acknowledge that every value is the product of a certain society, and that, in consequence, the claim that it contradicts other societies' values is meaningless. In this context, "justice" means the justice of a certain society. To that society, such justice is true and legitimate, but it is not justice in the universal, overarching sense, and in other environments and cultures, it may seem utterly unjust. Indeed, it appears that only through such

6. David Gurevitz, "The Meaning of Justice in the Age of Frivolity" [Hebrew], *Alpayim* 9 (1991): 167.
7. Richard Rorty, *Contingency, Irony, and Solidarity* (Cambridge: Cambridge University Press, 1989), 7.

relinquishment of absolute justice can we attain harmony both inside and outside our society.

The question for us is whether Judaism can abide such soft conceptions, which anchor justice, and perhaps truth too, in social norms? To my mind, there is a Jewish spiritual outlook that can accommodate the pluralistic mindset while setting its own boundaries for it.

RABBI NAḤMAN AND THE UNANSWERABLE QUESTIONS

In one of his better-known discourses, Rabbi Naḥman of Breslov detects a contradiction at the very base of human experience.[8] He refers to this contradiction as "conundrums without answers" or "conundrums from the void" (*kushiyot mehaḥalal hapanui*).

Rabbi Naḥman opens with the assertion that "due to His mercifulness, the Lord, blessed be He, created the world, for he wished to reveal His mercifulness." It is a difficult claim. As the poet Yehuda Amichai wrote in his poem *El Malei Raḥamim*, "Know that if not for the God-full-of-mercy / There would be mercy in the world, / Not just in Him."[9] Had God created a better world, perhaps there would be no need for mercy toward Him and us. Yet I think Rabbi Naḥman really claims not that the Holy One, blessed be He, created the world so He would have someone to whom to show mercy, but rather that the fundamental note of creation, the thing it reveals, is mercy. It is not mercy evoked by a specific, concrete condition – for instance, a person in a difficult situation; rather, mercy is linked to the basic paradox of creation as a whole, and specifically to human existence. Rabbi Naḥman explains this conflict through the kabbalistic idea of *tzimtzum*:

> This constriction (*tzimtzum*), which made way for the void (*halal hapanui*), will be comprehensible only in the Messianic Age,

8. Rabbi Naḥman, *Likkutei Moharan, Kamma* 64. For a lucid portrayal of this discourse and its basic ideas, see Eliezer Malkiel, *Wisdom and Simplicity* [Hebrew] (Tel Aviv: Yediot, 2005), chap. 5. See also Rabbi Shagar's commentary on this discourse in his *Expositions on Likkutei Moharan*, vol. 2, 270–89.

9. Yehuda Amichai, "God Full of Mercy," in *Yehuda Amichai: A Life of Poetry, 1948–1994*, ed. and trans. Benjamin Harshav and Barbara Harshav (New York: HarperCollins, 1995), 31.

as one must note that it comprises two diametrically opposed aspects. The *ḥalal hapanui* came about through the constriction, for He withdrew His divinity from there, so to speak, and no divinity remains there, so to speak. Were that not the case, it would not be a void, everything would be infinitude (*ein sof*), and there would be no space in which to create the cosmos. But the truth is that there is nevertheless divinity there, too, for indeed nothing can exist without His vitality. That is why the void will remain utterly inscrutable until the Messianic Age.

According to Rabbi Naḥman, *tzimtzum* is a paradox: On the one hand, in order for the world to exist, the Holy One, blessed be He, must withdraw from the cosmos. On the other, it is impossible for anything to exist without God. Conceptions of God's infinitude and unity, to the effect that "the entire world is filled with His glory" (Is. 6:3), imply that nothing exists outside of Him, and, consequently, that there can be no existence devoid of divine vitality. In any event, the reality of the *ḥalal hapanui* is at the root of all the metaphysical contradictions that cannot be resolved in a rational manner.

How does this tie in to the question of postmodern justice? I contend that the aforementioned contradiction[10] is among the conundrums for which Rabbi Naḥman said there is no solution. Let us revisit the ethical dilemma raised above: Do we have the right to intervene and impose our values on, for instance, Druze who harm a woman for betraying the laws of the sect? As noted, we can always employ – indeed, we cannot avoid – the reflexive point of view, which looks at everything in context. To fully embrace this outlook is to concede that my truth possesses no more value than the truth of a member of any other culture, and that I have no right to intervene in his world. It is a point of view embodying the perspective of the divine infinitude, which can contain all opinions. Yet I am still a specific person with my own specific truth, an individual who believes in his truth and who thus cannot deny it, nor does he wish to do so.

---

10. See p. 106.

The paradox can also be expressed by way of the dichotomy between two perspectives. On the one hand, there is a perspective of equanimity, which involves the nullification of all traits and values in the face of the divine infinitude, and disregards *tzimtzum* and the formation of the *ḥalal hapanui*. On the other hand is belief in oneself and one's values, from the perspective of our relativistic existence in a world where God is concealed and the *ḥalal hapanui* exists. This paradox encapsulates the paradoxical nature of *tzimtzum*: On the one hand, the Holy One, blessed be He, constricted Himself in order to make room for the cosmos and for man; on the other, "I the Lord change not" (Mal. 3:6), and the all-consuming divine infinitude is still present.[11]

Coping with this contradiction requires the belief that one's truth is a manifestation of God despite its relativity. The Lord is in everything; as the Hasidim say, "no place is empty of Him."[12] He is omnipresent, including in my own existence and values, which are thus a certainty. True, one can always ask, "But don't other people and other societies have different values?" But that possibility must not diminish the fact that I, too, have a certainty that I am unwilling to relinquish, a truth to which I will dedicate myself, for which I am willing to die, even kill (the last is the most difficult and severe of actions).

How can the two points of view coexist? How am I to harmonize my acknowledgment of the relativity of my truth with the clear conviction that I will not compromise on that truth?

These conundrums have no solutions, and Rabbi Naḥman proposes silence as an alternative. He cites the midrash in which Moses challenges God over the cruel fate suffered by R. Akiva. "Such Torah, and such a reward!?" Moses cries out as the great sage's flesh is weighed out in the marketplace. But God responds, "Be silent, for such is My

---

11. Both Rabbi Shneur Zalman of Liadi and Rabbi Ḥayim of Volozhin explained that *tzimtzum* was not an absolute historical act, which is why one can move between a perspective that includes *tzimtzum* and one in which everything is infinitude, but they explained these two perspectives differently. See Tamar Ross, "Two Interpretations of the Doctrine of *Tzimtzum*: Ḥayim of Volozhin and Shneur Zalman of Liadi" [Hebrew], *Meḥkerei Yerushalayim BeMaḥshevet Yisrael* 2 (1981): 153–69.

12. *Tikkunei Zohar* 81b. Various hasidic writings played up this statement and greatly expanded its meaning.

decree."[13] In other words, the solution is not on the intellectual plane; it is a reaction, or, more precisely, an abstention – not evasion but, rather, an authentic expression of a human situation that acknowledges its own complicatedness and refuses to deny any of its constituent parts. The fact that we cannot substantiate our own values, and will always doubt their truth, must not prevent us from continuing to believe in them. At some point, I will stop asking – not because I have an answer, but because the answer no longer concerns me. It is the point where faith becomes absolute.

Rabbi Naḥman's greatness manifests in his power to turn paradoxes into a means by which to cleave to God. Such is the case with the example above: It is likely that were any of us – Jews influenced by Western culture – to encounter a Druze who intended to murder a family member for betraying the sect, we would not stand aside. Without devoting too much thought to it, we would use any means at our disposal – including killing the would-be murderer – in order to prevent the woman's death.

Why? On the absolute level, there is no answer. In another discourse,[14] Rabbi Naḥman teaches that there are three possible responses to such paradoxical questions and situations: affirmation, denial, or a silence and deferral that reject the very premise of the question. Some questions not only have no answer, but require none – only faith. Paradoxical as it may be – and Rabbi Naḥman was singularly adept at formulating paradox – faith will persevere.

In the same discourse, Rabbi Naḥman also discusses disagreements, claiming that they too emanate from the *ḥalal hapanui*. In our context, such disagreements are represented as varying ethical standpoints. According to Rabbi Naḥman, it would be incorrect to state that one outlook is absolutely wrong and the other absolutely correct. Rather, the argument gives voice to a metaphysical dichotomy and requires me to adopt a dual point of view: While acknowledging that the competing ethical outlook is an expression of some aspect of the divine, I must staunchly adhere to my own outlook.

---

13. Menaḥot 29b.
14. Rabbi Naḥman, *Likkutei Moharan*, Kamma 6.

In comparing Rabbi Naḥman's stance with the aforementioned idea of "soft justice" – i.e., the postmodernist claim that justice does not derive from a constant metaphysical truth but is, rather, the product of social dynamics – we can establish that one must respect and grant significance to every opinion (this is the gist of Rabbi Naḥman's oft-repeated imperative to view others in a positive light) without diminishing one's respect for one's own opinion. Nor does Rabbi Naḥman posit a conclusive rational or Judaic mechanism for reconciling variant opinions. Instead he explains that it is precisely disagreement that clears the way for truth to manifest. In fact, he notes that the Torah is made up of discussions and debates.[15] Yet one cannot justify in this manner each and every opinion and ethical stance. Not every conundrum and argument derives from the *ḥalal hapanui*.

In the ethical context, the practical implication of Rabbi Naḥman's position is that it is incumbent on me to prevent a member of a different culture from harming another if I believe his action is immoral – even if his faith and culture compels him to do so, and even if, after the fact, I will be hard-pressed to justify the stance that spurred me to action, or to prove that it is preferable to the other's cultural outlook.[16]

One can extend Rabbi Naḥman's approach beyond questions of ethics and apply it to the human condition as a whole. Many people ask themselves whether their lives have value, even when they are fully aware that their very existence benefits another – supporting a dependent, educating someone, bettering the world, and so on. In the end, we all die, as do those whom we helped and who depended on us, and nothing remains. Yet we believe our actions carry eternal value. They are *our* actions, *our* faith, *our* truth, and their eternality is embodied in

---

15. See, for example, Rabbi Naḥman, *Likkutei Moharan, Kamma* 142; Rabbi Shagar, *In the Shadow of Faith*, 209–25.

16. Writings by rabbis in the Chabad movement often employ a similar argument to prove the unbreakable bond between the Jew and faith in God and the Torah. They point to the Jew's willingness to give his life to sanctify the name of heaven in a difficult hour and when it is a matter of principle, a willingness that constitutes "self-sacrifice beyond reason and logic," and they see this as proof that a Jew's soul cleaves to its Jewishness and to God. Of course, these writings do not acknowledge the relativity of this faith, and see it as an absolute truth.

their very presence in the here and now. Like the postmodernist, Rabbi Naḥman knows that the ultimate metaphysical questions transcend language and logic. But unlike the postmodernist, who deduces that these questions are thus meaningless, Rabbi Naḥman uses this knowledge to open up the possibility of faith. Like many other religious thinkers long before him,[17] he knows that absolute statements overstep the range of possible language games, and that silence is no less human – and no less meaningful – than speech.

In summation, let us return to the question of boundaries in light of the idea of soft justice (which, as noted, is congruent with Rabbi Naḥman's metaphysical stance), and apply it to the question of honor killings, female genital mutilation, and widow burning. One can describe two possible approaches: The first sets a boundary based on one's ingrained sense of morality, even if one cannot find absolute, universal justification for it; the second requires negotiating between the Western worldview and the worldview that justifies such actions, and acknowledges the respective values that undergird the two clashing outlooks – for instance, the value of family versus the value of the sanctity of life. Such dialogue can yield boundaries that are acceptable

---

17. The *Rishonim* and *Aḥaronim* were well aware of the relativity of every human utterance, but to defend the truthfulness of the faith they were forced to establish a hierarchy of truths. See, for example, the Maharal of Prague's concept of "truth due to," in his *Derush al HaTorah*. The test that established this hierarchy was not generally about content, meaning a thing's proximity to a certain truth content, but formalistic-ontological, relating to a thing's similarity to the divine unity. Sartre employed a similar device in *Existentialism Is a Humanism*, in which he defended himself against claims that existentialism was immoral. Another example is Rabbi Israel Salanter's approach to the question of man's capacity to attain truth. His problem was psychological; he did not believe man could purge himself of ulterior motives and arrive at the unadulterated truth (today this problem is framed as sociocultural – an inability to break free of social conditioning – rather than psychological): "For even after all his thoughts are purified, he cannot be sure the forces of his own psyche are not getting in the way" (Mordechai Pachter, ed., *The Writings of Rabbi Israel Salanter* [Hebrew] [Jerusalem: Dorot, 5733], 141). For a detailed analysis of Rabbi Salanter's point of view, see Rabbi Shagar, *On His Torah He Meditates*, 59 ff. It appears as if contemporary faith has been freed of the need to establish a hierarchy. While there are sources to that effect, they go beyond the scope of this footnote.

to both sides and, while preventing the killing, safeguard tradition and the absolute value that it assigns to family.

POSITIVE PLURALISM

The paradoxical nature of postmodernism, as described above, is a feature of postmodern pluralism, which is stark and comprehensive in its acknowledgment that all stances are the product of historical and social circumstances, of conditionings that have no absolute metaphysical justifications. It is this acknowledgment that generates postmodernism's paradoxes, contradictions, and despair.[18]

Yet I believe in pluralism, even if it differs from the pluralism of postmodernism: It is a positive pluralism, one of faith. The difference between the pluralism in which I believe and postmodern pluralism springs from the difference between uninspired relativism and a relativism open to inspiration; between a conception of postmodernism as an empty game and one that ascribes significance to it; between ascribing no weight or value to any opinion, including one's own, and seeing value in each and every opinion. Such a way of thinking deconstructs Rorty's dichotomy, mentioned above, between truth that is revealed and truth that is shaped or created. To me, the creative act reveals the divine through the human. All truths may be the product of human conditioning, but such conditioning constitutes the medium through which the divine manifests in the world. That is why the pluralist believer does not shy away from using the revelation metaphor; though he knows there are varying and conflicting revelations, the contradictions do not paralyze him. He is willing to concede that truth is a human construct, because he knows that human constructs are true creations, manifestations of God in a world that is "filled with His glory," not an empty, meaningless game.[19]

Indeed, I believe in the possibility of a positive, faith-filled pluralism. I am willing to open up to human creativity and see it as divine

---

18. As stated, the dilemma described here is rooted in the very nature of pluralism (which predates postmodernism) but is sharpened and amplified in the postmodern era.
19. For more on the relationship between faith and the question of truth as a human construct, see *On His Torah He Meditates*, 181–230.

inspiration, even though I am fully aware that creativity has many vectors, some of them contradictory. My encounters with various believers and nonbelievers will not weaken my belief, but rather strengthen it, for contending with the outside view of my faith has the power to free it of its subjectivity. Moreover, the process of becoming acquainted with alternatives to my own faith, and choosing it anew nonetheless, allows me to form a "face-to-face" bond that is more exalted than the superficial "back-to-back" relationship. Walking the path of the Hasidim and Rabbi Kook, I will be able to identify the divine in all things, without devaluing my own faith, but rather reinforcing it.[20] Traditional theological debates that sought absolute, transcendental criteria to determine which belief reigns supreme are meaningless in a postmodern world, but that should not impugn our perseverance in the faith of our fathers. We must see such faith as our home, self-evident and unquestionable, and thus in no need of such tests.[21]

I must take the ethical game as a given and play it, as I do the religious game: acting ethically and religiously out of a conviction that what I believe is true, but without going so far as to assert that faith in my own way renders other ways worthless. To turn my faith into something absolute, objective, and contextless is to fashion it into an ideology, an idol.[22]

The doubting of faith's universal absoluteness – postmodernism excels at this – has a balancing, productive role: It does not stifle our capacity to experience and believe in ourselves, but it does generate boundaries. The postmodern believer's awareness of the contradictions between various faiths, and of the paradoxes inherent in his own world, can stabilize him, rendering him more sensitive, ethical, and humble. The

---

20. Obviously, on an educational level, there is room to debate the correct age and developmental stage at which young people should be exposed to this more nuanced point of view. To my mind, young children are better suited to the ultra-Orthodox educational approach, which is based on a more inward-looking paradigm that does not often encounter the Other or an external perspective. Still, adhering to this approach in more advanced educational stages runs the risk of shaping an insular, rigid view of the world.
21. Furthermore, the very existence of faith and inspiration, which can strike at any moment, may bolster human solidarity. See below, chapter 10.
22. See *Tablets and Broken Tablets*, 399.

Muslim will remain Muslim and adhere to his faith. But if he, too, will adopt the reflexive point of view characteristic of the West, he will see me as a Jew, while I will see him as a Muslim and recognize his beliefs. Together, perhaps we will be able to generate human solidarity. This will come to pass when, on the one hand, "enlightened" Westerners stop trying to foist their values on all other cultures, and, on the other hand, fundamentalist Muslims cease their violent attempts to impose their own beliefs on the world.

However, the pluralistic aspect must be augmented by a universal dimension, meaning the knowledge that, beyond our various cultural differences, there is a universal truth shared by all humans, that "the earth is all of one piece."[23] The fact that there are elements and motifs that recur across various cultures, even those that are distant from one another, indicates a shared foundation that is inherent to our very humanity. That is why I can, for example, read and comprehend the words of a Chinese thinker who lived hundreds of years ago, and they will be relevant to me, even though we belong to vastly different cultures and epochs. This points to something that lies beyond our subjectivity and cultural perceptions. The world is not merely a collection of assorted cultures whose distinct contexts preclude intercultural communication; there is a common kernel of humanity. Indeed, this shared bedrock cannot be presented in an *a priori* manner; as we have seen, a pluralistic approach that promotes knowledge of, and respect for, the opinions of the Other is required if one is to locate the common motifs. Through pluralism, not only can I respect an ethical stance or article of faith that differs from my own, but I can dialogue with it, and in certain instances critique it.

By combining this universal point of view with doubt in the universality and absoluteness of any individual stance, every culture can accept other cultures as true alternatives that carry a kernel of truth. If more of us humbly acknowledge the limited capacity of the individual to utter absolute statements, perhaps we can establish justice and ethics alongside a renewed human solidarity.

---

23. Bava Batra 67a.

Chapter Seven

Mysticism, Postmodernism, and the New Age

THE NEW AGE MOVEMENT AND
THE POSTMODERN CONDITION

At first blush, postmodernism and the New Age movement appear to be antithetical to one another in both their content and their cultural vectors. Postmodernism is associated with alienation, intellectualism, and fierce criticism, while the New Age has been linked to excitement-seeking, spirituality, and mysticism. Postmodernism's standard-bearers constitute a relatively small intellectual elite, as opposed to those of the popular, unintellectual New Age movement, which bears folksy and even primitive characteristics, and whose devotees tend to hail from the "lower" social classes.

But despite these glaring differences, there is to my mind a strong connection between the recent mystical revival and processes

---

This essay is from a revised version of the second half of "Values and Faith in the Post-modern Age," in Rabbi Shagar's *Broken Vessels*. It was re-edited by Dr. Itamar Brenner and Dr. Zohar Maor for publication in *Tablets and Broken Tablets*, 54–66, with supplementary material from other drafts on the subject.

that ostensibly oppose it: postmodern pluralism, the deconstructive atmosphere that has taken hold in many disciplines, the end of ideology, and the loss of faith in grand narratives. Indeed, I think that the effects of postmodernism are what gave rise to the current spiritual renaissance. Mystical ecstasy is the flip side (the dark side, some would say) of postmodernism's dispirited rebellion. The social actualization of the postmodern age, which I attempted to describe in previous chapters, is evident in the New Age movement, among other phenomena. Thus, the New Age constitutes an additional, valuable perspective for elucidating postmodernism, despite being, on many levels, its socio-cultural inverse.

What characterizes the New Age movement? It appears that at its core is the mystical experience. Indeed, mysticism has become a hot commodity in our current cultural market. We have been inundated with diverse mystical literature: Eastern, Muslim, Indian, and so on, alongside our Kabbala and Hasidism. Add to this the resurgence of arcane practices and knowledge that were suppressed over two hundred years of secularization: witchcraft, magic, holistic medicine, and the like. All bookstores, including the most respectable ones, now devote at least a shelf or two to these genres.

Orthodox Judaism has also been profoundly affected by the New Age movement, with many youths – especially in Israel – studying meditation, yoga, reiki, tai chi, and various alternative-medicine disciplines. In some cases, the New Age is dressed up in Jewish trappings – in Jewish meditation courses, for instance, or when New Age ideas are harnessed to promote prayer or adherence to mitzvot. New Age terminology has suffused Jewish spiritual discourse, too, as we see with the substitution of "energy" for hasidic terms such as *or* (light) and *hayut* (vitality). We even see some openness to pagan myths, usually from the Far East. In fact, figures from such myths are sometimes identified, in one manner or another, with kabbalistic terms such as *partzuf* and *sefira*. The heretical works browsed on the sly by today's yeshiva students were not written by Aristotle and his disciples, nor do they deal with modern or postmodern philosophy; they are either translations from the Eastern spiritual canons – Buddhism, Taoism, etc. – or tomes that fuse New Age ideas and Eastern doctrines with Judaism.

Traces of this new spirit can even be found in the writings of contemporary kabbalists and hasidic leaders associated with mainstream Orthodox and ultra-Orthodox movements, including those of Rabbi Yitzchak Ginsburgh. His books deal with natural awareness, the body as a spiritual instrument, and even psychology, representing an attempt to pose a kabbalistic-hasidic alternative not only to Western psychology, but to techniques and conceptions of consciousness that bear the influences of assorted Eastern traditions.

Yet the New Age movement has not manifested only as a cultural revolution; right under our noses, colossal changes are taking place: some have been unfolding over hundreds of years, their significance only now becoming apparent to us, and others are in their infancy. Do the vast technological and scientific advances of recent generations have the power to revolutionize our very psychology as a species? Will human consciousness – how we perceive reality – change? And what of spiritual and physiological alterations of a magnitude that could give rise to a new kind of human? Are these advances destined to actualize the mystical consciousness in the concrete lives of the entire human race, thus fulfilling the vision of the New Age movement?

As noted, this movement has come on the scene at a time when academia is dominated by postmodern thought. We will begin by offering a few explanations for the link between the two phenomena, to then discuss several educational issues that arise from the New Age movement's influence on the religious community.

THE NEW AGE AS DESPAIR OVER
THE POSTMODERN CRISIS

The first explanation is superficial and circumstantial. It attributes the burgeoning interest in mysticism, as well as the larger worldwide religious revival, to the rootlessness and disorientation in modern and postmodern societies. The nonbeliever is terrified, critics say, of the nihilistic void opening beneath his feet with the death of the grand narratives, and his ensuing need for an all-knowing father figure leads him to a guru or a charismatic rabbi or mystic who can tell him what to do.

We can deepen this explanation by claiming that New Age mysticism is rooted in postmodernism itself, and in postmodernism's own depressive tendencies. The release from the oppression of religion and ideology brought not only anxiety but also despair: Religion's "murder" at the hands of secularism, and the destruction of the grand ideologies in favor of small narratives, brought guilt. As in the aftermath of many crimes, short-term relief soon gave way to lamentation over the loss of a home and the realization that there would be no turning back.

Furthermore, modern man learned that although he had won his freedom, he had no idea what to do with it. Freedom becomes fate, and man – as Sartre asserted – is "condemned to be free."[1] Freedom, it turns out, is no less oppressive than oppression itself. In the early twentieth century, people sought solace from freedom in various strains of fascism, but now that fascism's destructive consequences have made it unfashionable, the last resorts are folk religion and mysticism.

Indeed, it is common for people living in times of crisis to eventually cast their hopes on the supernal worlds. At first, full of pathos, they lament their loss, weaving absence into a lyricism of longing. But when that loses its appeal, they remain stranded in emptiness, where they are prone to reach out to the mystical or religious in the hope of filling the void.

THE NEW AGE, SCIENCE FICTION, AND POSTMODERNISM

However, there is another, deeper connection between postmodernism and the New Age movement. I will attempt to elucidate it with an alternative point of view that links the movement to core elements of postmodernism, such as the multiplicity of identities, the deconstruction of reality, and doubt about how we perceive reality. This perspective will help highlight postmodernism's mystical potential. I wish to demonstrate the point by focusing on fiction.

Several literary critics contend that modernist fiction is dominated by the epistemological.[2] The questions it poses are as follows: What is there to know of the world? Who knows it? How does he know it, and with what degree of certainty? The quintessential modernist literary

---

1. See Sartre, *Existentialism Is a Humanism.*
2. Brian McHale, *Postmodernist Fiction* (London: Methuen, 1987), 9.

genre is thus the detective story, whose protagonist, in his dogged quest for truth and certainty, seeks out knowledge, gathers evidence, and arrives at conclusions regarding various facts. Postmodernist fiction, on the other hand, is dominated by the ontological. The questions it poses are as follows: What is the world? What worlds exist? What happens when there is a conflict between various worlds? And so on. The quintessential postmodernist literary genre is thus science fiction.

What characterizes this literature, and what is the nature of its connection to postmodernism? Although science fiction is widely misperceived as dealing mostly with the advent of fantastical technological advances, its primary concern is that of changes in consciousness. Rather than emphasize the technology in the futuristic worlds it describes, science fiction highlights the mental developments that technology engenders. Alongside copious depictions of starships, exotic worlds, robots, powerful artificial intelligences, and time machines, the genre also features all manner of bizarre states of consciousness and shifts in awareness. In some cases, these altered states are the product of a world devoid of selves or – another classic science fiction trope – of a symbiotic-collective hive mind spanning the entire human race. Both phenomena are plainly expressions of a mystical awareness.

Another major theme of science fiction pertains to alternative modes of existence: The genre portrays countless alien worlds that are fundamentally different from our own. It also describes such profound changes in our world that merely thinking about them can trigger a mystical experience. Often, the cosmos is depicted in terms starkly reminiscent of kabbalistic literature: alternative universes, portals between worlds, worlds of *tohu* (chaos) and *tikkun* (rectification). Many of these worlds are home to a host of strange creatures that can be seen as mythical archetypes: Some live forever; others shape-shift, changing their appearance at will. These figures, once the staple of myths about the distant past, acquire a futuristic literary context that opens up readers to the symbolic, transhistorical experiences delivered by the original myths. Transposed into the future, these archetypes feel more realistic, since the future is a reality that can be imagined, that is bound to unfold. In other words, the fantastical must partake of the real if it is to engender a true mythic experience. Such a link can be attained through earnest belief in the myth (as in the ancient world), philosophical arguments that shore up the truth expressed by the myth (as in parts of the Greek philosophical canon), or – as in science fiction – by way of ostensibly scientific portrayals of the future.

Many science fiction stories take place in an epoch whose past is our future, while our present is often described as a prehistory characterized by savagery and ignorance. The advantage of such a perspective lies in its capacity to portray the present from the point of view of the future, while portraying the future as the past of an even more distant future. It forces the reader to reexamine his perception of time. In becoming past, our present assumes a mythical dimension, while the story's setting in the future imbues it with a sense of unreal reality that is absent from classic myths. Those fairy tales are obsolete, their fantasy a thing of the past, of a long-lost "golden age." Encountering the future, on the other hand, especially when set against a backdrop of advanced technologies (such as starships and robots), generates the excitement of knowing what has yet to transpire but is destined to become reality. This excitement generates a mystical experience. Thus, science fiction can perhaps serve as a kind of "mystical drug."

The use of motifs such as time travel, and the creation of worlds that amalgamate conflicting elements of our own,[3] disrupts our normal consciousness, subverts our sense of reality, and posits an unfamiliar mode of humanity. All are distinctly postmodern experiences that, in this context, can clearly promote a mystical outlook.

Science fiction has further mystical dimensions. What, for example, is the cultural significance of the popular subgenre of robot stories?[4] Why do we find them so attractive? It seems as though the

---

3. See, for instance, the connection between empire and advanced technology (including sophisticated robotics) in Isaac Asimov's *Foundation* series and the role of fundamentalist Islam in the context of futuristic science in Frank Herbert's *Dune* series, both of which create a weird fusion of past and future. This amalgamation of futuristic technological advances and ancient beliefs and social structures is quite alienating.

4. Alongside the robots are the robot-human hybrids – the cyborg and the human robot – so these stories, in fact, depict both man-machines and machine-men. For example, Roger Zelazny's novel *Lord of Light* (New York: HarperCollins, 1967) contains a "Pray-Machine." The description is more than merely an ironic representation

effect is generated by infusing the mechanical world with human elements, and injecting the human world with the mechanical. It is a potent expression of the postmodern multiplicity of identities and its effect of shattering the homogeneous identity and replacing it with a motley assortment of identity fragments. The diversity, complexity, and strangeness of our carnival of identities are compounded by fusions and struggles between human and robotic identities, as well as by other bizarre identity amalgams such as anthropomorphized animals. These combinations break through the limits of humanity itself, and therein is their appeal. The reconciliation – or, at the very least, the status quo – that these stories aim to establish is broader than that of "ordinary" fiction: It is reconciliation not only on the human plane, but between man and beast, and perhaps even between man and machine. This, too, disrupts the rationalism of the modernist story, bearing the kernel of a profound mystical experience engendered by the effacement of boundaries.

Science fiction describes profound psychological changes in humankind. One example is the question of what humankind's inner world will look like in a reality devoid of risk, a virtual reality in which people can live forever – climbing mountains, experiencing earthquakes, and even passing through flames – by way of perfectly safe "brain machines," without imperiling themselves in the real world. Reading such tales can induce a state of mystical excitement, not unlike the one brought on by hallucinogens, which open one up to entirely foreign psychological vistas. The excitement may indicate that the change is not merely psychological; at some point, the psychological differences between contemporary and future man become epistemological – engendering an ability to gain a new kind of knowledge of reality – and even ontological, when the posthuman comes on the scene.[5]

---

of the mechanical nature of our prayers (although the story certainly contains an element of criticism); it explores profound theological implications: Are the effects of prayer contingent on the precise performance of a sequence of actions, as if by machine? Can mechanical prayer be "real"? In examining these questions we come dangerously close to the idea of prayer as magic.

5. Should science fiction's predictions be taken as indications of what the future holds, like Jules Verne's books, which augured things that seemed impossible not long ago?

Mysticism thus pervades science fiction, whether explicitly or as a byproduct of the alienation felt by the reader while identifying with a story's protagonists.

These ideas tie in to theories of the French thinker Jean Baudrillard, who claims that the main hallmark of postmodernism is simulation. Unlike the problem of signification, which deals with the relationship between images and "basic reality," simulation "bears no relation to any reality whatever: it is its own pure simulacrum."[6] As the literary scholar Avraham Balaban writes, "Instead of a world signified by images, we are left with a world consisting only of images, phantasmagorical reflections of a reality that does not even exist."[7] This phenomenon of culture and awareness stems from technological advances that enable the clever mass production of images that no longer uphold the outmoded distinction between "essence" and "appearance." Such postmodern descriptions clearly resemble the effect of science fiction's depictions of the future: a release from the bonds to one exclusive reality. At bottom, this release is characterized by a mystical consciousness.

Moreover, postmodern philosophical and creative works deconstruct the once stable bases of consciousness and society, enabling – encouraging, even – the establishment of fantastic fiction as well as mysticism and the New Age. The mystical experience, which is also based on denying the world and ascending to a more rarefied plane of existence, becomes possible only by establishing the prospect of alternative realities. This supports my assertion that postmodernism can serve as a mystical aid.

In summation, despite the seeming gulf between the two phenomena, the New Age is a deeply postmodernist movement. It, too, relies on the shattering of the grand truths into slivers of truth, a deconstruction that allows the mystical consciousness to emerge.

I tend to believe that the imagination of science fiction authors indeed divines future vectors of the human spirit, and that the answer to the question is affirmative.

6. See Jean Baudrillard, "Simulacra and Simulations," in *Jean Baudrillard: Selected Writings*, ed. Mark Poster (Redwood City, CA: Stanford University Press, 2001), 173.

7. Avraham Balaban, *A Different Wave in Israeli Fiction: Postmodern Israeli Fiction* [Hebrew] (Jerusalem: Keter, 1995), 73.

FROM POSTMODERNISM TO MYSTICISM:
DECONSTRUCTION AS AN EXPANSION OF THE VESSELS

Science fiction provides a glimmer of humankind's apotheosis at the end of days. The creation of alternative worlds – entirely human constructions, as the reader is well aware – recalls the kabbalistic vision of created beings acquiring the power of divine creators and becoming full partners in the act of Creation. Science fiction authors create new worlds, and, consequently, so do their readers.

In light of the various processes described above – relating to both postmodernism and the New Age movement – one is reminded of the following description by Rabbi Kook:

> Why does the shattering of the vessels occur? For, as the Godhead provides according to Its capacity, while the recipient is limited, the benefit would thus be limited as well. That is why He provides influence without limit, according to His aspect... even though the created recipient cannot receive it without shattering completely, and then rebuilding himself through his desire to return to his unbounded source.... And thus the created can make himself and attain the perfection of a creator, and transcend the limitations of the created.[8]

The passage depicts the kabbalistic idea of the shattering of the vessels as a process that endows created beings with the creative freedom of the Creator. It contains several motifs, some modern (the created become creator) but also postmodern – the shattering enables a reconstruction of reality. Postmodernism denies man's capacity to create *ex nihilo*, while offering a far more enticing proposition: to create new permutations out of reality itself.

Rabbi Kook's statements draw on the kabbalistic notion that man's task is to purify and broaden the vessels, thawing them of dogmatic rigidity so they can contain the light of infinitude. It emerges that man's central role is to construct reality.

---

8. Rabbi Kook, *Orot HaKodesh*, vol. 2, 627.

Indeed, one can discern a similar process in postmodernism. As we know, deconstruction aims to shatter all the vessels, claiming that reality in its entirety – facts as well as metaphors and language – is nothing but a human construct. Furthermore, human creative works are never brought forth *ex nihilo*, but are always adaptations of elements from earlier works, which is why every such creation can be deconstructed and then reconstructed differently. On a kabbalistic level, we might say that this shattering of the vessels is not final, but instead purifies the vessels, allowing man to use their shards as building blocks for a new world. Truly, the role of deconstruction is to dismantle the vessels and make them supple, thus opening up new pathways for inspiration and illumination.

In his tale "Trust in God," Rabbi Naḥman of Breslov tells of a "warrior" who is none other than the *tzaddik* (i.e., Rabbi Naḥman himself) and can fix anything.[9] It is no accident that this *tzaddik* can only fix things, not create them out of nothing: Unable to create *ex nihilo*, created beings can only fashion new things out of the shards of the vessels, employing bricolage, the merging of diverse styles and available ingredients.[10]

It is important to note that the shattering of the vessels – when the overarching truth is gone and only language games remain – can lead to nihilism and moral paralysis. To avoid such a state, we must imbue our language games with inspiration. Therein is another link between postmodernism and mysticism. There is actually little distinction between the postmodern outlook and New Age mysticism, between the philosophy of language games in which there is no absolute truth – not because we have not discovered it, but because there is no "material"

---

9. Kaplan, *Rabbi Nachman's Stories*, 485–89.

10. The term "bricolage" was formulated by several French thinkers of the twentieth century. The anthropologist Claude Lévi-Strauss was the first to use it to describe spontaneous activity resulting from early experiences in a person's consciousness. See Lévi-Strauss, *The Savage Mind* (Chicago: University of Chicago Press, 1966). Later, postmodernist thinkers expanded the connotations of the term, with Derrida employing it to express the idea that every use of language relies on previous uses. See Derrida, *Writing and Difference* (London: Routledge Press, 1978), 95–278. It is bricolage in the Derridean sense that is evoked here.

from which to fashion such a truth – and a mystical conception that all is truth and all is God, that "no place is empty of Him."[11] The difference between a mystical consciousness and a secularized, postmodern consciousness lies in one's willingness to open up to inspiration, to break out of one's bewildered paralysis in the face of the countless possible language games – in other words, to go beyond the anthropological stance of studying a tribe without joining it. The self-consciousness of the postmodern observer prevents him from joining in the dance of the tribespeople, because, so he asks himself, "Why this dance and not another?"[12] The search for a reason and a preference clashes with the realization that there can be none; there is no stable base beyond games of social construction – hence the risk of nihilism. If postmodern man, however, can choose one of the options despite being aware that it is socially constructed, the very absence of absolute truth will be able to imbue his choice with mystical elation. This absence lends flexibility to the once rigid conception of truth, freeing one's consciousness to experience a variety of syntheses that were impossible prior to the postmodern crisis. In a religious context, postmodernism enables one to accept the yoke of the kingdom of heaven in a whole new sense, to see in faith an absolute decision with the capacity to create a new vessel by which to reveal the divine light.

---

11. *Tikkunei Zohar* 81b.
12. One is reminded of Buridan's ass, a hypothetical creature that, placed equidistant from a bale of hay and a pail of water, will perish of hunger and thirst because it cannot decide whether to eat first or drink.

Chapter Eight

Love, Romance, and Covenant

QUESTIONS AND DISTRESSES

A while back, I ran into a friend who serves as a rabbi in a Jerusalem synagogue. He related to me three questions that he is often asked by young couples who are about to get married. The first, most difficult question relates to family planning, namely using contraceptives to put off having children. The reasons for such a move are many: academic studies; a desire to strengthen the bond between husband and wife; and even fear that they are incompatible, leading to a desire to see how the relationship will unfold before the arrival of children who could complicate a breakup. The second question, which pertains to the wedding ceremony, was whether the bride and groom could place a ring on one another's fingers. The third relates to the days of ritual impurity during and after

This essay is based on a talk given at an event organized by Yeshivat Siaḥ Yitzḥak and Yakar in Jerusalem in Spring 5765. It first appeared during the author's lifetime under the title "Love, Romance, and Covenant," in Rabbi Shagar, *The Two Lights: Family Equality from a New Jewish Viewpoint*, ed. Zohar Maor [Hebrew] (Efrat: Yeshivat Siaḥ Yitzḥak, 5767), 303–17. Edited by Dr. Zohar Maor for publication in *We Will Walk in Fervor*, 271–86.

the menstrual period – the rules governing the separation between husband and wife and to what extent those rules can be bent. These are, of course, the questions of couples who have already decided to tie the knot; the most difficult questions of all are the ones raised by singles: How does a couple decide to marry? What expectations are legitimate and what are not? What is the determining factor – one's emotions or one's intellect? What is the procedure – should one compromise? And finally, why is it so hard to find a suitable partner?

I will not endeavor here to answer these weighty questions, some of which I have addressed elsewhere. Rather, in this chapter I will attempt to get at the root of the questions – the conflict between Jewish family life, the conception of family, and the ethos of the Jewish family, as constructed by halakha (or the spirit of halakha), and the conception of family in the modern world, which instills us with fantasies and expectations of our romantic partner.

The young religious men and women who ask such questions are motivated by a certain conception of romantic love. This conception is a relatively recent "invention," a system of expectations regarding one's future family that, as noted, derives largely from one's cultural milieu. The idea that the relationship between husband and wife is shaped independently of our social and cultural surroundings is incorrect.[1]

Halakha, meanwhile, shapes the marital relationship via its own values and conceptions, which differ significantly from those of romantic love. People for whom halakha is not the be-all and end-all may feel alienated by it and have trouble fulfilling its dictates. Hence the resistance – or, at the very least, the lack of identification and understanding – that arises in many young men and women in response to the halakhot governing married life. For better or worse, we are citizens of multiple worlds. We are immersed in an environment, and partake of a lifestyle, whose values are often quite distant from those of Judaism. This state of affairs gives rise to many conflicts, and causes people to feel trapped and sometimes experience harsh disappointments.

Thus, the questions with which I opened emerge from a profound dissonance between Western-modern conceptions and the

---

1. See, for example, Yoram Yovel, *Is It Love?* [Hebrew] (Tel Aviv: Keshet, 2004).

thrust of halakha. The question of the ring, for instance, is the question of equality. "If he can, then why can't I?" the bride asks. The desire for equality also underlies the second question, that of family planning. As opposed to the traditional wife, the modern bride does not see raising children and caring for her family as her sole purpose. She, too, wishes to pursue self-actualization through higher education and a career. Yet halakha – ostensibly at least – considers procreation and the raising of children to be the purpose of the family and the goal of sexual relations, and thus poses difficulties for those who wish to lead a marital life that defers childrearing.[2]

The problem is not just the changes in lifestyle and the challenge of raising children while studying and developing a career, but also the conflict – no less acute than the one mentioned above – between intimacy and family life. Let us look to Passover for an example. The Jewish festivals are family affairs, not romantic ones. They are not about seclusion in nature or honeymooning in a hotel room, but rather about the family hubbub: uncles and cousins, their spouses and grandchildren. What is a young couple to do if they seek solitude in the vineyards or wish to graze among the lilies, as described in the Song of Solomon, which we read during Passover? I sense strongly that there is something deeply Jewish about the holiday hubbub and commotion.

What will happen when, even absent the extended family, the couple is surrounded by children? The Torah considers children a blessing, the more the merrier: "Your wife shall be as a fruitful vine in the innermost parts of your house; your children like olive plants around your table" (Ps. 128:3). Are we willing to forgo this blessing? But what if its price is intimacy, not only between husband and wife, but between parents and children?

Naturally, the question of intimacy yields further questions: What of entertaining guests? One question I am occasionally asked by newlyweds is whether they should invite guests for their Shabbat eve meals or spend them together, alone, in the cozy quietude of their homes.

---

2. For more, see Rabbi Shagar, "The Mitzva of *Ona*," in *We Will Walk in Fervor*, 17–58. Of course, a man may also defer having children in order to pursue self-actualization.

The question of intimacy also touches on the third question: that of ritual impurity. Do the various prohibitions imposed on the couple while the wife is forbidden to her husband disrupt and impair their intimacy?

This issue raises another conflict that puts the tension between romance and halakha in sharp relief: the sexual urge, which *Hazal* termed *yetzer haarayot*, and which we will refer to by its modern designation – eros. Whenever *Hazal* spoke of a *yetzer*, or "urge," without elaboration, they referred to the sexual drive. According to one widely known tale, the Men of the Great Assembly even tried to eradicate it.[3] But *Hazal* did not doubt its indispensability: "Come, let us render gratitude to our forebears, for had they not sinned, we should not have come into the world," Resh Lakish asserted.[4] They also maintained that one must worship God with "two impulses, the evil impulse as well as the good impulse."[5] The attempt by the Great Assembly to destroy the urge was doomed:

> Then they said, "Since the time is propitious, let us pray that the tempter of sin [may be delivered into our hands]." So they prayed, and it was delivered into their hands. They imprisoned it for three days; after that they sought a new-laid egg for an invalid in the whole of the Land of Israel and could not find one. Then they said, "What shall we do? Shall we pray that its power be but partially destroyed? Heaven will not grant it." So they blinded it with rouge. This was so effective that one does not lust for his relatives.

The sages were well aware of the necessity of the sexual urge, embodied in the image of an egg used as medicine. Sexual vitality was apparently seen as an antidote for the patient's weakness, perhaps for all weakness. But why did Heaven not grant their request to curtail its power? It turns out that it is incumbent upon man to tell right from wrong; the divine totality often brooks no compromise.

---

3. Sanhedrin 64a.
4. Avoda Zara 5a.
5. Mishna Berakhot 9:5.

So how did the sages contend with the threat? Even though they conceded the indispensability of the sexual urge, they still sought to harness it to good works – the mitzvot of procreation and marital relations – and through them to justify it. Nothing is further from their point of view than the prevailing conceptions of romantic love in our society. We are hostages to romantic concepts of eros, and many couples object when told that its sole justification is that it is a mitzva. On the halakhic level, therein lies the problem with family planning: *Ḥazal* made sexuality subservient to the mitzva of procreation, and the distinction between the two raises a variety of issues. As noted, in this chapter I do not discuss halakhic questions but instead examine ideas of romantic love and possible Jewish alternatives to it. In the final section of the essay, I will attempt to demonstrate that the postmodern criticism of romantic love, of all things, posits an exciting point of view that could be quite compatible with Jewish conceptions of couplehood.

ROMANCE AND JUDAISM: CHAOS AND RECTIFICATION

What is evil about the libido, and why did the sages refer to it as the "evil urge"?

Let us discuss romance in modern culture and the contrast between it and marriage. We will begin with a passage from the Israeli sociologist Eva Illouz:

> But as the centrality of religion declined during the closing decades of the nineteenth century and the beginning of the twentieth, romantic love was inevitably carried along by the new wave of secularization. Themes of selflessness, sacrifice, and idealism were more and more brushed aside. Romantic love ceased being presented in the terms of religious discourse [as it had been before, during the Victorian era] ....[6]

Illouz quotes the historian Karen Lystra:

---

6. Eva Illouz, *Consuming the Romantic Utopia: Love and the Cultural Contradictions of Capitalism* (Oakland: University of California Press, 1997), 29.

> Especially during courtship, it can be shown that romantic love contributed to the displacement of God by the lover as the central symbol of ultimate significance.... [Lovers] were making deities of each other in the new theology of romantic love.[7]

Indeed, over time romantic love has practically taken on the status of a religion all its own.

Our conceptions of romance are an outgrowth of the major characteristics of mid-twentieth-century American culture: individualism, self-expression, a new ethics of pleasure, consumerism, leisure, and so on. The catalyst for these conceptions was the cinema. The boundaries between film and real life were blurred, and men and women constructed entire fantastical worlds based on what they saw at the movies. The romantic expected the love of his life to make herself known to him as if in a mystical vision. Yet, according to Illouz's description, romance deviated from the norms of morality, as it certainly did not sanctify such principles as loyalty, stability, and generosity. Thus, romantic love became a force that threatened the social and moral order while acquiring, precisely due to its menacing nature, the aura of a supreme value. It served as a utopian model of the individual's sovereignty and, as such, was perceived as conflicting with society. "It stood for such values as disinterestedness, irrationality, and indifference to riches. Ironically, however, in popular literature, love was supposed to magically bring economic security, and abundance."[8]

One can detect powerful reverberations of this idea in the allegories of Freud (and even more so among his rebel students), who considered sexual restraint detrimental to the autonomy of the individual. Several of his contemporaries agreed, including the philosopher Bertrand Russell, who opined that "love is an anarchic force which, if it is left free, will not remain within any bounds set by law or custom."[9]

---

7. Karen Lystra, *Searching the Heart: Women, Men, and Romantic Love in Nineteenth-Century America* (Oxford: Oxford University Press, 1989), 8.
8. Illouz, *Consuming the Romantic Utopia*, 9.
9. Ibid.

It is precisely this modern conception of romantic love, and of the eros at its core, that can lead us back to the world of the Jewish sages, for whom libido was *the* quintessential evil urge.

The sexual urge is indeed a power, negative and boundary-breaking, a force of chaos – that is its nature and thence its appeal. There is an inherent contradiction between it and culture. Put in the terminology of Hasidism, it represents a clash between the world of *tohu*, or chaos, and the world of *tikkun*, or rectification, which is also the world of Torah. Only through negation can the infinite be represented, as Maimonides taught.[10] Indeed, one can say that that is the deep source of the world of chaos. The conflict between libido and culture can thus be conceived as a conflict between infinite, spontaneous freedom and deliberate suppression. Hence Freud's pessimistic conclusion regarding chronic dissatisfaction and "the uneasiness of culture."[11]

Therein is the root of the romantic assault on the institution of marriage. Wedlock is often portrayed in American popular culture as the enemy of love and a threat to the thrill of passion. Sartre referred to it as a prison. Even if one willingly enters into this problematic institution, one must often revitalize one's marital relationship with all manner of contrivances and, especially, thrilling experiences.

The affectionate bourgeois marriage, it is claimed, is a myth, hypocrisy, the product of convenience rather than feeling. The convergence of romantic love and marriage generates a contradiction between the values engendered by that love (fervent feeling, idealization of the beloved, selfless emotion) and those required for a successful marriage (day-to-day partnership, dealing with a less than perfect spouse, the juggling of love with familial and professional responsibilities).

Freud's conception of the conflict between culture, which he considered an expression of the superego, and the id, the instinctual forces of the subconscious, as well as the conception of sexuality as a negative, boundary-breaking force, is synonymous with Ḥazal's identification of the sexual urge with the evil urge. The argument between Freud and

---

10. *Guide of the Perplexed* I:58–60.
11. This is the literal translation of *Das Unbehagen in der Kultur*, the German title of Freud's famous work *Civilization and Its Discontents*.

the romantics in this regard is thus a dispute over the status of culture, on the one hand, and the value of boundary-breaking romanticism, on the other, echoing the prophets' age-old battle against sexual, idolatrous wantonness. The pagan temple was the abode of the sacred prostitute, and pagan festivals and rites called for debauchery and the suspension of everyday sexual mores. Contrast that with the Jewish holidays, where the family takes center stage.

Marriage would thus appear to be a feature of the constricting, oppressive world of rectification (*tikkun*). But is that indeed the case? Did the sages, who also perceived a conflict between the sexual urge and Torah (the world of rectification), indeed see this opposition as inherent? Did Freud in fact echo them in positing pessimistically that "culture" is intrinsically repressive and discontenting? The Freudian point of view is seemingly foreshadowed in the words of the *Amora* R. Yitzḥak: "Since the destruction of the Temple, sexual pleasure has been taken [from those who experience it lawfully] and given to sinners, as it is written, 'Stolen waters are sweet, and bread eaten in secret is pleasant' (Prov. 9:17)."[12]

Even R. Yitzḥak, who does not ignore the conflict between libido and law, and the dissatisfaction that is the lot of the law-abider, considers the situation temporary. The conflict is not intrinsic and necessary; it is merely one consequence of the destruction of the Temple. In any event, rather than content themselves with fighting wantonness and suppressing it in the name of the law, the prophets and sages created an alternative, a rechanneling of the sexual urge, an eros that, instead of effacing the tension and suppressing desire, would raise them to a place of holiness. Here is a passage by Rabbi Joseph B. Soloveitchik that can help us elucidate at least one aspect of *Hazal*'s struggle with the issue:

> The third level of sexual life, *redeemed sexual activity*...spells a new relationship between man and woman. It places sexuality on a new plane.... This eternal quest of the unique, lonely individual to flee his solitude and to share his personal existence with

---

12. Sanhedrin 75a.

others finds fulfillment via the carnal medium. God, somehow, employs the flesh as an instrument of His will.... "*Vehaadam yada et Ḥava ishto*, Adam knew his wife Eve" (Gen. 4:1); "*vayeda Adam od et ishto*, Adam knew his wife again" (4:25). The Hebrew term *vayeda* in its sense of knowing each other sexually connotes the metaphysical element involved in the sexual function. The term *vayeda* points toward an act of cognition or recognition. The I recognizes the personal existence of the you.... If you should inquire as to the essence and meaning of the institution of marriage, I would say that through marriage the miraculous transition from the I-it contact to the I-you relationship occurs. Marriage personalizes sexuality as the joint experience of the I and the you.... Basically the same drive that brings man to God makes him quest for his companion.[13]

The preceding statements stem, of course, from a modernist worldview that does not separate romanticism from sexuality or identify sexuality with the evil urge. Yet, as opposed to the romantics, not only does Rabbi Soloveitchik not see a conflict between sexuality and marriage, but he believes that the redemption of sexuality is attained through marriage, through the raising of the relationship from I-it to I-you. Thus, he identifies the marital relationship with the ancient conception of covenant.[14]

Employing terms from dialogic philosophy, Rabbi Soloveitchik describes sexuality not only as a force that does not conflict with intimacy, but as intimacy's actualization. Although he allows for the existence of a conflict between sexuality and culture, he limits it to "the life of the flesh" (Lev. 17:11). To use hasidic and kabbalistic terminology, this is the grand mystery depicted as the sweetening of the *gevurot*, the *dinim* or severities, associated with the left side, by incorporating them within the *ḥasadim*, or kindnesses, of the right side. Untempered *gevurot*, manifest as passion, are *tohu*, chaos, and thus shatter the vessels. Hence the disappointment, emptiness, and discontent so often inseparable from the

---

13. Rabbi Joseph B. Soloveitchik, *Family Redeemed* (Jersey City: Ktav, 2002), 94–95.
14. For more, see Rabbi Shagar, "Modesty and Shame," in *We Will Walk in Fervor*, 261–70.

sexual experience: Pleasure becomes pain. Denial cannot exist on its own. Only when the relationship encompasses body and soul, when each partner acknowledges the presence of the other through the encounter and the gaze, can sexuality become presence, reality, and redemption from loneliness. Otherwise, it yields nothing but frustration and exponentially deepens each partner's solitude.

Let us revisit the meaning of Ḥazal's move to define sexual relations as a mitzva. Rabbi Soloveitchik dealt with this issue at length elsewhere in his writings. On numerous occasions he described the overcoming of the sexual urge, through the laws of family purity, as an injection of holiness into the relationship between husband and wife.[15] Halakha's role is to shape a different order of relations. It seeks to redeem the relationship from banality and secularization, and mold it into a system of purification and festive invitation; to recast sexuality as a sacred instrument of excitement and pleasure. If one fails to recognize that these are two distinct approaches to sexuality, and attempts to approach halakha using the terminology of Western eroticism, he will be unable to cope with these laws, and will perceive them as oppressive. The restraining of the urge, and the ensuing sense of alienation, is what sanctifies and safeguards one's libido. I wish to dwell on this point.

Does the fact that the Torah presents fecundity as the purpose of marriage, and places the raising and educating of children at the center of its conception of the family, preclude intimacy in the Jewish family? On the contrary. When they coined the blessings of the marriage ceremony, the sages imprinted their views about the family in the halakhic currency of prayer. What is the import of the blessings uttered under the wedding canopy, which often go unnoticed by us? What promise do they hold? To what do they aspire? "Blessed are You, Lord our God… who created joy and gladness, groom and bride, mirth, song, delight, and rejoicing, love and harmony and peace and companionship." Happiness and friendship are clearly crucial; yet "companionship" here is nothing like that of Western romantic love.

In this context, I like to quote the Slovenian postmodernist thinker Slavoj Žižek:

---

15. See, for example, Joseph B. Soloveitchik, "Catharsis," *Tradition* 17, no. 2 (1978): 38–54.

The way – the only way – to have an intense and fulfilling personal (sexual) relationship is not for the couple to look into each other's eyes, forgetting about the world around them, but, while holding hands, to look together outside, at a third point (the Cause for which both are fighting, to which both are committed).[16]

The blessings of the wedding speak to the companionship and solidarity generated by two companions in faith. Our primary objective is to overcome nihilism (which feeds and perpetuates our negative image of sexuality) and open up to faith in the Other, which is also faith in God.

The romantic metaphor for intimacy is one of self-discovery. But the self cannot be grasped, and neither can the Other, the object of love. At best, the self will briefly flicker into view, always through its attributes, which may bear the imprint of the other's uniqueness. Like the hidden God who reveals Himself only through His actions – "You cannot see My face, for man shall not see Me and live" (Ex. 33:20) – so too the self. The very attempt to grasp something obstructs intimacy. Paradoxically, only through distraction can the self be discovered. It flutters in the corner of the eye, it peers through the lattice, and its presence is rarely if ever enduring and direct. It cannot be a goal, and therein is the pitfall of romance: In becoming an object, it thwarts itself, as with all strivings of the ego. That is how one should understand the deeper intention of the sages in portraying the mitzva as the objective, fecundity as the goal, and family life as the purpose. It is also how one can overcome the sexual urge's innate flaw and the attendant disappointment, about which R. Yoḥanan said in the Talmud: "There is a small organ in man which satisfies him in his hunger but makes him hunger when satisfied."[17] Although it is a goal, the mitzva is not an achievement to be pursued. Rather, it is a state of mind that yields an action, the medium through which solidarity and companionship are manifest. Its purpose is to reveal through distraction, through the paradox of modesty, which exposes by concealing.

---

16. Slavoj Žižek, *The Puppet and the Dwarf: The Perverse Core of Christianity* (Boston: MIT Press, 2005), 85.
17. Sanhedrin 107a.

This is a vastly different ideal of marriage from the romantic conception that places eros at its core. Its objective is to sweeten desire and maintain it with gladness and friendship.

But can husband and wife be friends, too? This may seem like a strange question. Isn't there friendship between them? Yet with time, relationships become increasingly complicated and onerous, grudges accrue, passion makes way for hostility, and friendship fades. The intimacy posited by the Jewish approach offers relief from marital anguish.

The Jewish model of intimacy can be characterized as standing next to, rather than face-to-face with, the Other. But we must not conflate this shared outward gaze with ideas that co-opt the family in order to fulfill common goals, a view prevalent among certain rabbis. It is not about mere functionality, for a shared vocation does not imply a shared function. It is about a partnership in carrying out the mitzva itself, in its most profound sense – its faith. A faith partnership engenders the deepest of intimacies, the only intimacy, in fact, that possesses the power to deliver us from solitude. Romantic intimacy, at bottom an intimacy of ego and sexuality, cannot effect such a transformation. This may be the meaning of holiness in this context, where it plays a central part.

Thus, *Ḥazal*'s subsuming of sexuality in fecundity emphasizes an immanent aspect of sexuality itself. The only way to maintain it is by not turning it into a goal, for that distorts it. Sexuality is dispelled among those who pursue it or are enticed by it.

In the postmodernist context, one prominent author offers the following description:

> It is not chance that Umberto Eco chose love to define the postmodern: "I think of the postmodern attitude as that of a man who loves a very cultivated woman and knows he cannot say to her, 'I love you madly,' because he knows that she knows (and she knows that he knows) that these words have already been written by [the popular romance author] Barbara Cartland. [He] loves her in an age of a lost innocence." In other words, the postmodern romantic condition is characterized by the ironic perception

that one can only repeat what has already been said and that one can only act as an actor in an anonymous and stereotypical play.[18]

Here we see how our desire to grasp the Other causes the Other to elude us, not only in the personal, private context, but also in the general sense: The world of romance, as a whole, has lost its charm.

When we evoke the power of the directive, the shared gaze at a third point, we encounter the full power of the inherent gap between the self and the Other, a chasm that appears to dissolve the dream of attaining intimacy. Can I forge an inner bond with an Other whose very otherness is what sets him or her out as a stranger; who stands facing me and blocks my path; whose gaze ensnares me, keeping me from forgetting myself and attaining sweet abstraction, objectifying me with its abrasive, crushing scrutiny? One is reminded of Kierkegaard, who left his beloved fiancée – in order to love her. Only in her absence could he love her, only through abandonment. In yearning, one invokes the absent beloved, so that the yearning is greater even than one's love. Rabbi Naḥman of Breslov taught that this dynamic also characterizes the relationship with God, that longing is the essence because of its piercing infinitude.[19] Corporeality, by definition, entails imprisonment and diminishment. Therefore, there is no hope for love, and the path of longing and self-denial is the only viable mode of existence. This, by the way, is the difference between the doctrine of *hitbodedut*, the positive practice of self-seclusion, and loneliness.[20] By virtue of its absence, a Hasid's self-seclusion is a presence and a fullness. Rabbi Shneur Zalman of Liadi interpreted the Hebrew word for "bride," *kalla*, as connoting both *kilayon*, or "yearning," and *keleh*, "prison."[21] Longing is the only alternative to the limitedness of physical reality.

18. Illouz, *Consuming the Romantic Utopia*, 179.
19. See, for instance, "The Parable of the Heart and the Spring," in Kaplan, *Rabbi Nachman's Stories*, 359.
20. For example, see *Kuzari* III, opening.
21. Rabbi Shneur Zalman of Liadi, *Likkutei Torah*, Song of Songs 1a.

One may dismiss this Kierkegaardian progression as an attempt to replace reality with unreality, the existing world with a spectral one. But the truth is not nearly so straightforward. Yes, the self-deniers and ascetics do not live in "this world." Yes, the Hasid who escapes to the desert and lives a life apart from humanity is indeed in a state of self-imposed aloneness. But he is not lonely; his life may be a life of the World to Come, yet it has a presence and tangibility that often surpass those of reality. In this context, I like to quote the distinction drawn by the psychoanalyst Jacques Lacan between the Real and reality, which are not necessarily identical.[22] Plato already taught us that matter is but a fleeting shade of an idea.

Yet the mitzva drags the Hasid back into the community and makes him marry. But the marriage is not effected only through coercion. The deeper secret is that the mitzva becomes an environment that engenders the meeting between selves, and profound solidarity and intimacy. It is the way out of the Kierkegaardian conundrum.

Here is Freud:

It can easily be shown that the psychical value of erotic needs is reduced as soon as their satisfaction becomes easy. An obstacle is required in order to heighten libido; and when natural resistances to satisfaction have not been sufficient men have at all times erected conventional ones so as to be able to enjoy love.[23]

R. Meir made a similar point regarding the laws of family purity:

R. Meir used to say, "Why did the Torah ordain that the uncleanness of menstruation continue for seven days? Because being in constant contact with his wife, [a husband might] develop a loathing toward her. The Torah therefore ordained: Let her be unclean for seven days in order that she shall be

22. See above, chapter 2.
23. Sigmund Freud, *On the Universal Tendency to Debasement in the Sphere of Love* (Worcestershire, England: Read Books, 2013), 16.

beloved by her husband as at the time of her first entry into the bridal chamber."[24]

As I have elaborated elsewhere, the sexual urge cannot be fully actualized, because seizing it robs it of its pleasure.[25]

Casting fecundity as the goal of the relationship is different, however. It does not create an obstacle with the purpose of heightening libido; neither is it a "paradoxical intention,"[26] whose purpose is to create a spontaneous immediacy by diverting the intention. This point harks back to the words of Rabbi Soloveitchik: It is a practice that establishes an I-you relationship – one that cannot relapse into an I-it relationship – by tuning both parties to a common ideal that envelops them (this idea ties in to the kabbalistic concept of *or makif*, or "surrounding light") and bestows upon the I-you relationship an element of eternity. The process is one of Hegelian "sublation." The chaos of sexuality, which first appears as the antithesis of marriage, as something to be suppressed by marriage, is ultimately synthesized with it, raising it up so that the relationship becomes an intimate partnership of body and soul.

I wish to end this section with a note. You may have noticed that *Hazal's approach to* sexuality differs from Rabbi Soloveitchik's. *Hazal*, as we pointed out, enlist sexuality in the service of the mitzva. These days, that outlook is prevalent mostly in the ultra-Orthodox world. It is not about self-imposed solitude, but rather about the bustle and gladness of the mitzva. Conversely, Rabbi Soloveitchik's treatment – which applies a modern I-you intimacy, which did not exist in the time of the sages, to the man of faith, who is redeemed through the relationship – is clearly an attempt to incorporate modern sexuality and intimacy into the Jewish world. I would characterize this progression as Hegelian: Chaotic sexuality is retroactively made an essential part of the mitzva. In this context, the mitzva may inhibit and suppress, casting romantic intimacy

---

24. Nidda 31b.
25. See "Modesty and Shame"; *We Will Walk in Fervor*, 161–170.
26. This term was developed by Viktor Frankl in his *Man's Search for Meaning* (Boston: Beacon Press, 2006) and elsewhere.

as its antithesis. Yet the latter, too, is bound for failure. The synthesis is the third stage, where romantic intimacy is subsumed in the mitzva, which in turn becomes a medium for engendering intimacy, as in Rabbi Soloveitchik's description.

To my mind, despite the conflicts plaguing it, the religious Zionist movement is currently at this sensitive juncture – perhaps only fleetingly. I think the movement has forged a unique synthesis between sexuality and holiness, intimacy and the religious imperative. A nonreligious friend used to say he envied religious Zionist youth, the young men and women who had not lost their grace (and had largely retained their innocence as well), as opposed to, on the one hand, the gruffness and alienation prevalent in the ultra-Orthodox world, and, on the other, the promiscuity of the secular world, which in effect eradicates grace.

THE POSTMODERN CONDITION: MARRIAGE AS "NONLITERAL *TZIMTZUM*"

The postmodernist takes an overtly ironic stance on modern conceptions of romance. As in other areas, romantic love undergoes a process of privatization – a passage from the general to the private and specific, from the enduring to the fleeting. It is no longer about a big love, a love of one's life, but rather about brief, passing pulses, flashes of intimacy. Even the "value" of permissiveness has changed, no longer founded on the expectation that it can make one happy. People have learned that permissiveness has broken its promise; no viable alternative to the family has been invented. The postmodern conception of happiness is ironic, a denial of any eternal, solid model, of the grand narrative. Wherever there is no truth, everyone is right. The demand for equality is founded not on everyone's equal rights, but rather on the idea that in a place devoid of a certain right, no individual can demand that right, claiming priority over another. Permissiveness, as an objective, is not about the grand, romantic freedom so much as it is about a small, "hip" freedom. There is no expectation of redemption.

The glamour of Hollywood is perceived as inflated, insipid, and saccharine. I have childhood memories of a female cousin voraciously reading pulp romances, thrilled by the expectation that she, too, would one day find the love of her life. These days, who still reads such passé literature?

The question is whether postmodernism is too cynical to be compatible with the covenant. To my mind, not only is there an interesting confluence in this area between the postmodernist and the Hasid, but Jewish family life is in fact easier in a postmodern atmosphere.

"Soft postmodernism," as I have explained elsewhere,[27] is not cynical. It allows for an encounter, if one that is specific, haphazard, unpretentious. The postmodernist does not discount the role of chance in the world and in his life by linking them to a metaphysics. On the contrary, he accepts randomness and, forgoing the need for security, guarantees, justifications, and rationalizations, accepts the singularity of the encounter. The question of whether things "could have gone differently," which keeps the modernist (and us) awake at night, is of no consequence to him. It is a metaphysical "nonsense" question, and he, like Wittgenstein, answers it with a shrug.

What, then, is the guiding principle of postmodernism? It is, in fact, an absence of guiding principles; it is randomness. The critical question, however, is whether that absence, that emptiness, must persist. Does randomness necessitate arbitrariness? This is the question that separates hard postmodernism from soft. The hard postmodernist barricades himself in a position of absence and denial before sliding into meaninglessness and nihilism, truthlessness and relativism, flattening reality and then shattering it to bits. He deconstructs the subject, denies its unity, and turns the subjective point of view into a crossroads in the game of power discourses, which itself lacks any center or overarching intelligence.

The soft postmodernist, meanwhile, translates nothingness into equality, freedom, and even virtue. This is not to say that he speaks of equality out of a belief in the exalted value of all things, or that he believes in a freedom whose purpose is to facilitate the actualization of that which is absolute in every individual. His motives are not moral in nature. The values of equality and freedom are, to him, nothing but a reflection of the ancients' stoicism. To couch the idea in hasidic terms, it

---

27. See above, chapter 5.

correlates with the divine perspective of *sovev kol almin*,[28] or "surrounding all worlds," where the light of God encircles all things equally. The divine point of view sees no difference between up and down, or between light and dark – "the darkness is even as the light" (Ps. 139:12), according to the hasidic interpretation of the verse "For I the Lord change not" (Mal. 3:6). In comparison to the divine infinitude, everything is equally valueless, which is the exact claim of the postmodernist. Freedom, for instance, is a rule of fair play in a world where no absolute value can be invoked to foist something upon me.

Soft postmodernism distinguishes between randomness and arbitrariness; the former doesn't entail the latter. This type of postmodernism requires a willingness to forgo *the* truth in favor of a local truth, a specific justice, and a comportment that does not reach beyond itself. It is a twofold concession: Not only does the soft postmodernist surrender the truth; he also relinquishes the very need for it. For example, what happens when we accept ourselves, in an act of renunciation, when we accept our rootedness and contingency as total and definite? Again, it is a twofold concession: We surrender both absoluteness and the need for it. The second concession, which does not make a big fuss over the first one, marks the moment of release from angst. It is then that ecstasy sets in.[29] This is not an ecstasy of truth, but rather an ecstasy of life itself. It reflects precisely the truth of life, the joy of life, infiniteness itself, and it is made possible by surrendering the need to seize, to justify, to call out infinity by name. To be precise, the truth is a manifestation of life – not a prerequisite for it.

Postmodernism accepts life as is. This equanimity is also apparent in its approach to the family: The postmodernist will accept his wife in the same vein. Paradoxically, this equanimity is identical to

---

28. [Ed. note: According to Kabbala and Ḥasidut, the divine revelation includes two modes: *Memalei kol almin* (filling all worlds) is the Divine Presence enlivening every creature. It is revelation that we can grasp and understand. *Sovev kol almin* (surrounding all worlds), on the other hand, is a light too sublime to enter the world, and thus incomprehensible. Nevertheless, it hovers above the world, so we can intuit it occasionally. See above, pp. 95–96.]

29. See Gur-Ze'ev, *Toward Diasporic Education*, 198 and elsewhere; and Carlo Strenger, *The Designed Self* (Hillsdale, NJ: Analytic Press, 2005), 151–52.

that in Hasidism: Every individual life, in and of itself, encompasses the fullness of life. Every woman is *the* woman, and every man *the* man. This marvelous paradox necessarily casts the betrothed woman as *the* woman, preserving her uniqueness. The same is true for the man, of course.

Against this backdrop of randomness there is an encounter, but it is the opposite of the arbitrariness generally associated with randomness: an encounter, a friendship, and even gladness and ecstasy over the experience of life in itself.

The irony of soft postmodernism can deliver us from the sexual urge, because it possesses the capacity to ironize the libido without seeking to deny it. The urge exists, just like everything else, so the postmodernist will not stoke it and strengthen it by denying it; hence the preference for friendship over romance. In such a context, romance will be perceived as an obscene metaphysical urge. That is why it has become a religion with adherents and clergy, an expression of a quest for the absolute.

The postmodernist can enter a covenant, but of a different sort. It is not a metaphysical covenant but rather an adult one, between two who are destined, and who have decided, to walk together. The lack of pretense is precisely the thing that can breed – out of freedom, tenderness, and deep mutual caring – love, companionship, and friendship. Specificity, and the release from overarching need, leads to acceptance of oneself and of the Other as fleeting rather than absolute beings, and facilitates a mature, affectionate friendship, "love and harmony and peace and companionship."

The question is whether such is a covenant of the elderly, passionless and devoid of youth's ardor. It only takes a small nudge for atheistic ecstasy to morph into profound religious fervor, into faith and cleaving, on the condition that it retains its humbleness and equanimity. My faith and love spring from equanimity, from accepting my life as is, without preconditions. It is a faith that does not try to vault over itself, a security that arises from devotion that grasps at nothing.

Such a love will refrain from hurting the Other, and will uphold the covenant. I often tell young couples contemplating marriage that they must accept each other as they are, without either partner trying to change the other. The self-sacrifice of accepting and respecting the other as is – that is the covenant, and the only thing that lends totality to a marriage. A wise man once said that marriage begins at the moment we discover that the person we married is not the person we thought we married.

Another hasidic term that can be applied to these ideas is *tzimtzum*, "constriction" or "contraction." In Kabbala and Hasidism, *tzimtzum* refers to the original divine action, in which *ein sof*, or the divine infinitude, evacuated a space within Himself in which to create the cosmos. But did He really constrict Himself? Did He truly detract from His infiniteness, imprison part of Himself, and recede, leaving behind the vacuum known as the *ḥalal hapanui* (literally, the "empty space," or void)? Hasidism explains that the doctrine of *tzimtzum* should not be taken literally, because it is inherently paradoxical. God is at once present within the *ḥalal hapanui* and absent from it: As Maimonides wrote in *Guide of the Perplexed*, "He exists, but not through an existence other than His essence."[30] His infinitude enables Him to seem finite, with a finitude that is itself infinite. The *tzimtzum*, too, the process of creating a particular cosmos, can give hidden expression (and Hasidism indeed interprets the doctrine of *tzimtzum* as a description of the hiddenness of God) to the infinite absoluteness that determined that universe's identity. It is this process that differentiates a prison from a home. The walls of my home are not barriers that bear down on me, imprisoning and limiting me; rather, they are my identity; they delineate the place of my intimacy, my covenant. They do not make me finite; they are me; I am that I am, finite-infinite.

Marriage can thus be described as a nonliteral *tzimtzum*, and it is there, in the ability to sustain a paradox, that we can find an antidote to our aversion to commitment, brought on by the Sartrean position, which sees the *kalla*, or bride, as a *keleh*, a prison, and denies the possibility of covenant. If we succeed in seeing the specific, our choice, as an expression of the infinite, it will no longer constrict us. The discovery of the Divine Presence in a marriage can recast our calculated, principled

---

30. *Guide of the Perplexed* I:57.

choice of a partner as an expression of the infinite through randomness (as in Purim).[31]

I would like to see marriage as the true avant-garde of our era, the coming together through a simple covenant, "according to the law of Moses and Israel." The true rebellion is the Orthodox one, to be a gull in a world where no one consents to being duped, to commit when everyone avoids commitment. It is an act of self-sacrifice, but so is every covenant.

31. See Rabbi Shagar, *Chance and Providence.*

Chapter Nine

Self-Actualization and Society

We often occupy ourselves with the tension and contrast between self-actualization and development, on the one hand, and the needs of society, on the other. How much should we devote to society and how much to our own personal and spiritual growth? This tension has been discussed in various contexts over the ages by many Jewish and Western thinkers. In light of their ideas, I will attempt to sketch the optimal relation between the two demands.

This essay originally appeared in Rabbi Shagar's *Tablets and Broken Tablets*, 251–71. It was based on a talk delivered in 5755 at Midreshet Lindenbaum, an institute for women's Jewish studies in Jerusalem, where he was teaching at the time, in memory of one of their students. Rabbi Shagar prepared the talk for publication in a book in her memory which was not ultimately published. Edited by Dr. Zohar Maor, this essay is based on his draft, plus additions from notes prepared before the talk, a draft for another talk for Yom Kippur 5755, which also dealt with the relationship between the individual and society, and a draft for a third talk about repentance and society, delivered during Elul 5765.

Rabbi Naḥman of Breslov phrased the problem in typically incisive fashion: "Any time one hears another person while praying, meaning that one hears and senses that there is another person present – that is not good. For while praying, one must imagine that there is no one present other than oneself and the Lord, blessed be He."[1] According to Rabbi Naḥman, when I am praying, the presence of another constitutes a distraction, since his gaze removes me from my place of solitude, where I am sincere. My being-for-others, in Sartre's terms, causes me to see myself as the Other sees me – as an object rather than a subject. Furthermore, the other's gaze generates reflexivity, and consequently duality, in me. It externalizes me, blocking my path to an outpouring of the soul, to an encounter with my own inner self. The worshipper must elude this alienated consciousness in order to retain genuine inwardness. Yet halakha requires a quorum of ten for prayer. The obvious tension between that requirement and Rabbi Naḥman's statement epitomizes the conflict between self and society.

The discussion of this tension dates back to Ḥazal. The Yerushalmi's assertion, "When one is engaged in the needs of the community, it is as if one is studying Torah,"[2] deals precisely with this issue. One who studies Torah for himself, who is steeped in his own spiritual world, cleaves to the *Shekhina* and has nothing but the blessing of God's closeness. One who is forever occupied with the needs of the community would appear to be the Torah scholar's opposite, yet Ḥazal equate one with the other.

We find the opposite statement in the following midrash: "One who concerns himself with the needs of the community forgets what he has learned. Said R. Yehoshua b. Levi, 'R. Yehudah b. Pedaya taught me sixty laws concerning the plowing of a gravesite, and I have forgotten them all, because I concerned myself with the needs of the community.'"[3]

---

1. Rabbi Naḥman, *Likkutei Moharan, Tinyana* 103.
2. Y. Berakhot 37:1.
3. Exodus Rabba 6:2. The plowing of a grave is a noteworthy example, for it too is a community need. For another example, see the story of R. Shimon b. Yoḥai's emergence from the cave, which deals with the purification of the city (Shabbat 34a).

Torah study takes precedence over all mitzvot – except those that cannot be fulfilled by someone else – including manifestly social ones such as performing an act of charity, attending a funeral, and visiting the sick. Personal perfection does not come before pressing social requirements, even if attending to them entails a high spiritual price, like the one paid by R. Yehoshua b. Levi, who, says the midrash, forgot the Torah he had learned.

This question sometimes takes on a halakhic aspect. For instance: May one teach Torah to others who are on a lower level, or is it permitted – perhaps required – to avoid teaching others, devoting one's time instead to advanced studies? Rabbi Moshe Feinstein deliberates the question.[4] He cites Rabbi Moshe Sofer, the *Ḥatam Sofer*, claiming that when R. Akiva defined the commandment of "love your neighbor as yourself" (Lev. 19:18) as "a fundamental principle of the Torah,"[5] he meant it specifically in the realm of Torah and mitzvot – that in spiritual matters, no person takes precedence over another. But when it came to matters of the world, the *Ḥatam Sofer* wrote, R. Akiva opined that "your life takes precedence."[6] But Rabbi Feinstein disagrees, contending that in Torah matters, the individual takes precedence over others. "And it is clear," he writes, "that even when one already knows one tractate and even an entire *seder*, his study of other *sedarim* takes precedence over teaching others that same tractate…in studying the Torah, too, he is forbidden to teach others before studying himself." But in conclusion, he writes, "I have instructed that every Torah scholar, despite having his own needs…is required to spend time teaching others, even if in so doing he neglects his own studies." This ruling represents an attempt to balance self-perfection with social obligations.

These are, of course, only a few examples of the halakhic debate on this topic. It is a complex debate, both in the works of Ḥazal and in those of their successors throughout the ages. Below we will discuss some of the statements of these rabbis, interwoven with selections from secular thought on the matter.

---

4. Rabbi Moshe Feinstein, *Iggerot Moshe, Even Ha'Ezer* 4:26.
5. Y. Nedarim 9:4.
6. Bava Metzia 62a.

EXTREME WITHDRAWAL

Perhaps the most prominent rabbi who went to the extreme of prefer-
ring his inner life over communal involvement was Rabbenu Baḥya in
Duties of the Heart. He preached extreme withdrawal from society to the
point that, for him, the mitzvot of the Torah, which seek to maintain
the world, are the only barrier to utter seclusion. Yet he does require
the withdrawal of select individuals. Their task is to remind the masses
of their true purpose. To his mind, "It would not, however, conduce to
the improvement of the world that all human beings should practice
asceticism, for this would lead to the abandonment of civilization,"[7]
which is precisely why the world needs a few "genuine abstainers" to
serve as exemplars for the rest of humanity. He describes these elect as
"individuals who live in accordance with the highest type of asceticism,
so that they resemble the spiritual beings. They renounce everything
that distracts them from the thought of God. They flee from inhabited
spaces to the deserts or high mountains, where there is no company,
no society…. The love of God delights them so much that they do not
think of the love of human beings."[8]

Such asceticism stems from Rabbenu Baḥya's existential stance,
which is apparent in his emphasis on the "duties of the heart," meaning
inner duties, as opposed to the "duties of the organs" – one's external
commitments. The contrast between internal and external is thus parallel to the opposition between self and society. Meaningful contact with
the self, with one's truth and intimate sincerity – and, by extension, with
God – requires inner concentration and self-immersion, in a state of
tranquility and solitude. Such inwardness is not merely an internalized
externality; the difference between the two states is ontological, as the
Rishonim taught. Internality can never become a thing, an object standing before me, external to me – as opposed to the Other, who is always
an external reality to me. That is why society will, by definition, alienate
me from myself, distancing me from my innerness. The problem is not
merely a shortage of time or attention, but an inherent contrast stemming

---

7. *Duties of the Heart*, vol. 2, "Gate of Abstinence," chap. 1, 293.
8. Ibid., chap. 3, 303.

from the fact that solitude is a prerequisite for inner concentration, for cleaving to and finding the self, a self that is not social.

And indeed, Rabbenu Baḥya writes, "A sage, it is related, was wont to pass the first half of each day in the company of his fellowmen. But when he was alone, he would declare, 'Oh, for inward light,' by which he referred to duties of the heart."[9] Seclusion from others was, to this sage, a prerequisite for apprehending the light, which, hidden within the heart, is antithetical to social interaction.

This existential approach has many equivalents in Kabbala and Hasidism, often expressed through the argument that the source of the "I" is the root of the soul in the supernal realms, while culture (or nature) only endows man with the accouterments of selfhood. Every human being has an authentic kernel, the source of his soul, and he must thus be loyal to himself above all.

Rabbi Menaḥem Mendel of Kotzk (also known as the Kotzker) emphasized inner truth, and in his final years he completely withdrew from society, even from his own Hasidim. In expositions and tales, he gave voice to the conflict between inwardness and extroversion, between individual and society, inherent in the tension between "I" and "you" described by more than a few Western thinkers. First, there is his famous aphorism: "If I am I because I am I, and you are you because you are you, then I am I and you are you. But if I am I because you are you, and you are you because I am I, then I am not I and you are not you."[10]

According to this existential outlook, the "I" precedes the "you." Only after the individual discovers himself as a human subject, as a soul, can he acknowledge that the Other, the "you," also has a soul. The Kotzker teaches us that there can be no real "you" without an "I" first. The same idea is expressed in more extreme fashion in the following story, which not only calls for the "I" to take precedence over the Other, but bespeaks a profound aversion to society:

---

9. Ibid., vol. 1, introduction, 27.
10. Martin Buber, *Tales of the Hasidim: The Later Masters,* trans. Olga Marx (New York: Schocken, 1961), p. 283. See Rabbi Shagar, *A Time of Freedom,* 185.

An old Jew once lost his snuffbox made of horn, on his way to the House of Study. He wailed: "Just as if the dreadful exile weren't enough, this must happen to me! Oh me, oh my, I've lost my snuffbox made of horn!" And then he came upon the sacred goat. The sacred goat was pacing the earth, and the tips of his black horns touched the stars. When he heard the old Jew lamenting, he leaned down to him, and said, "Cut a piece from my horns, whatever you need to make a new snuffbox."

The old Jew did this, made a new snuffbox, and filled it with tobacco. Then he went to the House of Study and offered everyone a pinch. They snuffed and snuffed, and everyone who snuffed it cried: "Oh, what wonderful tobacco! It must be because of the box. Oh, what a wonderful box! Wherever did you get it?" So the old man told them about the good sacred goat. And then one after the other they went out on the street and looked for the sacred goat.

The sacred goat was pacing the earth, and the tips of his black horns touched the stars. One after another the people went up to him and begged permission to cut off a bit of his horns. Time after time the sacred goat leaned down to grant the request. Box after box was made and filled with tobacco. The fame of the boxes spread far and wide. At every step he took, the sacred goat met someone who asked for a piece of his horns.

Now the sacred goat still paces the earth – but he has no horns.[11]

While the Jews enjoyed their boxes and snuff and righteous sneezes – perhaps even uttering a blessing on the tobacco – the sacred goat was left hornless. The goat, of course, symbolizes the Kotzker himself. I think the story is a truthful depiction of the tension between the public's superficiality and herd mentality, and the man of spirit (like the rebbe), who is forced to sever his own connection with heaven in order to satisfy the needs of his flock.

---

11. Martin Buber, *Tales of the Hasidim: The Later Masters* (New York: Schocken, 1961), 288.

I AND THOU

This existential stance is by no means straightforward or self-evident –
not philosophically, and certainly not from a psychological standpoint.
Does the "I" indeed precede the "thou"? Can the self construct and find
itself solely within the bounds of its own selfness?

Many modern psychologists opine that the "thou" precedes the
"I." The famous developmental psychologist Jean Piaget claimed that a
child's "I" emerges through interaction with others,[12] that the self is
shaped by contact with what is not-self. The idea that it is precisely the
encounter with the Other that creates my "I" is Hegelian. The interaction
with the outside world enriches the inner one, and those who choose
to sink into themselves are destined to sag and atrophy. The outer provides material that the inner requires, that the inner fashions into its
own world, which is why one who pursues inwardness while ignoring
the Other is bound to fall apart. Furthermore, there is much danger in
the pursuit of inwardness, for one runs the risk of turning the self into
an idol, a fetish. In the religious context, and as opposed to certain
hasidic approaches, the importance of a mitzvah lies not in the subjective experience of closeness to God that one may derive from it. Rather,
as Rabbi Ḥayim of Volozhin wrote in *Nefesh HaḤayim*,[13] mitzvot have
objective significance, for they are the will of God, and by fulfilling God's
will, one participates in the rectification of the upper and lower worlds.
According to this approach, not only does the "thou" precede the "I," it
is a prerequisite for it.

Yet the relationship between "I" and "thou" can exist in two
modes. According to the first mode, it is precisely the recognition
of the existence of a "thou" – as an objective, valuable reality that is
external to and independent of me – that generates an "I" with value
and dignity. Without it, one develops a stunted, infantile personality
full of feelings of inferiority and lacking in objective perception and
confidence. Some advocate an objective I-thou relationship, deeming
alienation an essential step toward the formation of a complete, independent self. According to this conception and derivative psychological

---

12. Jean Piaget, *Six Psychological Studies* (New York: Random House, 1967).
13. *Nefesh HaḤayim*, gateway 1, chap. 4, and elsewhere.

approaches, the relationship with the Other is founded on respect but devoid of intimacy. However, there is also a second mode of existentialist discourse, which, when it does not fall into narcissism, can conceive of the Other as intimacy. There, the "I-thou" relationship is between two subjects, two interdependent souls. Although such dependency may breed insecurity and controlling behavior in both parties, under optimal conditions each side can imbue the other with confidence. Such a relationship can facilitate dialogue between subjects, a "fusion of horizons" of sorts, to borrow a hermeneutical term from the German philosopher Hans-Georg Gadamer.[14]

According to the first existential approach that we examined, the "I" precedes the "thou" (and sometimes even opposes it); according to the second, the "thou" precedes the "I." It would appear that the ideas of Martin Buber could resolve the tension between these two options, for he prioritizes neither "I" nor "thou." Instead, each enables the other. The dialogic condition emerges not from resistance, as Piaget suggested, but from connecting with the Other, through some affinity. The actualization of an affinity to a "thou" transcends both the rigid conception of selfhood that Franz Rosenzweig portrays[15] and Rabbi Soloveitchik's conception of slavery as existential loneliness and the exile of speech.[16] Interest in the Other derives from one's capacity to go beyond oneself and establish a real affinity; it depends on one's trust in the Other. For Buber, dialogue expresses the discourse and spirit that develop between two persons through conversation. The Other is not the subject of my speech; he is partner to it.[17]

For Buber, the "I" is not a given; it emerges through an affinity. Thus, when we address the Other as an "it," an object, we establish a certain kind of "I"; when we turn to the Other as a "thou," a subject,

14. See Hans-Georg Gadamer, *Truth and Method*, trans. Joel Weinsheimer and Donald G. Mar (London: Continuum, 1975).
15. Rosenzweig, *Star of Redemption*, 74–82.
16. Rabbi Yosef Dov Soloveitchik, *Divrei Hagut VeHaarakha* (Jerusalem: World Zionist Organization, 1982), 358.
17. This notion is reminiscent of Rabbi Naḥman's idea that Torah homilies are a shining of the countenance. See Rabbi Naḥman, *Likkutei Moharan, Kamma* 27; Rabbi Shagar, *Expositions on Likkutei Moharan*, vol. 1, 242–43, 334–337.

we establish ourselves as a more exalted "I," one that is also free of objectification. In effect, according to Buber, by relating to the Other as a subject we establish our own "I" as subject. I-thou relations are an expression of the world of speech, which is a coupling or convergence that defies description in the terms of the world of "it."[18] According to Buber, a true, profound society emerges through the special relationships formed between many "I-thou" pairs, while at the center of all affinities lies the affinity to the divine: "The extended lines of relations meet in the eternal *Thou*. Every particular *thou* is a glimpse through the eternal *Thou*."[19]

Rabbi Tzaddok HaKohen of Lublin expresses similar ideas of the divine in his *Dover Tzedek*:

> There are three known manners in which one can encounter the Lord, and they are called "I," "Thou," and "He." One encounters the Torah through the secret of "Thou." It is known that it is a loftier level than "I" among the attributes of the Lord, blessed be He, but when it comes to the attainment of *human* attributes, one first apprehends that the Lord, blessed be He, is opposite one, and only then can one apprehend that the Lord, blessed be He, is in fact inside one's heart and mind. And not until the *Shekhina* is speaking from one's throat can one use the title "I."[20]

The "Thou," God's presence outside man, precedes the "I" – the divinity within man. Only through the objective apprehension of the "Thou," the divinity that is entirely outside oneself, does the "I" – subjectivity, which is identified with the *Shekhina* – emerge. Rabbi Tzaddok identifies the level of "Thou" with Torah study – as well as with the free choice and striving upon which the Torah is founded – and the "I" with prayer, the realization that everything is in the hand of heaven: "in the secret of 'Thou,' where we realize that the Lord, blessed be He, is in

---

18. Martin Buber, *I and Thou* (Edinburgh: T. & T. Clark, 1944).
19. Ibid., 75.
20. Rabbi Tzaddok HaKohen of Lublin, *Dover Tzedek* (Har Berakha: Mekhon Har Berakha, 5768), 184.

fact inside our hearts and minds, and that everything comes from Him."[21] Yet when Rabbi Tzaddok discusses the three levels of divinity – their order is "Thou," "I," and "He" – he is speaking of man. The first stage is autonomy (free choice) and the ability to stand and be present in front of the Lord, blessed be He. Only afterward can one attain subjectivity and identify divinity with it. It is then that man loses his freedom, discovering that all his decisions and actions come from the Lord, blessed be He. The highest level, however, is "He," the hidden root, the World to Come, the utopian and concealed. That level is revealed in the human will, the attribute of *sovev kol almin*, or "surrounding all worlds," which justifies everything. Here freedom reemerges, for only if man chooses with his deep, authentic will can he align himself with the supernal will. This alignment is the source of the release and self-acceptance that trigger ecstasy. The level of the individual is not subjectivity, but something beyond it. It is freedom – "will has no reason."[22] The higher "I," above consciousness, may be the goal, but one cannot attain it without first standing opposite the Other, and without gaining the authenticity of the second stage.

The first stage is thus "Thou" – the divine "Thou" that constructs human endeavor out of freedom. Freedom, in turn, enables the "I," authenticity, which entails a loss of freedom. At the final stage, we return to the higher "I," beyond consciousness, where we find a higher freedom.

I AND HE

In the relationship between the individual and the Other, sometimes the other's presence manifests not as "thou" but as "he," as transcendence. In fact, for Rabbi Tzaddok, the presence of the "thou" is already a manifestation of the transcendent. The French Jewish thinker Emmanuel Levinas developed a social and ethical system centered on the encounter with the other's transcendence, with the absolute as it is revealed in the other's countenance. For Levinas, subjectivity arises from my

---

21. Ibid., 191.
22. See Rabbi Tzaddok HaKohen, *Tzidkat HaTzaddik*, section 198; Rabbi Shmuel MiSochachov, *Shem MiShmuel* I, *Noaḥ* 5675. This stance is similar to the postmodernist conception, which we will describe below.

commitment to the ethical imperative and the responsibility imposed upon me by the revelation of the absolute in the countenance of the Other. As Ze'ev Levy describes this view, "philosophy is … the troubled consciousness of the self, caused by the Other…. The ego that is seemingly steeped in the sense that it is alone in the world is 'roused out of its tranquility,' 'disturbed' by the Other, forced to emerge from its self-totality, meaning from its former sense that there is none but it, and take responsibility."[23] Social responsibility, dignity, and morality begin with responding to the Other, who transcends me. Society, for Levinas, is founded upon the awe of the absolute that is revealed in the face of the Other; not on love, meaning a sense of closeness and intimacy.

While responsibility means moving beyond the self, only through responsibility can I attain selfhood. As Levinas writes: "To be Me/Ego, thenceforth signifies being unable to escape from responsibility, as if the whole edifice of creation stood on my shoulders."[24] Subjectivity is in fact the relinquishment of the freedom to do as I please: "Freedom would therefore signify the acceptance of a vocation to which I alone can respond."[25] A similar idea was propounded by Rabbenu Baḥya, who explains that in dedicating oneself to the Lord, blessed be He, one is released from the angst generated by the subject's confinement within himself.[26] However, for Levinas, this devotion is manifested as responsibility toward the divine inherent in the human Other.

For instance, if a man leaves his family because he is attracted to another woman, his guilty conscience should not be interpreted on the psychological level; one must go to its source, as Martin Heidegger did. For Heidegger, it is infinity's call to the finite, the standing in the eye of the infinite, that generates pangs of conscience. Like the title of Heinrich Böll's book about the Nazis' crimes, the question is "And where were you, Adam?" For Levinas, too, it is the betrayal of the Other, of the responsibility that the Other's presence entails, that keeps one awake at

---

23. Ze'ev Levy, *Otherness and Responsibility: A Study of Emmanuel Levinas' Philosophy* [Hebrew] (Jerusalem: Magnes Press, 1997), 85–86.
24. Emmanuel Levinas, *Humanism of the Other* (Champaign: University of Illinois Press, 2013), 33.
25. Levinas, as quoted in Levy, *Otherness and Responsibility,* 87.
26. *Duties of the Heart,* vol. 2, "Gate of Humility," chap. 5, 89.

night. As soon as I have spoken to someone, stood face-to-face with him, I can no longer ignore him. To fail to respond to the Other is to fail to respond to being. Therefore, Levinas says, the individual cannot disregard his social responsibility – not only to ensure the health and safety of the Other, but to respect his difference and otherness.

I AND WE

In contrast to the first existential stance that we discussed, which gives precedence to the self and grapples with the tension between individuality and social requirements, the communal point of view begins with "we." In more radical versions of this outlook, the community has a spiritual essence, or spirit, that emanates from its individual members' souls. On the national level, for example, Rabbi Kook and others speak of the "spirit of the nation," while the Maharal of Prague refers to the "form of the nation." According to such ideas, individuals are parts of a single body, and the existence of such a communal or national organism is evident in the collectivity of its creative endeavors. When a teacher faces a class, for example, we clearly see that the interaction between the students generates a collective dynamic that is fundamentally different from the sum of their individual reactions.

The positive and true aspect of the communal outlook is manifest in our sense of solidarity and patriotism, of companionship and affinity for those next to us; in how the singing of "*HaTikva*" moves us and makes us feel connected to generations of Jews. These feelings issue from a shared reservoir, from the place where our individual personalities melt away, fusing with a larger collective.

One expression of the communal point of view, where the "we" precedes the "I," is in social psychology, which recognizes that individuals conduct themselves differently among others than when alone. Another, profound manifestation of such a viewpoint is Jungian psychology, based on the idea of the collective unconscious. Dream symbols, for example, are described by this outlook as archetypes shared by all of humanity.

Each of these attitudes has its own implications, of course, but what unites them is the idea that the individual is not an island, but rather part of a collective. It is not just about the individual's influence on another individual – which can be perceived as taking place apart from other influences – but about all individuals being part of a single body, a united essence. One need not conceive of this body as the spirit of a nation; language is a powerful example of something that transcends our private selves (we speak it but do not create it), predates our private existence, and clearly shapes our world and images.

Despite the tendency to identify Rabbi Kook's and Maimonides' worldviews with such a communal ideal – Rabbi Kook due to his assertion that the community precedes the individual, and Maimonides in that he posits the community as a prerequisite of faith[27] – both can be seen as prime examples of a perspective that begins with "I" but is later inverted, granting preeminence to social engagement.

When it comes to Maimonides, the reason is clear: His ideal was an intellectual cleaving to God, which can be achieved only by the individual. Maimonides can thus be said to advocate an intellectual aristocracy. In the introduction to his commentary on the Mishna, he explicitly states that the sole purpose of the laity is to facilitate the individual sage's actualization; basically, it serves as his society, keeping him company.[28]

Still, Maimonides concludes his *Guide of the Perplexed* with an analysis of the following verses:

> Thus said the Lord: Let not the wise man glory in his wisdom, let not the mighty man glory in his might, let not the rich man glory in his riches; but only in this should one glory, in his earnest devotion to Me, for I the Lord act with mercy, justice, and righteousness on earth; for in these things I delight, says the Lord. (Jer. 9:22–23)

Maimonides explains that the first verse describes the virtues of man, the loftiest of which is wisdom, i.e., knowledge. Yet even that is not his ultimate purpose:

---

27. See Rabbi Shagar, *This Is My Covenant*, 99–100, 104–107.
28. See *Maimonides' Introduction to His Commentary on the Mishnah*, trans. F. Rosner (Lanham, MD: Jason Aronson, 1995), 91–106.

Thus the end that [the prophet] sets forth in the [second] verse may be stated as follows: It is clear that the perfection of man that may truly be gloried in is the one acquired by him who has achieved, in a measure corresponding to his capacity, apprehension of Him, may He be exalted, and who knows His providence extending over His creatures as manifested in the act of bringing them into being and in their governance.... The way of life of such an individual, after he has achieved this apprehension, will always have in view loving-kindness, judgment and righteousness, through assimilation to His actions, may He be exalted.[29]

Many have noted this sudden shift in Maimonides' narrative, which throughout the preceding chapters portrays the apprehension of God as the ultimate end, and all of one's social existence as a means. Ultimately, it seems, some social interactions are a means, material underpinnings that can be acquired only through contact with the world. But another kind of social interaction is a goal in itself – when an enlightened person rectifies society by infusing it with divine insight, thus perfecting providence.

A similar reversal is apparent in the ideas of Rabbi Kook, who conveys, in passages that bear the hallmarks of personal experience, the deeply felt tension between society and the pursuit of existential spiritual completeness:

The individual can attain virtue only from within himself, from his essential, inner self, and not from without, for coincidences do not yield true happiness. And yet, are not the Torah and the mitzvot, which come to man from without, the essence of happiness? Indeed, upon examination, we find that one attains through Torah and mitzvot only what is already latent in one's soul.[30]

29. *Guide of the Perplexed* III:54, 638.
30. Rabbi Abraham Isaac Kook, *His Chambers: Personal Chapters* [Hebrew] (Ramat Gan, 1998), 24.

Society, the environment, and practical life lie across my path like stumbling blocks, preventing my holy passion – which is imbued with the sacred light of the awe of God and basks in innate love – from revealing itself all the time, from striving in all the attributes. Whenever I am in the company of people I become embarrassed.[31]

As with other issues, Rabbi Kook's personal experiences carried over to his formal writings, where one can find the same tension, along with a proposed solution:

The greater a person's stature, the more he must search for himself... so that he must engage in solitary reflection... until finally his soul is revealed to him... and then he will find his happiness... in becoming even-tempered and uniting with all of creation, and in lowering himself to the extreme edge of humility, to the point where any being in the depth of his self is annulled... then he will comprehend every fragment of truth... wherever it may roam. And he will gather everything to him without a trace of hatred, jealousy, or competition.

One whose soul radiates within must often engage in solitary reflection. The habitual company of others, who are typically coarser in spirit than he, dims the scintillating light of his higher soul.... It is very difficult to tolerate society, meetings with people who are fully immersed in an entirely different world.... And yet, it is precisely this ordeal that burnishes and elevates one.[32]

Rabbi Kook opens with solitary meditation, but, as we see in the first passage, it is a prerequisite for facilitating a more profound, nuanced approach to society and other people. The suffering that an individual endures due to his encounters with society becomes cathartic, enabling

---

31. Rabbi Abraham Isaac Kook, *Eight Notebooks* [Hebrew] (Jerusalem: Raanan family, 5764), notebook 8, 281.
32. Rabbi Kook, *Orot HaKodesh*, vol. 3, 270.

him to refine his social interactions. My capacity to accept the Other, even if through anguish, bonds me to him.

THE POSTMODERN COMMUNITY

In conclusion, let us examine the issue of the relationship between self and society from a postmodern point of view. According to postmodern conceptions, community cohesion, nationality, and all other social structures are fictions, a means of exerting control and power. Post-modernism assumes the pivotal role played by discourse as a shaper of interactions, but it challenges the unity of discourse, the idea that it has a fixed center. Postmodernism strives to deconstruct and dissolve that center.

I wish to discuss two thinkers whose ideas can help us understand the postmodern perspective on the relationship between the individual and the community. Employing these ideas, through the conception of prayer, I will attempt to outline the ideal relationship between individual and society, bringing us back to the quotation from Rabbi Naḥman with which we opened. Here is the anthropologist Clifford Geertz:

> To see ourselves as others see us can be eye-opening. To see others as sharing a nature with ourselves is the merest decency. But it is from the far more difficult achievement of seeing our-selves amongst others, as a local example of the forms human life has locally taken, a case among cases, a world among worlds, that the largeness of mind, without which objectivity is self-congratulation and tolerance a sham, comes.[33]

The fact that I experience myself from the inside, as a subject, but see the Other from the outside, as an object, is the source of the foreign-ness and alienation between people. We saw above that it is also what

---

33. Clifford Geertz, *Local Knowledge: Further Essays in Interpretive Anthropology* (New York: Basic Books, 2000), 16. For more on this statement by Geertz, see the following works by Rabbi Shagar: *We Will Walk in Fervor*, 345; *At the Handles of the Lock* [Hebrew] (Efrat: Yeshivat Siaḥ Yitzḥak, 2004), 78–79; and *In the Shadow of Faith*, 98–99.

alienates the existentialist from society. Geertz proposes a process that is meant to overcome this gap. It includes three imperatives: that we "see ourselves," "see others," and "see ourselves amongst others."

With the first, the individual perceives himself from the outside, "as others see [him]," as an object. Indeed, seeing my "self" as others see me is enlightening, because it releases me from my subjectivity. Afterward, one sees the Other from the inside, as "sharing a nature" with him, and realizes that the Other, too, experiences himself as a subject.[34] With the dual effect of self-awareness and decency, these two steps close the gap between self and Other. The third point of view places the individual not across from the Other but alongside him, "a case among cases." In his own eyes, the individual is no longer an "I." Nor is he a "you." He is a "he." It is an external viewpoint that generates the humility typical of the postmodern world – overcoming hubris, and instilling in the individual the knowledge that he is nothing special. Such unpretentiousness often breeds a lowliness that borders on modesty, based on the knowledge that the self is "random." "But on this man will I look…on him who is poor and of a contrite spirit" (Is. 66:2), the prophet says. A society that arises out of such an outlook will be tolerant, giving space to its individual members. To my mind, it represents a distinctly secular worldview, for it posits that our existence is random and meaningless. It is informed by the trauma of communism, which forced it to forgo totality and togetherness, to settle for a simple coexistence of decent human beings.

To better grasp Geertz's social theory and the alternative that I am proposing, we will employ kabbalistic terms to describe various facets of God's presence in the world.

I have already suggested that postmodernism expresses the perspective of *sovev kol almin,* or "surrounding all the worlds" – the divinity that transcends the universe. The other perspective, *memalei kol almin,* or "filling all worlds," is the opposite of *sovev,* in that it describes a reality that is not random but is instead steeped in meaning, and even generates a powerful mutual responsibility based on a perception of

---

34. This point of view can be compared to the attribute of mercy, which encounters the Other not as an objective reality but as a subject. It constitutes the ability to encounter the other's intimacy.

the unity of creation and of the other's godliness. On its own, however, the *memalei* point of view poses great danger: In the spiritual context, it can give rise to stagnation and dogmatism, because it "contains" divinity in limited, constricted vessels; in the social context, it can create a suffocating embrace of the Other that overlooks the other's uniqueness.

That is why *sovev* – with its equanimity and the reflexivity that generates relativism – must augment the *memalei* point of view. *Sovev* may be corrosive, but it engenders tolerance. Spiritually, forgoing the need to constrict God in a vessel leads to a sense of release and ecstasy, to a true encounter with the divine infinitude. Geertz's third stage thus offers us a nonessentialist view of society, which has clear advantages. Nonetheless, although I certainly do not underestimate the tolerance and freedom inherent in such a perspective, it can lead only to a social existence *alongside* others, while Judaism aims for an existence *with* others. That is, for example, the purpose of communal prayer. The ideas of Franz Rosenzweig can help us understand how such prayer is generated, and why it does not necessarily deny the individual his freedom:

> But originally, the song for several voices is of the same tone and rhythm, and, beyond the content of the song, whatever it might be, there is the form of unanimity. Moreover, the content is itself nothing other than that which establishes this form. One does not sing together in view of a specific content, but rather one seeks a common content in order to be able to sing together.... What is it that is established first? It can only be the community of the song, and this community not as a fait accompli, not as an indicative, but as a fact established at the moment.... And this invitation could not be an imperative...rather the invitation itself must be placed under the sign of the community, the one who extends the invitation must himself be invited...and in return, the farthest, the whole world, is not external to him, but a fraternal reality that sings in unison with him the praise and the act of thanks.[35]

---

35. Rosenzweig, *Star of Redemption*, 249.

At the center of Jewish prayer is the uttering of "we," which depends on trusting the Other. Such a quorum need not be based merely on the collective idea, according to which an individual exists only as part of the community. Rather, Rosenzweig's explanation enables us to create a "we" that accepts the postmodern pursuit of freedom and an open field, but, as opposed to postmodernism, does not settle for being alongside others. The utterance of "we" can arise from a profound partnership, but one that is not only the result of shared interests, inflated egos, or a conceited patriotism. Rather, it must arise out of a focal point of shared *kavana*, or intention – "How could the two separate realities find each other if not in the unity of that before which they sing?"[36] – and faith in the other's sincerity. The knowledge that his soul and his freedom drive him to be a partner to me, to my values, my faith, my Judaism – even my searches – generates a powerful sense of partnership, unity, and solidarity. And beyond the feeling, there is a true unity of souls. The communal song is not the sum of its singers but a coalescence of voices. Its special challenge is to create harmony without drowning out the uniqueness of each individual voice. I must not forget myself in myself, but rather remain attuned to the Other, to adapt myself to him out of faith that his freedom will adapt itself to me. The awesome experience of merging is why communal song holds such powerful sway over us, and it is the secret reason for the sense of purification and exhilaration that it so often engenders in us.[37]

If the above is true of communal song, then it is doubly true of communal prayer. Prayer, too, reveals that element of the "shared I" that retains the freedom of all its individual participants. I perceive the Other with the same earnestness with which I perceive myself, and consequently, through the inner freedom that I grant him, I see him as

---

36. Ibid., 250. For a similar idea, see Joseph B. Soloveitchik, *The Lonely Man of Faith* (New York: Doubleday, 1992), 43–66.
37. Rabbi Hayim of Volozhin, in *Nefesh HaHayim* (gateway 1, chap. 20), explains that "by bending one's lips, which is the [soul] aspect of *nefesh* of *ruah*, one elevates the words higher and higher with one's voice, until the root of the soul." Through speech, man connects with his deepest source, his beginning, the root of the soul where everything is one.

my partner, as one with me. We partake of the same existence and, no longer strangers to one another, "We are all one man's sons" (Gen. 42:11).

However, it is important to emphasize – once again, in light of Rosenzweig – that such harmony persists in prayer only because it exists in the world of what ought to be, not in the world of what is. It anticipates a redeemed, harmonious world but does not make it truly manifest in our lives:

> [I]t is not yet possible for the community or for the man in the community to pray only for the coming of the Kingdom; this prayer is still obscured and blurred by all sorts of other supplications: the forgiveness of sins, the ripening of the crop, in short, all that the rabbis designate with great profundity [as] the needs of a solitary man. For there are the needs of the solitary man. If the individual were already really united with the whole world as he anticipates this in the praise and thanks, then he would have renounced all his needs. They are the sign that he is only anticipating in the praise and the act of thanks, the deliverance from the bonds of need, within the bond that in general joins the soul and the world, and therefore that Redemption remains absolutely to come, that it is a future.[38]

In the world of what is, we can never fully overcome the tension and dissonance between individuals, the "a man is a wolf to another man" mentality. Yet through our faith in the faith of the Other, in his subjectivity and sincerity; by creating a shared center toward which all can aspire, we can draw from the future community of prayer and harmony to go beyond the solitude of the individual.

---

38. Rosenzweig, *Star of Redemption*, 251–52.

Chapter Ten

Seventy Bullocks and One Sukka: The Land of Israel, Nationalism, and Diaspora

T he Talmud describes the festival of Sukkot as one in which all of the nations of the world stand before the Lord, blessed be He, and are granted absolution:

> R. Elazar stated, "To what do those seventy bullocks [offered during the seven days of the festival] correspond? To the seventy nations…" R. Yoḥanan observed, "Woe to the idolaters, for they had a loss and do not know what they have lost. When the

---

This was essay compiled from drafts from 5753 and 5765 as well as parts of a draft written before Passover 5765. Edited by Yishai Mevorach and Dr. Zohar Maor for publication in a book of sermons by the author for Sukkot, *In the Shadow of Faith*, 113–32.

173

Temple existed, the altar atoned for them, but now who shall atone for them?"[1]

This description relates to the words of the prophet Zechariah regarding the nature of Sukkot at the end of days: "And it shall come to pass that every one who is left of all the nations that came against Jerusalem shall go up from year to year to worship the King, the Lord of hosts, and to observe the festival of Sukkot" (Zech. 14:16).

One gets the impression that Sukkot is a universal festival – one that encompasses all the nations of the world. Yet it appears as though the Jewish people retains its unique status: The nations are granted absolution only when standing before God by virtue of the Temple rituals, which are exclusive to the nation of Israel. Furthermore, the site of the celebration is the Temple, "the place that the Lord your God shall choose" (Deut. 15:5), in Jerusalem, the capital of the Jewish people.

Can universalism and Jewish particularism coexist? Does the festival of Sukkot truly equalize all nations, or is it perhaps meant to emphasize the uniqueness of the Jewish people? In the Midrash,[2] we read the following: "It is like two people who went before a judge, and we know which of them won the trial only according to who emerges with a spear in hand.[3] So, too, Israel and the nations…. We know Israel won only when they emerge from before the Holy One, blessed be He, with their palm branches and citrons in hand."[4]

To my mind, the writings of the Maharal of Prague, which deal with the relationship between the people of Israel and the Land of Israel, posit a profound, nuanced universalism that does not preclude uniqueness, even if founded upon Jewish particularism.

1. Sukka 55b.
2. Leviticus Rabba 30:2.
3. The translation of the Aramaic באיין as "spear" appears in the *Arukh*. See the *Matnot Kehuna* commentary on Leviticus Rabba op. cit.
4. The midrash contains a typical barb: The "victory lap" with spear in hand was a Roman custom, so it is ironic that the Jews' victory over the nations is expressed by way of a similar image.

BACK IN ITS PLACE

The Maharal, who was ahead of his time in many of his ideas, also anticipated secular viewpoints about nationalism:

> The Diaspora is itself conclusive proof of the Redemption, for there can be no doubt that the Diaspora constitutes a divergence from order, as the Lord, blessed be He, put every nation in its proper place, and put the Jewish people in its proper place, which is the Land of Israel. Exile from one's place is a total divergence. All things that are moved from their natural place cannot persist in a place that is unnatural for them; rather, they must return to their natural place. For were they to remain in a place that is unnatural for them, the unnatural would become natural, which is an impossibility.... Indeed, for the Jewish people themselves... the appropriate place, according to the natural order, is the Land of Israel, as their own masters rather than under another's mastership. Like every other natural thing, each has its place... and each is its own master. Were they to remain in the Diaspora forever, it would...become natural. This is because only things that are natural persist, for the nature that the Lord, blessed be He, granted to every single thing sustains that thing until it is perpetuated....
>
> Dispersion is also unnatural, and just as each and every thing returns to its place, so, too, the disjointed and scattered parts become one again...which is why every dispersal is bound to coalesce. Thus, the dispersal of the Jewish people among the nations is a divergence from nature, for since they are a single nation, it would be proper for them to stand together and be one...and it would seem that their dispersal, more than any other, is utterly unnatural...therefore, the Diaspora can teach us of the Redemption.[5]

---

5. Maharal of Prague, *Netzaḥ Yisrael*, chap. 1.

Today, there is a consensus as to the natural right of nations to self-determination, and political-territorial independence forms the basis of international law. This opinion was presaged by the Maharal. Throughout his writings, he employs Aristotelian science, which constitutes the physical underpinning of his metaphysics, and here he applies it to international politics. This science teaches that every object aspires to be in its natural place. The rock, for example, aspires to return to its source, the earth, which is why, when thrown into the air, it falls back down (we now know, of course, that what compels the rock is gravity). Aristotelian science, according to the Maharal's interpretation, asserts that chance occurrences cannot persist, for they are a divergence from the nature of a thing, and thus by definition must cease if the thing is to return to its natural state. Based on these assumptions, the Maharal discusses a certain order, a necessary causality by which each nation is assigned a territory. He also emphasizes that dispersal and enslavement run counter to this order, and that every nation must by nature return to its proper place. It emerges that the fulfillment of the national idea is guaranteed because it partakes of the natural order. Thus, to his mind, the dispersal and Diaspora of the Jewish people are themselves irrefutable proof of the coming Redemption: The Jewish people lost its independence, was exiled from its land and scattered to the ends of the earth, but this state of affairs cannot persist, for it contradicts the natural order dictating that nations are destined to be gathered to their proper place.

The Maharal's conception of the nature of nations is linked to another insight: Gratuitous hatred, or *sinat ḥinam*, by dividing a nation, when by nature it would tend to coalesce, is the quintessential diasporic sin. For him, gratuitous hatred is not merely exile's cause, as *Ḥazal* asserted,[6] but also the punishment and the exile itself:

> For they were given the First Temple by virtue of the three patriarchs…and the Second Temple was parallel to the community of Israel itself…. Therefore, gratuitous hatred negates the power of the community of Israel, which is called the community of

6. Yoma 9b.

Israel because it connects and unifies Israel. Thus, it is said that the Second Temple was destroyed solely by gratuitous hatred.[7]

He adds:

> For the exile is the dispersion and division of the Jewish people. When they are divided among themselves as well, they increase the division and dispersion beyond what the Lord, blessed be He, assigned them.[8]

The Maharal's ideas about the unity that derives from the natural order of nations, and his conception of the sin of gratuitous hatred, profoundly influenced Rabbi Kook, in terms of both Rabbi Kook's opposition to separate communities[9] and his positive outlook regarding a Jewish national movement whose standard-bearers were heretics and sinners.[10]

---

7. Maharal, *Netzaḥ Yisrael*, chap. 4.

8. Ibid., chap. 25.

9. See Rabbi Kook, *Orot*, 73; Rabbi Kook, *Eight Notebooks*, notebook 2, 283.

10. In fact, the national unity described by the Maharal and later by Rabbi Kook is metaphysical. The Maharal transposed Aristotelian physics to the realm of ideas, to encompass such entities as nations. This reflects the Maharal's conception of nature not only in the sense of the physical world, but also in an immanent sense: certain essential features of a thing are not part of its physical nature. Thus, the causality he describes should be understood to exist on a metaphysical or even theosophical-kabbalistic level. There is no doubt that the above quotation posits an Aristotelian formulation of kabbalistic ideas, expressed by Nahmanides (e.g., in his commentary on Lev. 18:25) and Rabbi Abraham ibn Ezra (e.g., in his commentary on Ex. 23:20), regarding each nation's ministering angel and connection to its land, including the Jewish people's connection to the Land of Israel.

The metaphysical law regarding the cohesion of the nation lies beyond matters of ethics and religion. It expresses the world's metaphysical causality, which precedes adherence to Torah and mitzvot and is thus essential to the very existence of the nation. Hence the capacity, manifest in Rabbi Kook's approach, to form an alliance with secular Jews: "There are no end of negative physical and spiritual ramifications to the nation's splintering ... even though a full schism cannot, and will not, come to pass. To think of it is to think of all-out idolatry, which we are certain cannot endure" (Rabbi Kook, *Eight Notebooks*, loc. cit.).

The Maharal's statements have many implications, of which we will discuss only a few. They are relevant to our contemporary ability to maintain a partnership with the secular world and its values, especially since Jewish identity and connection to the land – once common denominators of religious and secular Zionism – have been eroding in recent years. To my mind, the Maharal's ideas pose an alternative basis for uniting the nation, via a connection that depends not this or that action, but rather on the Jewish people's metaphysical cohesion.

The question we face today is: Are parts of the Israeli left fated to be rejected by the national religious community, just as the Haskala (Jewish Enlightenment) movement was rejected by the Hasidim in Europe? Although as a rule they never abandoned other Jews, even criminals, the Hasidim waged a fierce battle against those who supported the Haskala, the so-called *maskilim*. This fact is driven home in the following statement by Rabbi Shneur Zalman of Liadi, in the *Tanya*:

> Even those who are distant from the Lord's Torah...we must draw in with strong cords of love, and perhaps that will bring them closer to the Torah.... Even those to whom one is close and whom one's reprimands failed to sway from their sins – one must love them despite the commandment to hate them. For both are true: One must hate the evil in them and love the good buried in them, the divine spark they carry.[11]

The problem was that the hasidic idea of belonging to Judaism hinged not on the performance of this or that action, so that "even those who are distant from the Lord's Torah" could partake of Jewish identity. Rather, it depended upon a Jew's belonging to the Jewish intimacy, to the inner Jewish spark, and identifying with the Jewish world and the things it represents: belief in the Holy One, blessed be He, and His Torah, and acceptance of His mitzvot, even if one does not fulfill them in practice. Upon concluding that the *maskilim* had severed their bonds with that intimacy, the Hasidim inferred that these Jews had been cut off from Judaism itself, and proceeded to wage all-out war against them.

---

11. *Tanya*, pt. 1, chap. 32.

To my mind, the author of the *Tanya*, who made no explicit reference to the Haskala, would have said that such a split entails *karet*, the
biblical punishment by which one is spiritually cut off from the Jewish
people. By extension, such an individual would no longer be a partner to
the Jewish intimacy. On the face of it, the law of *karet* would also apply
to present-day secular Jews. Indeed, for many secular Jews, identifying
as Jewish has nothing to do with belief in God and His Torah, nothing to do with Judaism, which at bottom is about Torah and mitzvot.
The sinner described in the *Tanya* still identifies with that intimacy; thus,
even if he is a thief and a scoundrel, so long as he attends synagogue to
hear the *Kol Nidrei* and recite the *Ne'ila* prayer on Yom Kippur, he is a
Jewish thief and scoundrel.[12]

Like the Hasidim, who founded their idea of the Jewish people's
cohesion on identification with a kernel of intimacy, many members of
Israel's national religious movement base this unity on national identification and residence in the Land of Israel. Both elements are absent
from the current discourse among many within the secular left. Is a
state of *karet* (disconnection) between the religious Jew and the secular leftist thus inevitable? In light of the Maharal's statements about a
unity rooted in the natural law of nations, which precedes any religious
or moral definition and is a prerequisite for the existence of the nation,
perhaps we can formulate an alternative approach that will enable us
all to shelter in a single sukka – even those who are not connected to
their Jewishness.

EXILE AS A NATURAL STATE

In clearly acknowledging that a nation by nature aspires to return to its
place, one must conclude that exile, the Jewish Diaspora, is a condition
for Redemption. As the Maharal writes, "Dispersion is also unnatural,
and just as each and every thing returns to its place, so, too, the disjointed
and scattered parts become one again." To his mind, the Diaspora is a
sign of the future Redemption. Further on, however, things get more
complicated, as he seeks to establish the possibility of Jewish existence
in exile despite his fervent faith in the Redemption:

---

12. See Rabbi Shagar, *A Time of Freedom*, 143–44.

And even though He made us downtrodden and wretched, it is our very wretchedness that reveals our elevated quality. The quintessential feature of the Jewish people's wretchedness is its dispersion among the nations, and it is indeed scattered to the ends of the earth. One may come to think this situation implies a great shortcoming... for what greater shortcoming can there be in a nation than its being scattered to the ends of the earth, to the point where the nations say that it cannot even be described as a nation, that the Jewish people is no longer bonded to the divine?

On the contrary, however, we will provide clear evidence that the dispersion of the Jews throughout the world indicates its divine quality. When the Jewish people was in its land, it was in their proper place. And when you examine all things that have a place, it is clear that their respective places relate to them and are appropriate for them... to the extent that were a thing to depart from its unique place, it would be lost.... But when they are exiled from the land to a single place, this does not apply to the Jewish people, for the Jewish people is the crux of the world. As we have stated, the place relates to the owner of the place. That is why the Jewish people was dispersed all over the world – for it is fitting that a nation that is the entire world would have the entire world as its place.[13]

One can discern in these statements an attempt to contend with Christian dogma, which saw in the wretchedness of the exile and dispersion of the Jewish people evidence that it had been rejected by God, "to the point where the nations say... that the Jewish people is no longer bonded to the divine." In this argument, the Maharal tries to base the Jewish people's existence precisely on exile by defining the dispersion as inherent to it.[14] It emerges, then, that the law of nature associating each and every nation with a geographic location,

---

13. Maharal, *Netzaḥ Yisrael*, chap. 56.
14. [Ed. note (Yishai Mevorach): For more on the Maharal's ideas about the nature of existence, redemption, and exile, see Rivka Schatz, "Existence and Eschatology in the Teachings of the Maharal," *Immanuel* 14 (1982): 62–72.]

which was so clear at the outset, does not necessarily apply to the Jewish people. What is astonishing about the Maharal's approach is the implication that, because the Jews lack a single place that is unique to them, nature itself is unnatural to the Jewish people. Indeed, the entire world is their place, they are cosmopolitan, and their state of dispersion is a function of their virtue. According to the Maharal, the exile does not simply imply the future Redemption; it is, in and of itself, evidence of the virtue of the Jewish people. By nature, the Jew and the Jewish nation possess lofty spiritual aspirations, exalted yearnings, which is why the nation cannot seize on a specific location and see it as the be-all and end-all: "For it is fitting that a nation that is the entire world would have the entire world as its place." Its place is beyond geography, and its identity transcends the constricted boundaries of nationhood.

Moreover, this virtue is part of the spiritual development of the Jewish people, which was forged while they were exiled in a single land – Egypt. The Maharal adds, "And do not be troubled by the fact that the Jewish people were in Egypt, which is a single place. For at the time, the Jewish people had not acquired that lofty virtue, until they emerged from Egypt and the Lord, blessed be He, took them as His people." Later, however, after the process of their uplifting was concluded, "it is fitting for a thing that is the entire world to have all four points of the compass as its place."[15]

At the end of the day, Redemption itself, i.e., the ingathering of the exiles to the Land of Israel, is perceived by the Maharal as unnatural to the Jewish people. The Jew's authentic place is, in fact, in exile, and the Land of Israel is outside the sphere of his natural state. The same approach is apparent in the Maharal's reading of the following verses from the episode of the twelve spies: "And they spread an evil report of the land that they had spied out unto the Children of Israel.... And all the congregation raised their voice and cried; and the people wept that night" (Num. 13:32–14:1):

---

15. Maharal, *Netzaḥ Yisrael,* loc. cit.

All natural things yearn for their natural place. Were the land a natural place for Israel, and had they yearned for the land, it would have remained so for eternity. But in this case, the opposite was true: They wept for nothing, and did not want to go to the land. This shows that the land is not the natural place of the Jewish people, which is why they did not remain there... for "the favor of a place is in the estimation of its inhabitants" (Sota 47a), and everything yearns for its natural place; thus their weeping indicated that the land did not fully belong to them. They wept, showing that the land was not entirely theirs, and so they were exiled.[16]

This passage implies that exile is the ideal Jewish condition. One can see in it an augury of the ultra-Orthodox worldview that clashes with Zionist Orthodoxy's conception of a non-miraculous Redemption: namely, that there can be no natural political Redemption – only a miraculous one – for there is no natural mode of Jewish political existence, due to the contrast between faith and the Jewish people, on the one hand, and kingship and nature, on the other.[17]

Should we take the Maharal's "non-Zionist" statement as a divine decree, and conclude – as did, for example, Hermann Cohen and Franz Rosenzweig[18] – that the Jews' universalism means that their place is in exile? Should we take the sukka, in which we are meant to make our home for a week out of the year, as a symbol of the exilic nature of the Jewish people? Indeed, the sukka is, on the one hand, an expression of the Redemption, and on the other, a fleeting thing, "the fallen sukka of David" (Amos 9:11), a reminder of the Jewish people's supernatural existence in the desert. Or can we perhaps glean another option from the Maharal's statement?

The Maharal's unwavering belief in the ingathering of the exiles, as manifest in a statement quoted partially above – "for all components

---

16. Ibid., chap. 8.
17. For more on this tension, see the exposition on Israel Independence Day in Rabbi Shagar, *Broken Vessels*, 149–58.
18. Cohen, *Religion of Reason*, 253–68; Rosenzweig, *Star of Redemption*, 317–25.

have a single thing in common...every dispersal [including that of Israel] is bound to coalesce" – implies that it is the exile that establishes the possibility of the redemption of the people of Israel in the Land of Israel. The Jew, precisely because he is the "crux of the world," must divest himself of his particularistic nature and pass through the crucible of exile to the ends of the earth, if he is to one day regain that nature – which is tantamount to the Land of Israel – in a more exalted, rectified fashion.

The path from exile to redemption in the land is expressed by way of the mitzva of sukka. The sukka, a temporary dwelling that parallels the temporary exile, is also compared to the Land of Israel.[19] The Maharal's statement imbues the connection between the sukka and the Land of Israel, between the temporary dwelling and the permanent home, with special significance: We require a miracle if we are to earn a place on earth. But because the Land of Israel is the Jew's miracle, nature itself becomes miraculous.

This has two implications. First, the Jewish nature acquires a wondrous aspect that prevents it from sinking into the banality of the world; hence the Maharal's fantastical-utopian characterization of the end of time.[20] Second, critically, the path to the Land of Israel, to a government and territory, passes through exile. That exile is more than merely historical, a punishment for past sins; it cultivates the ability to gain a foothold in the land and take root in it. The Diaspora, befitting the Jewish people by virtue of its unique character, is what constitutes its connection to the entire world, and what enables the Jews to hold fast to their land without being confined to narrow-minded parochialism and staunch patriotism.

---

19. One is reminded of the statement attributed to the Vilna Gaon to the effect that there are only two mitzvot a person can enter with his entire body: settling the Land of Israel and dwelling in the sukka. See Rabbi Hillel of Shklov, *The Voice of the Turtledove* (Spring Valley, NY: Feldheim, 2002), 7. Rabbi Hillel was a student of the Vilna Gaon. [Ed. note: The authenticity of this work is disputed among scholars.]

20. See, for example, Maharal, *Gevurot Hashem*, first introduction; Gershom Scholem, "Concluding Statement," in *The Messianic Idea in Judaism: A Seminar in Honor of Gershom Scholem's Eightieth Birthday* [Hebrew] (Jerusalem: Israel Academy of Sciences and Humanities, 1981), 257.

It emerges that not only is the sukka informed by the worldly –
"'You shall dwell' (Lev. 23:42) implies [dwelling] in the same manner
as you ordinarily live"[21] – but the world subsumes "the fallen sukka
of David."

MODERATE NATIONALISM

The sukka, a diasporic, temporary dwelling that is also an expression of
the Land of Israel's harvest festival – incorporating the exilic and the
rooted – has the capacity to answer difficult questions that arise with
the Jewish people's return to the land.

What happens when the balance of power shifts, when the exiled
nation, scattered to the ends of the earth by virtue of its own exalted
quality, becomes sovereign over a defined territory? Now that it has
won dominion, must its collective historical memory of Diaspora and
defeat compel it to treat the other residents of the land with contempt
and hostility? Put in more concrete terms: Will the Jewish people's
return to "the international politics that it once relinquished against its
wishes and yet guided by an inner will"[22] lead it to treat the Other within
its midst just as it was treated by the nations of the world? Must power
corrupt us? Were that the case, we would lose our link to the world at
large, the characteristic that, according to the Maharal, turns the Jewish people into the "crux of the world." The Maharal's idea can yield a
fresh approach, saving the defeated-cum-victor from the trap that awaits
him; a path to the Land of Israel that passes through exile may soften
the Jewish people as it gains ascendancy, so that it yet belongs to "the
four corners of the earth."

The desire to establish a "softer" nationalism – one that makes
room for the Other, that does not look down on or disdain other nations –
can be traced back to the Torah. In contrast to the Maharal, who discusses all the world's nations, the Torah refers to the Other living among
the Israelites who inherit the land: "And if a stranger sojourns with you
in your land, you shall not do him wrong. The stranger that sojourns
with you shall be unto you as the homeborn among you, and you shall

---

21. Sukka 28b.
22. Rabbi Kook, *Orot*, 13.

love him as yourself; for you were strangers in the land of Egypt: I am the Lord your God" (Lev. 19:33–34). The Torah embeds the foundational Jewish experience of bondage in Egypt as a lesson for the present. But the memory of the Exodus, so pronounced in the Bible as to be the rationale for many of the mitzvot, is not merely a recollection of victory and redemption; it is also a remembrance of suffering and poverty. This memory is meant to foster sensitivity and awareness of the other's tenuous plight, and to prevent condescension toward him: "Therefore love the stranger, for you were strangers in the land of Egypt" (Deut. 10:19).

The Torah's objective in decreeing the memory of the Exodus is to establish a solidarity of the *defeated*, not the *victors*. Epic past triumphs are not meant to make us drunk with power; rather, they are to instill in us the faith that it is God "who gives you power" (ibid. 8:17), steering us away from the temptation to believe that "my power and the might of my hand have gotten me this wealth" (ibid.). Aggression exerts a powerful draw, and the Torah warns against it repeatedly in its passages of rebuke. Preoccupation with power and the pursuit of authority over others stem from a dearth of faith in the Lord, blessed be He, and fly in the face of that which the Torah seeks to impart to the nation as it inherits the land: memory and the sensitivity it engenders.

The message is clear: The insecurity of the Diaspora must deeply inform our confidence as the inheritors of the land. Otherwise, confidence will degenerate into hubris, into the sense that all is due to "my power and the might of my hand." Such a state of mind precludes faithful devotion to God and sensitivity to the suffering of the strangers in our midst – a quality we were dispersed to the ends of the earth in order to acquire. Thus, it is precisely the diasporic nature of the sukka – the very sukka in which God commanded us to dwell when we emerged from Egypt, "that your generations may know that I made the Children of Israel dwell in sukkot when I brought them out of the land of Egypt: I am the Lord your God" (Lev. 23:43) – where one surrenders one's power and puts his trust in God, that can facilitate an all-encompassing divine influx that includes the offering of seventy bullocks for the welfare of the world's nations.

Yet there is more to it. Both nationalism and universalism are necessary. Nationalism is rootedness in what one is, in an identity unique to the nation and the individual. However, if it is not to turn rigid and callous, it must be tempered by universalism, if only in order to introduce an element of doubt into it. Universalism subverts the preference for one national identity over another, as well as the very authentic existence of that identity. That is because universalism is the shared dimension, the common grounds for all of humankind. Put in religious terms, it is where we encounter the image of God. From this point of view, the human is the real, and nationalism merely a later, highly malleable construct.

Conversely, universalism must be augmented with nationalism. Universalism is an abstraction in that it "makes" all human beings identical, effacing the very real differences between people. Nationalism, for its part, emphasizes the other's difference and inimitability. True, in modern philosophy we encounter a different reading of universalism, one that is based on accepting the other's difference, on the fact that no two persons are comparable – each has his place in the world. But even this view of universalism requires nationalism, for universalism is at bottom a movement that denies identity. That is why it makes it impossible to pinpoint how one person is preferable to another. The individual's place is defined not through the acknowledgment of his specific and coherent identity, but rather by his inaccessible otherness. There is no internalization of his uniqueness, only of his incomparability to any other. Nationalism, meanwhile, marks a resurgence of the specific, immutable identity.

This insight, regarding the compounding of the nationalist and the universal, can also be read in the Maharal. While the Jewish people may be the crux of the world whose place is the entire world, he writes, it must retain its uniqueness and remain apart from the other nations:

> The survival of the Jews depends on their separation from the nations, to the extent that they are a complete nation unto themselves. For a thing that is complete unto itself stands apart, and if the Jews do not remain apart from the nations, they are not a complete nation unto themselves. Thus, the difference between the Jews and the other nations, the place where they stand on their own, utterly unconnected to the others, is what enables them to survive in exile.[23]

---

23. Maharal, *Netzaḥ Yisrael*, chap. 25.

THE REMAINDER OF JACOB

Among postmodernist thinkers, one can discern a new avenue for establishing universalism, in which the universal is no longer the result of a single "vessel" containing all people, however similar or alike they are, but rather the result of a *remainder* of humanity that cannot be contained in any vessel or order – including, for instance, a national order. That is the remainder about which Micah prophesied: "And the remainder of Jacob shall be in the midst of many peoples, as dew from the Lord, as showers upon the grass, which are not looked for from man, nor awaited at the hands of the sons of men" (5:6).

What is this remainder? It is the extra piece of the puzzle. Mathematically speaking, it is the remainder left without a "place" after a division. Socially, it is "a foreign body within the social texture, in all its dimensions."[24]

And what is the remainder of Jacob?

> The remnant of Israel, those who have remained faithful, the true people in the people…the man in Judaism is always somehow a remnant. He is always somehow one who remains, an inside whose outside was seized by the river of the world and driven off, whilst he himself, that which remains of him, remains standing on the shore.[25]

The Jew remains outside the existing order, "'the part that is no part,' not simply a nation among nations, but a remainder, that which has no proper place in the 'order of nations.'"[26] He abstains from that order by cleaving to the Torah. The Torah is the heterotopic space in which the Jew resides,[27] in that its order is an order of justice and integrity

---

24. Žižek, *Enjoy Your Symptom!* 122.
25. Rosenzweig, *Star of Redemption*, 427–28.
26. Žižek, *The Puppet and the Dwarf*, 131.
27. [Ed. note: The word "heterotopia" was coined by Foucault. In our context, it denotes the "other space," meaning a space – either linguistic or physical – that is other, not in the sense that it differs from adjacent spaces, but in that it does not exist on the same plane and in the same order as other spaces, and thus stands categorically apart. Below we will see that the heterotopic Jewish existence also deconstructs the existing

rather than an order of nature. In cleaving to the Torah, the Jew alienates himself from a world that relies on the natural order, and from the
spaces of all nations, thus, by dint of his very alienation, becoming Other.[28]

Jewish nationalism does not relate directly to that of any other
nation, for it exists unto itself, like the life of the Jew. It is its own place, a
self-contained whole, its borders a part of itself. Rosenzweig described it
as an existence whose eternity stems from having "the universe entirely
in itself."[29] Jewish nationalism is its own system, and as such it does not
compete with others. In fact, the Other is not even on its horizon, so
that it does not compare itself to him in any way.[30] It is utterly foreign
to those who are "a remainder in and of themselves."[31]

The Maharal also employed the idea of the remainder. In interpreting the unity of Israel, he used the same terms with which he
interpreted the unity of God.[32] To him, Jewish nationalism has no object,
just like the concept of God's unity.

In the Maharal's terms, the Jewish people is "pure form," whereas
other nations are "form embedded in matter" and have an object outside
themselves. Jewish nationalism is without "objectuality"; it is what it is,
and requires nothing outside itself – an essence, content, or purpose – to

order of peoples and nations. See Michel Foucault, preface to *The Order of Things: An
Archaeology of the Human Sciences* (New York: Vintage Books, 1994), xv–xxiv; and
Michel Foucault, "Of Other Spaces: Utopias and Heterotopias," *Architecture/Mouve-
ment/Continuité* 5 (1984): 46–49. On this use of the term in subsequent scholarship,
see Peter Johnson, "Geographies of Heterotopia," *Geography Compass* 7, no. 11 (2013):
790–80.]

28. See *In the Shadow of Faith*, 63–83.

29. Rosenzweig, *Star of Redemption*, 324.

30. [Ed. note (Y.M.): Jewish diasporism, too, should be identified with the remainder, as
it constitutes a deferral of the world and settlement in a "non-place" – a borderless
castle in the sky. To be precise, the Jewish spirit seeks not diasporism, but rather the
place that is a remainder, that despite being in "nothingness" is everywhere. This
outlook contradicts the idea that diasporism is uprootedness and the denial of place.
This view lacks the insight that non-place is itself a place. See Gur-Ze'ev, *Toward Diasporic Education*. It is worth noting briefly that due to its paradoxical nature, Jewish
diasporism differs from Levinasian otherness and the Derridean gap.]

31. Žižek, *The Puppet and the Dwarf*, 131.

32. See, for instance, Maharal, *Netzaḥ Yisrael*, chap. 38; and Maharal, *Derekh Ḥayim*
"Introduction to the Mishnah."

define it. For that reason, the Jewish people's place is the entire world, and there is no specific place that defines it. Similarly, God's place is not the world, for, as the Midrash states, "He is the place of the world."[33]

The unity of God is a unity without content, whose definition is ontological; it is a self-sufficient existence, and so too is the existence of the Jews. This insight is also apparent in the idea of the *pintele yid* ("Jewish kernel") found within every Jew, according to Hasidism, where we can also discern a certain influence of the Maharal: the Jewish kernel is that which "describes" the Jew; it is his intimacy with his existence, which is being-for-itself[34] – "Let them be yours alone" (Prov. 5:17). It emerges that a Jew is not defined by a specific content, but rather through his very intimacy with his being-Jewishness. It is a closed loop in which existence feeds itself, requiring no external input. As noted, this dynamic is why Hasidism sees anyone who relinquishes that kernel, that intimacy, as having been cut off from his people. The Maharal would likely not have identified with this assertion.

It is worth adding that, as "pure form," the Jewish people is a foreign body among the nations. Yet this is precisely what allows it to contribute to the collective. It "is not simply a foreign body, an intruder which disturbs the harmony of the social bond: precisely as such, [it] is what 'holds together' the social edifice by means of guaranteeing its fantasmatic consistency."[35] First, the remainder invades a society that is not its own, thus crumbling all orders; it exists but cannot be positioned in any order. Consequently, it "disturbs the harmony of the social bond," subverting it by positing absolute otherness and difference. This pure difference becomes the basis for the universalist consciousness precisely because it undermines the consensus. In the Maharal's terms, it subverts the laws of nature, which serve to judge the Other or the group of others. Here is how Slavoj Žižek formulated the same insight: "It is as if

33. [Ed. note (Y.M.): Genesis Rabba 68:9. See also Rabbi Tzaddok HaKohen of Lublin: "The Jewish people has no place in the world, like the Lord, blessed be He, who is the place of the world while the world is not His place ... for [Jews] have no purchase in any specific place ... as it is stated, He gave Jacob the World to Come and Esau this world" (*Kometz HaMinḥa*, part 2, section 10).]
34. For more on this Sartrean term, see p. 80.
35. Žižek, *Enjoy Your Symptom!* 123.

the universal and the particular paradoxically *change places*: what one encounters in the center instead of the universal is a kind of 'particular absolute'... while the various universals are all of a sudden reduced to the role of species of an impossible-unfathomable genus."[36] The encounter with the remainder grants each and every individual a place and personal space. Universalism, in this case, constitutes in fact rejection of unity and uniformity. It emerges not from a view of the similar, but because of the inability to unearth a yardstick capable of determining that one person is preferable to another. The remainder signifies that individuals are incomparable.

But there is another aspect to the existence of a remainder. As noted, the Maharal emphasizes that while in exile, the Jewish people must remain apart from the gentiles and safeguard its uniqueness by retaining its language, dress, and customs. This demand is the immediate practical implication of conceiving of the Jews as a remainder: "The survival of the Jews depends on their separation from the nations. ... For a thing that is complete unto itself stands apart." On the face of it, the demand for difference alienates one's surroundings. But there is another way of looking at it: Even if it leads to apartness, the being-for-itself mode of Jewish existence need not result in alienation. On the contrary, it has the capacity to bring out the human in every individual. Humanity itself, like Jewish existence, can be defined as life for itself, without an object, a mode of being that is not defined by that which lies outside it. The presence of the Jew can evoke the realization that what makes one human is not a certain idea or identity, but rather the very fact of one's humanity. As such, the Jew uncovers a profound bond to all that is human, and highlights that humanity through his very existence.[37]

---

36. Ibid.
37. [Ed. note (Y.M.): There is an apparent contradiction between the above description of the Jewish people as "pure form" and the assertion that this state of being is applicable to all of humanity. The discrepancy can be reconciled through the fact that the passages above dealt with nations and peoples, in which context "pure form" is a category exclusive to the Jewish people, while the discussion here pertains to individual people in general, not nationalism. The individual Jew, as a member of the Jewish nation, can expose what is common to all people: their very being.]

This marks a reversal in the approach to the universality embodied by the remainder: At the outset, the crumbling of the national order led to the acknowledgment that no individual can be given precedence over the other, an acknowledgment that grants the Other a place by virtue of an inability to judge him. But such a universality undermines rather than facilitates unity. However, when the humanity of every individual becomes the basis for a universal connection and a granting of personal space, human unity can be accomplished.[38]

The remainder, broken down into constituent, inaccessible parts, is the blessing that reveals the humanity latent in everything, "as the showers upon the grass."

We oscillate between universalism and nationalism, between humanity and covenant. It is a fertile opposition, where the loss of one pole immediately damages the other. In order to establish worldwide solidarity, the world needs a pure nationalism that is not defined through the relations between the nations, a remainder of Jacob.

The dichotomy between the statements "Lo, it is a people that shall dwell alone and not be reckoned among the nations" (Num. 23:9) and "it is fitting that a nation that is the entire world would have the entire world as its place" is expressed through the festival of Sukkot: On the

---

38. [Ed. note (Y.M.): It appears that Levinas aimed for a similar place: "What identity does it cling to? One that refers only to itself and ignores all attributes: one is not a Jew by being this or that. Ideas, characters, and things can be identified insofar as they differ from other ideas, characters, and things.... A person is not who he is because he was born here rather than there, and on such-and-such a day, or because he has blond hair, a sharp tongue, or a big heart...he just is who he is. In the same way, one is just a Jew.... 'You are born a Jew; you don't become one'" (Emmanuel Levinas, *Difficult Freedom: Essays on Judaism* [Baltimore: Johns Hopkins University Press, 1990], 50). A Jew's Judaism is beyond all definition. It is what it is, a premise that serves as a basis for one's attributes, just as one's human self precedes one's attributes. But this insight does not lead the Jew to withdraw behind his Judaism. On the contrary, Levinas writes of a difficult ethical dilemma that arises. Because it is pure essence without attributes, Judaism is an "absolute sense of identity... alien to any sense of introspection or complacency. Instead of just paying attention to the outside world, it exhibits a perpetual attentiveness.... It listens and obeys...a Jew is accountable and responsible for the whole edifice of creation.... Far from being a serene self-presence, therefore, Jewish identity is rather the patience, fatigue, and numbness of a responsibility – a stiff neck that supports the universe" (ibid.).]

one hand, "You shall dwell in sukkot seven days; all that are homeborn in Israel shall dwell in sukkot" (Lev. 23:42) – exclusively the homeborn in Israel; and on the other, "And it shall come to pass that every one who is left of all the nations that came against Jerusalem shall go up from year to year to worship the King, the Lord of hosts, and to observe the festival of Sukkot." Finally, the festival of Sukkot represents the Jewish dichotomy between Diaspora and homeland: The Land of Israel's harvest festival, with the sense of stability that it induces, is celebrated in the sukka along with the exile.

An Individualist Religious Thinker, Without Grand Narrative

Rabbi Shalom Carmy

Among the Israeli religious writers loosely associated with postmodernism, Rabbi Shagar enjoys special prestige. One reason is his devotion to the close reading of classical Jewish texts – not only the hasidic works that play a large role in his thinking, but the standard halakhic literature, the Talmud and its medieval and modern analysts. It is not irrelevant that he devoted his career primarily to the teaching of Talmud along with other classical texts. Several books of halakhic-conceptual analysis by Rabbi Shagar have appeared, on subjects like martyrdom and the Sabbatical year.[1] This aspect of his work plays little role in the present volume. Yet it is a vital part of his contribution.

The precise manner in which Rabbi Shagar integrated talmudic study and philosophical reflection is open to criticism. My revered

---

1. For example, see Rabbi Shagar, *Loving You unto Death*, on martyrdom; and *Shemitta*, on the Sabbatical year.

mentor Rabbi Aharon Lichtenstein expressed reservations about its subjectivity and the danger of subordinating the logic of halakhic discourse to theological speculation. Many who are sensitive to these complaints, as I am, continue to find value and enjoyment in Rabbi Shagar's insights and in his approach to Talmud.[2] For us, the fact that he incorporates this essential element of Jewish thought, and has something important to say about it, fortifies his standing as a serious partner in religious study.

Rabbi Shagar left behind a legacy of discourse rather than a system, partly by choice and partly by fate. Like Pascal, his early death closed off the possibility of producing a comprehensive treatise. His characteristic immersion in dialogue with the texts is not intended to be exhaustive, as would be the case in academic research, and it often makes his thinking hard to follow. The book before you is more straightforward in its argument than most of his work, and is therefore well suited to serve as an introduction. At the same time, the fragmentary nature of Rabbi Shagar's writings intensifies one's sense of his sincerity, which is confirmed by those who knew him. Despite his frequent resort to postmodern jargon and even more characteristic reliance on the esoteric vocabulary of Hasidism and mysticism, he seems committed to meeting his audience at eye level, so to speak. There is little reason to suspect him of an offstage agenda. The problems he addresses are real to him, and if his writing is sometimes opaque in terminology or argument, it is his best effort to deal with the questions that engage him as he struggles to develop his views.

Rabbi Shagar's map of contemporary Orthodox discourse may be configured slightly differently from the one English-language readers are accustomed to. At the risk of gross simplification: Americans tend to begin by dividing modernists from *Haredim*. The former are considered more engaged with the modern world, as measured by openness to secular education, celebration of the accomplishments of secular Zionism, and the like. Within the modern camp, there is a more nationalist orientation, arrayed beneath the banner of Rabbi Kook, and an outlook more devoted to the cultivation of the individual, identified with Rabbi

2. See my article "'The Covenant Function' and the Encounter with God" [Hebrew], *Netuim* 17 (5771): 195–99.

Soloveitchik. To see the world from Rabbi Shagar's perspective, it may be useful to contrast the collectivist ideology associated with Rabbi Kook and his disciples with the legalistic or behavioral theology most astringently championed by Professor Yeshayahu Leibowitz. The former founds the religious way of life on the national project; the latter envisions a world where the individual's religion is defined entirely in terms of the decision to obey God or withhold obedience. Both approaches are insensitive, from Rabbi Shagar's religious point of view, to the individual's search for meaning. On this map Rabbi Soloveitchik appears, very much in light of his *Halakhic Man* rather than later works such as *The Lonely Man of Faith*, as a legalist with a somewhat broader, denser, and richer sense of individual humanity and human striving than that subscribed to by Leibowitz.

When I refer to Rabbi Shagar as a kind of individualist, it is because his deepest impulse is to rebel against religious systems that, in his view, compel the individual to subjugate his or her experience to anything external, be it the destiny of the collective, as it is for many religious Zionists, or the austere and external authority of the law, as is the case for the Leibowitzian.

How Rabbi Shagar perceives the current state of Jewish religious thought matters for two reasons. First, because he does not reflexively oppose "modern" positions to "*haredi*" ones, we should not be surprised when at crucial points he finds more to recommend in *haredi* positions than in typically "modern" doctrine. Second, and perhaps more important, when Rabbi Shagar himself makes extreme or one-sided statements, it is necessary to know what position he is arguing against, and therefore to what degree he offers a desirable corrective to popular ideas and how his own should be subjected to correction.

II

What is Rabbi Shagar's relation to postmodernism? As a thinking religious individual, not a professor, he (thankfully) makes no attempt to comment exhaustively on so-called postmodernism. His strongest relations are to French authors like Sartre, Lacan, Baudrillard, Foucault, and, to a lesser extent, Levinas. He learned a great deal from the late Wittgenstein, especially *On Certainty*, and he shows familiarity with standard Jewish and non-Jewish German writers like Buber, Rosenzweig, Heidegger, and Gadamer, as well as a variety of studies on recent social trends. Not all these thinkers come under the postmodern rubric, but even those who preceded it exerted a degree of influence on postmodernism.

Much ink has been spilled on the meaning of the postmodernist label. Rabbi Shagar has much to say about modernity and postmodernity. For example:

> [M]odernity believed in the existence of an absolute truth. This belief led to a demand for coherency and the resolution of all contradictions in a given language, be it historical, psychological, biological, or religious. (p. 58)

> Modernity saddles the individual with responsibility for himself and his world, so he can no longer rely on what is external to him. He must show initiative and create his own values and conceptions. Hence modern values – at least in their accepted sense – are secular values. They place the individual in the center, shifting God from His once preeminent position and even rendering Him irrelevant. (p. 42)

Correspondingly, postmodernism is "a mode of life and a state of consciousness" (p. 85) deriving from "a loss of faith in grand narratives, in metaphysical goals, and in comprehensive theories…the historical accounts that were largely constructed in order to justify one side or another, and with it their belief in an exhaustive moral and intellectual harmony upon which one could base one's life" (p. 86). Postmodernism is belated insofar as it is aware of the modernist project and is disillusioned with it.

Rabbi Shagar's use of postmodernism can be subsumed under three main categories: epistemological, metaphysical, and in the description of contemporary social phenomena. In all these areas, but especially in the first two, he tends to endorse the mentality arising from postmodernism.

What do we know in the religious realm? For modernity, it was deemed possible, by believers and atheists alike, to arrive at some demonstrable and universally compelling truth about God, if only the investigation were carried to its ultimate conclusion. Like Rabbi Soloveitchik, Rabbi Shagar does not advance formal arguments against such attempts; like him he takes it as a cultural given that religious commitment nowadays is generally not grounded securely in "objective" proofs, available equally to all rational inquirers. For Rabbi Shagar, the fact of religious pluralism, the lack of agreement about religious truth, carries a great deal of weight. For the disappointed modernist, the upshot is skepticism and despair of reaching truth. Rabbi Shagar holds that postmodernism shows a way to sustain robust religious commitment.

What can we say about God? The modernist, who aspires to transparent rational comprehension, is bent on formulating true religious doctrine. Rabbi Shagar, relying on Wittgenstein and others, denies that human language is capable of formulating such truths. Therefore the modernist project here too ends at an impasse. Again, Rabbi Shagar maintains that postmodernism allows for robust religious confidence in the absence of the kind of rational certainty sought by the modernist.

Whether and why there has been a radical change regarding these two questions can be disputed. After all, Jews have constituted a minority wherever they have been for millennia, so religious pluralism is hardly new to us. The marginalization on principle of conventional proofs of metaphysical truths goes back to Kant, offhand an eminent Enlightenment modernist, though one so minded may discover in him postmodern elements. And Maimonides, among many others whom Rabbi Shagar read through a Wittgensteinian lens, rejected transparent definitions in religious philosophy, though without elaborating a general critique of language as did Wittgenstein. Rabbi Shagar responds to these questions, and lists plausible reasons for the uniqueness of the late-twentieth-century predicament and therefore the urgent need for his postmodern remedies. See in particular chapter 5.

The nature of religious faith is central to the opening chapters. The second half of the volume focuses on contemporary culture and social relations. Here Rabbi Shagar functions as both diagnostician and therapist. Tackling a broad range of problems, he argues convincingly that we confront genuine novelty in contemporary consciousness, so Jewish thought must go boldly where it has not gone before, both in our analysis of the social world and in proposing fresh ideas about how to live our lives in light of these new experiences.

The book thus moves from more abstract philosophical questions to areas of pressing, concrete concern. This progression is logical. In what follows, I will comment briefly on some of Rabbi Shagar's themes in that order, highlighting particularly apt passages. Nevertheless, the interests of many readers may incline them in a different order.

III

Chapter 1, "Uncertainty as the Trial of the *Akeda*," is one of the most difficult sections in this book. Rabbi Shagar starts out by gesturing at several questions perennially discussed by moderns and intertwined, though not identical, with the question that interests him, as implied by the title of his essay. The necessity of analyzing a variety of earlier texts also complicates his exposition.

Shagar first questions the relationship of religion and morality, whether one should obey God when His commands counter conventional morality, whether God can command unjust actions. He is equally unhappy with the views he ascribes to Kierkegaard, Leibowitz, and Rabbi Soloveitchik, according to which God stands above ethics, so His command trumps the ethical, and with the view he attributes to Rabbi Kook, which posits a harmony between the divine command and natural morality. The nineteenth-century Reform rabbi Abraham Geiger taught, contrary to the biblical text that praises Abraham's willingness not to spare his only son, that the true lesson of the *Akeda* is that Abraham did not do as God had originally commanded. This upending of the Torah has become virtually an article of faith among liberal Jewish spokespersons. Whether or not Rabbi Shagar was familiar with Geiger's role in this innovation, he seems obviously aware of the approach. What is important is that he clearly rejects it. He does not justify disobedience to God. What, then, does he advocate?

Before returning to this question, Rabbi Shagar raises the one that is really at the heart of his thinking: "How can a person be sure such a command really comes from God?" (p. 4). And his answer is that Abraham indeed cannot know with certainty, contra Maimonides, who inferred from Abraham's willingness to kill his son that the true prophet does not doubt his mission. Rabbi Shagar wends his way through a number of midrashim in which Satan challenges Abraham's commitment, and notes that ultimately Abraham is unable to justify his action by referring simply to the fact of divine command. For Rabbi Shagar: "The lesson is clear: A conceited, all-knowing religious stance renders the trial, and with it the entire religious endeavor, a sham" (p. 13).

Rabbi Shagar repeatedly insists that he is not a relativist; the kind of uncertainty he locates in Abraham, and in all robust religious faith, in no way diminishes the absoluteness of commitment. In chapter 6, he spells this out explicitly as a readiness to die and even kill for one's faith. Nor does he disdain the role of rationality in religious discourse. Much of his philosophy stands or falls on whether and how satisfactorily he explains this position.

What about Abraham, or at least the midrashic Abraham Rabbi Shagar exhibits, who can be depicted neither as laudably disobedient and rebellious nor as "conceited [and] all-knowing" in his obedience? It is crucial for Rabbi Shagar, as for Kierkegaard and for Rabbi Soloveitchik, to exclude the kind of harmonious reading familiar from popular invocations of Rabbi Kook's approach. So he concludes: Abraham must obey, but he refuses to give away his human feelings and ethical obligations. "[O]ne is under no obligation to turn a blind eye to an injustice, even a divine injustice" (p. 16). In the effort to define his position, Rabbi Shagar adopts the term "protest." He continues: "It is precisely through the act of protest that one expresses religious fervor, and, perhaps, retroactively justifies one's obedience."

The word "protest" may not be the exact one needed, as none of the sources cited by Rabbi Shagar convincingly portrays any attempt on Abraham's part to object to the command, even to pray for its abrogation, or any expression of reluctance or divided loyalty. One could have chosen another term – submission, surrender, acceptance, and faith all come to mind – but none of these words would be perfect either. So we are left with "protest," even though this term, in its ordinary sense, is inadequate.

What Rabbi Shagar argues plausibly is that Abraham's resolute-ness in fulfilling the command is independent of rational justification. The idea that ultimate commitment cannot be argued for and made universally comprehensible is in keeping with the postmodern theme of this book. It may also appeal to students of the *Akeda* who are not fully on board with the particular exegesis of the chapter.

In formulating his approach to the *Akeda*, Rabbi Shagar could have gotten some help from Rabbi Kook, who holds in a responsum that when faced, like Abraham, with a command that contravenes natural morality, a prophet must clarify whether the voice he hears is indeed that of God.[3] Kierkegaard and Rabbi Soloveitchik place the religious above the ethical without annihilating the latter.[4] The distinction between the two spheres in Kierkegaard's *Fear and Trembling* emphasizes the incom-municability and particularity of the religious command, which sounds very much like Rabbi Shagar's opposition to modernist rationalism and universality. In any event, Shagar does not engage with these texts, perhaps because he disagrees with other aspects of Kierkegaard's book and is therefore disinclined to become entangled in his formulations. It should be noted that a reader who differs with Rabbi Shagar's analysis of Abraham as a biblical-midrashic character might nonetheless find it valuable in understanding the philosophical issues involved.

Like the opening essay, chapter 2, "My Faith: Faith in a Post-modern World," begins by contrasting Rabbi Shagar's outlook with the collectivism of much religious Zionism, for which the relationship to

---

3. Rabbi Abraham Isaac Kook, *Mishpat Kohen* (Jerusalem: Mossad HaRav Kook, 1985), no. 144, p. 343. See further my "Paradox, Paradigm, and the Birth of Inwardness: On R. Kook and the Akeda," in *Ḥazon Naḥum: Studies in Jewish Law, Thought and History Presented to Dr. Norman Lamm on the Occasion of His Seventieth Birthday*, ed. Yaakov Elman and Jeffrey Gurock (New York: Yeshiva University Press, 1997), 459–78; and the important works of Yehuda Gellman, such as *Abraham! Abraham! Kierkegaard and the Hasidim on the Binding of Isaac* (Aldershot: Ashgate, 2003).

4. On Rabbi Soloveitchik, see my "Pluralism and the Category of the Ethical," *Tradition* 30, no. 4 (1996): 145–63. At that time I could not quote from his most careful discus-sion of the *Akeda*, in *The Emergence of Ethical Man* (Jersey City, NJ: Ktav, 2005), a work presumably unavailable to Rabbi Shagar. I have discussed this further in an essay for *Studies on the Thought and Writings of Rabbi Joseph B. Soloveitchik*, ed. Dov Schwartz (Yeshiva University Press, forthcoming).

God is first established via membership in the Jewish people, on the one hand, and with Leibowitz's reduction of religion to normative obedience, on the other hand. Against these views, though with the awareness that peoplehood and law are essential components of religious life and that he is speaking for a certain kind of Orthodox Jew and not for all, Shagar insists upon the primacy of an individual religious worldview. In this chapter, the major obstacle to faith is the existence of a scientific worldview that makes no room for what is not grasped by science. Rabbi Shagar's prime example is divine providence: the believer seeks the hand of God in events that science regards as indifferent manifestations of scientific laws. Another is faith in the redemption of the world. Rabbi Shagar's fundamental move, following Lacan, is to separate the Real, which is pre-linguistic and thus not subject to scientific categorization, from other perspectives. The spiritual apprehension of the world is no less real than the physical description. Is this subjectivity? Shagar claims that the very question "bespeaks a dichotomy between the subjective and the objective that is dissolved by faith" (p. 32). The attempt to treat such apprehension conceptually, "for instance, by trying to demonstrate its objective truth" (p. 33), destroys the reality.

Is this approach overly dependent on the adoption of Lacan's theories? I don't think so. In the background stands Wittgenstein, as Rabbi Shagar explicitly acknowledges, whose later philosophy emerges from sustained reflection on ordinary language, including religious language. Against the "foundationalist" orientation (Shagar would call it modernist) – according to which all truths should be indubitable, demonstrable propositions, or inferences from them – Wittgenstein observed that competent knowers assert with certainty many propositions about themselves and their surroundings without presupposing a potential appeal to some process of inferential confirmation. Religious believers, when speaking of divine intervention or the future state, are not typically making the kinds of assertions that invite empirical verification. Something deeper is at work. In fact, Rabbi Shagar stresses that the most profound believers are those with no need or interest in confirmation via nonreligious "objective" demonstration. A Shagarian who did not care for Lacan could develop an alternative theory to accommodate these fundamental insights.

A great danger in this approach is that such a faith, emanating from the bowels of one's selfhood, would not be religious faith, but merely an act of egocentric self-anointment; in Rabbi Shagar's words, "the tendency to turn oneself into the yardstick of reality" (p. 34). Appealing to Lacan enables Shagar to speak about different levels of reality, so what is experienced at one level is not evident at another. Later in the essay, he distinguishes between different paths to religious faith. The reader can evaluate the success of these strategies. In closing, Rabbi Shagar reminds us of the role of observance and tradition in stabilizing our religious life, at a practical level, and as constitutive of language and communication, along Wittgensteinian lines.

Chapter 3, the draft of a conference lecture on "Religious Life in the Modern Age," ponders how the Orthodox should respond to non-Orthodox ideologies. Like many, Rabbi Shagar is unhappy with what he calls "universalizing" tendencies in Rabbi Kook, meaning the tendency to subsume the Other into an Orthodox narrative. Like many, he is extremely sensitive to a larger philosophical situation: We believe in our own beliefs – virtually a tautology – though others do not. At the same time, it seems almost as certain, with regard to our deepest beliefs and commitments, that we cannot triumphantly demonstrate them to others, and thus must regard them as logically contingent. Following Wittgenstein and many great witnesses of religious thought, including Rabbi Naḥman and John Henry Newman (who is not mentioned), Rabbi Shagar knows that the most lively and committed believers are simply not preoccupied with the question of justification. Writing from a postmodern perspective, he states: "I no longer feel the need to justify myself to the Other or, conversely, to recognize him in me" (p. 44). Shagar also knows that cultures, even those distant from one another, share foundations that make it possible for one to understand others. Whether this suffices at the communal or institutional level will become important in chapter 6.

Rabbi Shagar seems to believe that the postmodern confidence enabling one to live without attempting to justify one's commitments entails an abandonment of the claim to their truth; he argues that the term "truth," in any case, has too many meanings to be utilized in these contexts. What does it mean, on this view, when an individual changes his or her beliefs? Is this an act of self-destruction? One reason I have alluded to English-language writers is that one may fully endorse the fundamental insights of this chapter without taking over Rabbi Shagar's metaphysical or even epistemological formulations.

In this essay, Rabbi Shagar also contrasts Orthodoxy with Conservative Judaism. Orthodoxy is aligned with postmodernism, in his opinion, because, in his opinion, "the Orthodox *posek* has inexhaustible options for maneuverability in his interpretations.... He can extract whatever he needs from the text through interacting with it" (p. 55). Much of the Conservative worldview, however, is informed by an academic standpoint "subordinate to the objective, ethical, and historical conditions that gave rise to halakha" (ibid.). Here Rabbi Shagar broaches a crucial question for any Orthodox thinker: Given the availability of manifold interpretive tools, can Orthodoxy – or any other coherent legal system – dispense with objective content in favor of unlimited flexibility? A thorough account would require Shagar to explain the difference between what the *posek* needs and what he wants, and to discuss how the *posek* is trained. On the spot and elsewhere in the book, he makes comments about the role of tradition and the nature of language that mitigate this problem at a practical level. Surely any generalization about Rabbi Shagar's approach to halakhic decision-making and analysis would have to reflect his halakhic writings as well, just as theoretical pronouncements about scientific method proposed by a practicing physicist cannot be evaluated without examining his or her scientific work. As to Conservative Judaism, I wonder whether its leading exponents see themselves as strictly bound to *Wissenschaft* in their legal deliberations.

At the end of the lecture, Rabbi Shagar commends the ḥaredi community for its "self-acceptance," even as he bemoans its rigidity: "I have no need to prove to others, or even to believe, that my faith is the truth or the Good; it is sufficient that it is I and the way I am" (p. 64).

If the earlier essays in the book open Rabbi Shagar to the charge of subjectivity and treating self-identity as a religious and ethical oracle, chapter 4, "Freedom and Holiness," explores the tension between these ideals in a way that seeks to balance them. After surveying concepts of freedom in Jewish sources and various philosophical systems, including Maimonides, Spinoza, and Sartre, Rabbi Shagar doubts the postmodern notion that man can be as God and create truth or holiness: "It appears that, in spite of everything, something will always remain beyond the grasp of human freedom, a residue that cannot be manufactured by humans" (p. 82). And he sums up: "Postmodern freedom can lead to holiness when it maintains an aspect of inspiration. It can express the infinite in man and in reality, the miracle that lies beyond natural law. It can also protect the holy from that which would ossify or limit it" (p. 84).

The postmodern thesis of chapter 5, "Living with Nothingness," may be familiar by this point. Yet the essay contains striking social insights. In short, Rabbi Shagar identifies a fundamental gap between older forms of power analysis, or materialism, and the present state: the hierarchical structure of class domination that was capitalism, according to Marx, versus the decentered discourse of power in Foucault; old-fashioned greed for ownership and its prerogatives versus the sheer wastefulness of consumerism; even the replacement of the market, where human beings bought and sold products, with the impersonality of the supermarket checkout. Rabbi Shagar perceives an affinity between this experience of a pointless world and the faith of mystics and philosophers like Rabbenu Baḥya, who advocate "surrendering [the] very need for security, and … a willingness to accept the divine will, whatever it may be, and identify it as good" (p. 95). Of course he recognizes that much postmodern theorizing tends to cynicism and despair, and attempts to distinguish between hard and soft postmodernism, where the latter contains the potential of valid religious existence in the face of contemporary meaninglessness.

The everyday implications of the postmodern diagnosis and Rabbi Shagar's postmodern prescription are worked out in the following chapters. If our conception of justice is not based on universal, demonstrable principles, asks Shagar in chapter 6, "Justice and Ethics in a Postmodern World": "Does the democratic West have the right to preach its own ethics to peoples who, for reasons of religion or tradition, oppose it?" (p. 105). His examples are widow burning and female genital mutilation. His answer is that losing the external, objective "hard" idea of justice does not affect the firmness of our convictions: "[The Lord] is omnipresent, including in my own existence and values, which are thus a certainty" (p. 112). Though other people and societies have different values, "I, too, have a certainty that I am unwilling to relinquish, a truth to which I will dedicate myself, for which I am willing to die, even kill (the last is the most difficult and severe of actions)" (ibid.).

Rabbi Shagar focuses on whether "we" should refrain from imposing Western values on non-Western cultures but does not consider the scenario in which we Jews, with our commitment to circumcision, to traditional family structure, and so much more, are the aliens being judged by the liberal West. It may also seem paradoxical that he is willing, in principle, to take life in the name of his faith, but forbidden to "assert that faith in my own way renders other ways worthless" (p. 117). No doubt, one can speak in mystical terms of complementary categories according to which both universal equality and individual commitment can be justified, and there are other ways of dissolving the logical inconsistency. At a practical level of human relations, the difficulty nevertheless persists.

Chapter 7, "Mysticism, Postmodernism, and the New Age," is one of the most surprising contributions in this volume. At first blush, the attraction of postmodernism and New Age for the same people seems coincidence: the former is about alienation and skepticism, the latter about mysticism and the quest for excitement. One might think New Age is a sentimental escape from the disorientation of postmodernism. Rabbi Shagar argues that the two trends have much in common. Both assume a fluidity and changeableness of identity and a willingness to entertain multiple realities. He demonstrates the links between them in the course of examining the fascination of science fiction. His primary guide here is Baudrillard, who distinguished between signification, which deals with the relation between image and reality, and simulation, which bears no relationship to any reality whatsoever. Rabbi Shagar explores the implications for religious existence of such claims to creativity unbounded by reality.

Perhaps the most profound and relevant discussion in this book is chapter 8, "Love, Romance, and Covenant." The author presents the well-known philosophical and practical tensions between Judaism, with its overriding commitment to family obligations, and romantic intimacy. Faithful to rabbinic sources, he also stresses the necessary role of sexual romance in marital life; he cites sympathetically the work of

Rabbi Soloveitchik and others in articulating the value of interpersonal intimacy in a halakhic setting, and he understands perfectly that "The Jewish model of intimacy can be characterized as standing next to, rather than face-to-face with, the Other" (p. 142).

But Rabbi Shagar has more to say: In the postmodern world, he argues, the modern promise of romantic love, as an absolute oblivious to the world, transcending all other values, has been exploded. Intimacy is still valued, but without the unrealistic expectations. Equally important, with such disillusionment, and in opposition to the modern romantic model, one must recognize the locality and contingency in one's choice of a life partner. With these developments, the halakhic balance between intimacy and the religious imperative gains a newfound charm. In this chapter, Rabbi Shagar refers to his experience guiding couples and celebrates "religious Zionist youth…who had not lost their grace (and had largely retained their innocence as well), as opposed to, on the one hand, the gruffness and alienation prevalent in the ultra-Orthodox world, and, on the other, the promiscuity of the secular world, which in effect eradicates grace" (p. 146).

Chapter 9, "Self-Actualization and Society," intelligently addresses the age-old conflict between the desire for self-perfection and working for the benefit of others. The last section of the essay strikes a postmodern chord: Given that postmodernism – with Clifford Geertz as the primary interlocutor – regards all social structures as fictions, it threatens to reduce the social world to a series of relationships alongside others, where Judaism aims for an existence with others. Using hasidic sources and Rosenzweig, Rabbi Shagar explores the role of prayer in giving meaning to the life of the individual within the community.

The concluding chapter, "Seventy Bullocks and One Sukka: The Land of Israel, Nationalism, and Diaspora," is a discourse on this topic, heavily involved in texts of Maharal, *Tanya*, and others. Rabbi Shagar's goal is to establish a "'softer' nationalism, one that makes room for the Other, that does not look down on or disdain other nations" (p. 184). While the universalism reflected in the sacrifices of Sukkot is rooted in rabbinic literature, for modern readers the focus in this chapter echoes the interpretation of Sukkot in Rosenzweig's *Star of Redemption*, which reflects a non-Israeli perspective on the Jewish people's relationship to the world.

III

Our summary and examination of Rabbi Shagar's salient themes demonstrates the importance of his efforts to understand the present crisis for Judaism and for humanity. That is not to say that his theses are beyond criticism. The incomplete nature of his legacy is itself reason to deem it an invitation to further investigation rather than a set of solutions. It would indeed be ironic if his advocacy of postmodernism as an approach eschewing grand narratives engendered a philosophy according to which all intellectual and spiritual rivers flow through modernism and arrive at a formulaic postmodern destination. In particular, one must be wary of the solipsistic dangers in his sometimes unquestioning reliance on self-acceptance as a key to moral and religious truth and the concomitant downplaying of divine transcendence. That Rabbi Shagar himself seems intermittently aware of these problems – his deployment of Lacan's idea of the Real is an excellent example of his attempts to deal with it – does not exempt us from struggling with them on our own. I hope it is not out of place to suggest that the further study of Shagar's philosophical productivity and his problems might benefit from greater exposure to anglophone philosophy, by which I mean mainly the methods of analytic philosophy of religion and epistemology practiced by Plantinga, Alston, and many others, which put a premium on careful and precise formulation of argument. I would include the neo-Aristotelianism identified with Alasdair MacIntyre, whose concepts of tradition and practice, and whose analysis of our present social and intellectual predicament, overlap with Rabbi Shagar's concerns without depending on postmodernism.

The major questions that preoccupy Rabbi Shagar are central to our self-understanding in difficult and challenging times. Some of these questions have not been tackled by previous Jewish thought if only because contemporary conditions are unprecedented. Rabbi Shagar is both a pioneer in confronting these challenges and a teacher who brings to bear earlier sources, both hasidic and halakhic, and a selection of modern literature, philosophic and academic. His original spirit does not exempt him from criticism. To the contrary, the importance of the questions he struggles with and the great amount of study and thinking left undone make it imperative for us to treat his contribution with the same gravity and critical spirit that he brought to the task.

Works by Rabbi Shagar

WORKS REFERENCED IN THIS VOLUME

A Time of Freedom

זמן של חירות: דרשות לחג הפסח, ערך י' מבורך, אלון שבות תש"ע.

At the Handles of the Lock

על כפות המנעול: דרשות לימי התשובה וליום הכיפורים, ערכו א' ניר וא'
צוריאלי, אפרתה תשס"ד.

Broken Vessels

כלים שבורים: תורה וציונות דתית בסביבה פוסטמודרנית, דרשות למועדי
זמננו, ערך א' צוריאלי, אפרתה תשס"ד.

Expositions on Likkutei Moharan

שיעורים על ליקוטי מוהר"ן: ב, ערך נ' לדרברג, אלון שבות תשע"ה.

In the Shadow of Faith

בצֵל האמונה: דרשות ומאמרים לחג הסוכות, ערך י' מבורך, אלון שבות
תשע"א.

Loving You unto Death

אהבוך עד מוות: עיון רב־תחומי בסוגיית קידוש ה' במסכת סנהדרין ע"ד- ע"ה, ערך נ' סמט, אפרתה תשס"ד.

On His Torah He Meditates

בתורתו יהגה: לימוד גמרא כבקשת אלוקים, ערך ז' מאור, אפרתה תשס"ט.

On That Day

ביום ההוא: דרשות למועדי אייר, ערך י' מבורך, אלון שבות תשע"ב.

Shemitta

שיעורים בגמרא: שמיטה, ערך א' אברמוביץ, אלון שבות תשע"ה.

Tablets and Broken Tablets

לוחות ושברי לוחות: הגות יהודית נוכח הפוסטמודרניזם, ערכו ז' מאור (עורך ראשי), א' ברנר, נ' סמט וא' אברמוביץ, תל אביב ואלון שבות תשע"ג.

This is My Covenant

זאת בריתי: גרות, חילון, נישואין אזרחיים, ערך ז' מאור, עורכי המאמרים: ז' מאור, מ' פאלוך וא' דוקוב, אלון שבות תשע"ב.

To Illuminate the Openings

להאיר את הפתחים: דרשות ומאמרים לימי החנוכה, ערך י' מבורך, אלון שבות תשע"ד.

We Will Walk in Fervor

נהלך ברג"ש: מבחר מאמרים – יוצא לאור לקראת יום השנה הראשון להסתלקותו, ערך ז' מאור בהשתתפות ש"י דייטש, אפרתה תשס"ח.

OTHER WORKS BY RABBI SHAGAR

זכרון ליום ראשון: דרשות לימים נוראים, ערכו א' צוריאלי וי' מבורך, מהדורה שנייה מורחבת ומתוקנת, אפרתה תשס"ז.

הליכות עולם: הלכה והיסטוריה, ערך א' אברמוביץ, אלון שבות תשע"ו.

פור הוא הגורל: דרשות לפורים, ערך א' צוריאלי, מהדורה שנייה מורחבת, אפרתה תשס"ה.

פניך אבקש: דרשות שנאמרו בישיבת הכותל בשנת תשמ"ב, ערכו מ' ורדיגר וע' פוקס, אפרתה תשס"ח.

רעים האהובים: דרשות חתונה, בשיתוף עם הרב י' דרייפוס, ערכו י' מבורך וא' ניר, אפרתה תשס"ח.

שארית האמונה: דרשות פוסטמודרניות למועדי ישראל, ערך י' מבורך, תל אביב תשע"ד.

שובי נפשי – חסד או חירות: קובץ פרקי תשובה, ערך י' דרייפוס, מהדורה שנייה מתוקנת, אפרתה תשס"ג.

שיעורים על ליקוטי מוהר"ן: א, ערך נ' לדרברג, אלון שבות תשע"ג.

English Works

The Human and the Infinite: Discourses on the Mean-ing of Penitence, trans. Naftali Moses (Efrat: Yeshivat Siaḥ Yitzḥak, 2004).

Chance and Providence: Discourses on the Inner Meaning of Purim, trans. Naftali Moses (Efrat: Yeshivat Siaḥ Yitzḥak, 2005).

Index

A

Abraham, 2–19, 31, 200
absurdity, 59, 108
Adam, 139, 163
    sin, 79, 81–2
affinity, 45n9, 160–1, 164, 204
Ahab, 5
Akeda, 1, 4, 6, 8, 9, 13, 15, 18, 198, 200
Akiva, Rabbi, 112, 155
alienation, ix, xxii, 59–60, 83, 90, 119, 126,
    140, 146, 159, 168, 188, 190, 205–6
Alston, William, 207
Amalek, 97n, 99–101
Amichai, Yehuda, 110
Amital, Rabbi Yehuda, 46
anarchy, 70, 73, 81, 136
apologetics, xxi, 23–4, 52
argument, ix, xviii, xix, 10–4, 17, 27n17,
    47–8, 53, 87, 109, 113–4, 124, 134, 157,
    180, 194, 197, 207
Ark of the Covenant, xiv, 3
Aristotle, 73, 120, 176

Asimov, Isaac, 124
authenticity, 4, 6, 33–4, 43, 57, 78–80, 162,
Avin, Rabbi, 14, 15

B

Baal Shem Tov, Rabbi Israel, 57
Baḥya ibn Pekuda, Rabbenu 92–5, 156–7,
    163, 204
Balaban, Avraham, 126
Bar-Elli, Gilead, 53
Bar Kochba Revolt, 69
battle, xiv, 5, 138, 178, *see also* struggle
Baudrillard, Jean, 126, 195
Be'er HaGola, xii
Being, 30, 80–1, 96–7, 164, 189–91
Berman, Samuel A., 9
Betrayal, 79, 111, 113, 163
Bialik, Hayim Nahman, 47
Binding of Isaac, xxi, 1
body, 32, 48, 51–2, 56, 75, 121, 140, 145,
    164–5
Boll, Heinrich, 163

Brenner, Itamar, xxiii, 21, 105
Breslauer, S. Daniel, 47
bricolage, 128
Brisker method of study, xv
Buber, Martin, 4, 160, 161
Buber, Solomon, 4
Buddhism, 92, 120
Buzaglo, Meir, 45

C
Camus, Albert, 93, 95, 97
capitalism, 86, 89–90, 204
Cartland, Barbara, 142
certainty, xix, xxiii, 1–19, 23, 36–8, 57, 112,
    122–3, 197–201, 204–5
Chabad, 114
choice, xxii, 29, 34, 44, 64, 74–6, 79–83,
    96, 103, 129, 150–1, 161–2, 194, 206
    and freedom in the Bible, 68–72
Christian dogma, 180
cleaving, 29, 33, 77, 93, 113–4, 149, 154, 157,
    165, 187–8
coercion, 78, 144
Cohen, Aviezer, 41
Cohen, Hermann, 2, 28, 182
communism, 86
community, xxii, 23, 47, 60, 62, 69, 106,
    121, 144, 154, 164–5, 206
    Haredi, 203
    National Religious, xii–xv, 41, 43, 45,
        59–60, 178–9
    of Israel, 176–7
    Postmodern, 168–172
complexity, 87, 125
complicatedness, 113
compromise, xx, 42, 102, 109, 112, 132, 134
confinement, 32, 163, 183
Conservative Judaism, *see* Judaism
covenant, 23, 60, 70, 83–4, 191
    love, romance, and, 131–151, 205

D
death, 68, 113
    of God, 86
deconstruction, ix, xiv
Deleuze, Gilles, 89, 100
democracy, 105, 204
Derrida, Jacques, 89, 100, 128, 188
De Saint-Exupery, Antoine, 46
Descartes, Rene, 87
devotion, 6, 19, 56, 94, 149, 163, 165,
    185
Diaspora, 175–6, 179, 183, 185
    Jews of, xii
disagreement, *see* argument
divine
    command, 1–5, 11, 16, 18, 22, 27, 68,
        72, 76, 155, 178, 185, 198–200
    grace, 94
    infinitude, xviii, 77, 83–4, 95–6, 103,
        111–2, 148, 150, 170
    light, xviii, 95, 129
    revelation, 35, 37, 52
    supervision by, 35
    unity, 115
duality, 23–4, 28, 32–3, 36, 57, 63, 73,
    77n17, 80–3, 94, 154
Durkheim, Emile, 87

E
Eco, Umberto, 142
ecstasy, 92, 95, 101–3, 120, 148–9, 162,
    170
Eden, 71
education, 133, 194
Edward, Betsalel Philip, 32
Edwards, Dylan, 32
ego, 141–2, 163
Elazar, Rabbi, 173
Eliphaz, 9–12
empathy, 51

emptiness, 60, 122, 139, 147
enlightenment, 75, 118, 166, 169, 197
    Age of, 86
    Jewish, 178
Ephrathi, Jacob E., 7
epistemology, 108, 122, 125, 196, 203, 207
equality, 69, 98–9, 133, 146–7, 205
equanimity, 94–6, 99, 112, 148–9, 170
esoterica, xix, 38
eternal, eternity, 42, 45, 74–6, 114, 145–6, 182, 188
Eve, 81
exile, 158, 160, 175–7, 184, 186, 190, 192
    as a natural state, 179–84
existentialism, xxi, 33–4, 92–5, 97, 115n17, 160, 169
Exodus from Egypt, 69, 72, 185

F
faith,
    and science, 25–32
    and the Real, 32–6
    and tradition, 38–9
    as possibility, 36–8
    beyond words, 21–4
    loss of, 85, 88, 120, 196
    the nature of, 56–8
family, 52, 60, 69, 115–6, 138, 140–2, 146–8, 205
    planning, 131–5
    purity, 140, 144
fanaticism, 58
Far East, 120
fascism, 81, 86, 122
fate, 68, 81, 93, 122, 194
fear of God, 3–4, 9–13, 69, 76
Feinstein, Rabbi Moshe, 155
Fichte, Johann Gottlieb, 34
Foucault, Michel, 88, 187, 195

freedom, xvi, xx, 23, 26–7, 34, 38, 55, 98, 122, 127, 137, 146–9, 162–3, 170–1, 203–4
    and holiness, 67–84
    in the Bible, 68–72
    Maimonides and the paradox of, 72–7
    modern, 78–81
    postmodern, 81–4
Freud, Sigmund, 26, 87, 136–8
Fromm, Erich, 81
fundamentalism, 28, 46, 58–60, 118, 124n3

G
Gadamer, Hans-Georg, 160
Geiger, Abraham, 198
gentiles, 190
Geertz, Clifford, 168–9
Gibeon, 30
Ginsburgh, Rabbi Yitzchak, 121
Goldman, Eliezer, 26–7
gratuitous hatred, *sinat ḥinam*, 176–7
Great Revolt, the, 69
Guide of the Perplexed, 2, 4
guilt, 122, 163
Gurevitz, David, 108–9

H
halakha, xxi, 38, 42, 45–58, 65, 132–5, 139–40, 154–5, 193–5, 203–7
Halbertal, Moshe, 25
Ḥanukka, xii, 48, 54
ḥardal, 45n10, 59
ḥaredi Judaism, xiii, 58–9, 194
Harlap, Rabbi Yaakov Moshe, 24
harmony, ix, 3, 43, 71–3, 86, 110, 140, 149, 171–2, 189, 196, 198
Hasidism, ix, xi, xii, xiii, xvii, 60–1, 83, 117, 120, 137, 148, 150, 157, 178–9, 194
Haskala *see* Enlightenment, Jewish

Ḥayyim of Volozhin, Rabbi, 112, 159
Ḥazal, xi, 1, 3, 5, 6, 8, 134–5, 139, 142, 145,
    154–5
Hegel, Georg W.F., 30, 82, 145, 159
Heidegger, Martin, 30, 92, 163
Herbert, Frank, 124
heretic, 92, 120, 177
hesder, xv
heterotopia, 187–8
Hillel of Shklov, Rabbi, 183
Hirsch, Rabbi Samson Raphael, 42
holiness, xiii, xxi–xxii, 2, 28n19, 31, 39,
    42, 52n23, 67–84, 138, 140, 142, 146,
    203–4
home, 47, 62–3, 117, 122–3, 133, 150,
    182–4, 192
honor killings, 106, 115
hubris, 34, 82, 169, 185
humanism, 67

I

Ibn Ezra, Rabbi Abraham, 177
idealism, 135
identity, 9, 32–4, 46, 86, 91, 122, 125, 150,
    178, 181, 185–6, 190–1, 203, 205
ideology, vii, ix, xv, xxi, 26, 86, 92, 98, 102,
    117, 120, 122, 195, 202
idolatry, xiii, 5, 15, 70–1, 103, 117, 138, 159,
    173, 177
Illouz, Eva, 135–6
image of God, 186
individualism, vii, xiv, 68, 76, 88, 136,
    164
injustice, *see* Justice
insularity, 117n20
innocence, 4, 12, 29, 33, 57, 142, 146, 206
inspiration, 34, 82–4, 116–7, 128–9, 204
intimacy, xxii, 8, 22, 37, 46–7, 62–4,
    133–4, 139–46, 150, 160, 163, 178–9,
    189, 205–6

Isaac, 4, 6, 8, 13, 16
Isaiah, 71
Ishmael, 7
Israel, 151
    Jewish State, xv
    Land of, xv, 174, 177, 179, 183–4, 191

J

Jacob, 64, 187, 189
Job, 3, 4, 9, 10, 12, 13, 14, 70
Judaism, xx, xxii, 6, 120
    Conservative, 41, 43, 47, 53,
        55–6, 203
    Human Values and the Jewish
        State, 2
    Orthodox, ix, xxi, 41–3, 53, 55, 61–3,
        120, 203
    Reform, xxi, 41, 43, 47, 53, 55
    Ultra-Orthodox, xiii, xv, 58
Jungian psychology, 164
justice, 2, 3, 10, 16–7, 69, 86, 99, 148, 165,
    187, 199, 204
    and ethics in a postmodern world,
        105–18
Joshua, 30

K

Kabbala, xiii, xix, 38, 93, 120, 148, 150, 157
Kant, Immanuel, 28, 87
Kasher, Hannah, 2
Katz, Jacob, 43
Kaufmann, Yehezkel, vii
Kierkegaard, Søren, 2–6, 142, 144,
    198–200
King of Aram, 5
King David, 21
Kook, Rabbi Abraham Isaac, vii, viii,
    xiii, xix, 3, 24, 29, 31, 37–8, 42, 44, 79,
    83, 102, 117, 127, 164–7, 177, 194, 199,
    200, 203

L

Lacan, Jacques, xix, xxi, 32–3, 144, 195, 201–3, 207
language games, 49, 59n36, 89, 115, 128–9
leadership, xiii, 56, 121
legality, 11, 17, 195, 203
Leibowitz, Prof. Yeshayahu, 2, 22, 25–7, 42 195, 198, 202
Levi, Rabbi, 6, 7
Levinas, Emmanuel, vii, 162–3, 188, 191, 195
Levi-Strauss, Claude, 128
Levy, Ze'ev, 163
liberalism, xxii, 198, 205
liberty, 26, 38, 68, 78–9, *see also* Freedom
    as nothingness, 81–4
Lichtenstein, Rabbi Aharon, 194
Lifshitz, Rabbi Joseph Isaac, 33
literature, 136, 147
    hasidic, xv, 120
    Jewish, 47, 56, 193, 206
    modern, 207
    mystical, 120, 123
    New Age, 120, 126
    postmodern, xvi, 126
    science fiction, 123
loneliness, 138, 140, 143–4, 160
love, 3, 5, 10, 163, 178
    God's, 18
    innate, 167
    of God, 3, 5, 10, 18, 37, 64–5, 68, 77, 91, 94, 156
    romantic, ix, 131–51, 206
    the stranger, 185
    your neighbor, 155–6
loyalty, 78–9, 136, 157, 199
Luzzatto, Rabbi Moshe Ḥayyim, 30
Lystra, Karen, 135

M

MacIntyre, Alasdair, 207
Maharal of Prague, xiii, 29, 30, 78, 115, 164, 174–184, 186, 188–190
Maimonides, xviii, 2, 4, 16, 23, 30, 34, 35, 37, 48, 72–83, 137, 150, 165–6, 197, 203
Malkiel, Eliezer, 50
Maoism, 86
Maor, Zohar, 1, 21, 67, 105, 153, 173
Marcuse, Herbert, 30
marriage, 135–151
    as "nonliteral *tzimtzum,*" 146–151
Marx, Karl, 26, 87, 204
materialism, 60, 73–7, 89–90, 204
Meir, Rabbi, 144
Menaḥem Mendel of Kotzk, Rabbi, 157–8
mercy, 8, 93, 110, 165, 169n34
Messiah, messianism, xx, 26n16, 36–7, 110–1
metaphysical, 85, 88, 92, 98, 100, 109, 111–6, 139, 147, 149, 196–7, 203
Mevorach, Yishai, 173
Micah, 187
Midian, 15
Midreshet Lindenbaum, 153
mitzva, mitzvot, 17, 50, 52, 69, 76, 120, 155–6, 159, 166, 178–9, 183, 185
    of procreation, 135, 140–6
    of Sukka, 182–5
modernism, xii, xviii, 207
modernity, vii, xiii, xx–xxi, 28, 41–65, 85, 105, 196–7
Modern Orthodoxy, vii, xxiii, 2, 43, 45, 55, 58
modesty, 141, 169
morality, 17, 70, 115, 136, 163, 198
    natural, 198, 200
    of God, 17

Mordekhai Yosef Leiner of Izbica,
    Rabbi, 30
Moses, xiv, 39, 54, 112, 151
motivation, 73
Mount Sinai, 39, 54
multiculturalism, 44–5, 59, 105
multiple worlds, xix, 25–32, 35, 42, 60,
    82, 84, 94–6, 122–4, 127, 132, 148, 159,
    162, 168–9
Musar movement, 93
mystical freedom, 81–4
mysticism, xv, xix, 29, 31, 33, 38, 55–6, 92,
    101, 119–129, 136, 194, 205
myth, 120, 123–4, 137

N
Naboth, 5
Naḥman of Breslov, Rabbi, viii, xviii,
    21–2, 48–9, 55, 57, 64, 89, 99, 101–2,
    110–15, 128, 142, 154, 160, 168, 203
nationalism, viii, xiii, 173–92
    moderate, 184–6
nature, 3, 26, 29, 32, 70–4, 76, 80, 82, 84,
    133, 157, 175, 180–3, 188–9
Nazism, 86, 163
Neitzsche, Friedrich, 86–7
Neuhouser, Frederick, 34
New Age, xix, 101n33, 119–29, 205
Newman, John Henry, 202
nihilism, xviii, xx, 59n36, 68, 73, 96, 98–9,
    121, 128–9, 141, 147
nothingness, xvii, xix, 30, 45, 147, 188
    liberty as, 81–4
    living with, 85–103, 204

O
objectivity, xix, 14, 30, 32–3, 55, 78, 81, 117,
    159, 161, 168, 197, 201, 203–4
ontology, 28, 123, 125, 156, 189
Orthodoxy, *see* Judaism

Other, the, 157–64, 168–72, 184, 188–91,
    202, 206

P
paradox, 10, 13, 95–6, 99–102, 106, 108,
    110–3, 116–7, 141, 145, 149–50, *see
    also* Freedom
Pascal, Blaise, 194
pathos, 122
peace, 70, 140, 149
Peli, Pinchas H., 2
Piaget, Jean, 159, 160
Plantinga, Alvin, 207
Plato, 144
Pleasure, 31, 91, 97, 136, 138, 140, 145
pluralism, xiv, 44, 105–10, 116–8,
    120, 197
postmodernism, xiii, xvi, xviii, xix, xx,
    xxi, 82–85, 86, 92, 93, 97–8, 101–2, 105,
    108, 116, 119–20, 122, 126–8, 142, 147–9
    195–6, 205–6
    crisis, 81, 129, 207, *see also*
        postmodernism, despair
    criticism, xviii
    deconstruction, ix, xiv, xviii
    despair, 116, 121–2, 197, 204
    doubt, *see* skepticism
    hard/soft, xviii, xix, 97–99
prayer, xii, 16n27, 23–4, 27, 36n41, 120,
    125n4, 140, 154, 161, 168, 170–2, 179, 206
pride, 13, 71
problems, xix, 15, 47–8, 194, 198, 207
promiscuity, 70, 146, 206
prophecy, 4–6, 37, 70, 138, 166, 169, 174,
    187, 199–200
psychology, 25, 102, 121, 164

R
Rabinowitz, Dan, 106, 108
Ramat Gilead, 5

Rashi, 10
rationalism, 24, 102, 109, 125, 200
rationalization, 23–4, 51, 147
Real, domain of the, xix, xxi
reality, 12, 28–37, 42, 49, 51, 53, 59,
    64, 74–5, 80, 82, 84, 87–92,
    94–101, 109, 111, 121–8, 140,
    143–4, 147, 156, 159, 169, 170,
    201–5
reason, 57, 64, 82–3, 87
reconciliation, 125
redemption, 81, 94–5, 146, 172, 176, 181,
    182–3, 185, 201
    personal, 38, 139–40
    the Redemption, End of Days, 36,
        127, 174–5, 179, 182
reflection, 57, 167, 193, 201
religious fervor, 16, 77, 149, 199
religiosity, xx, 12, 56, 103n34
relativism, xviii–xix, 59n36, 96,
    98, 105, 108–9, 112, 116, 147,
    170, 199
relinquish, 44, 76, 95, 102–3, 109–10,
    112, 148, 163, 184, 189, 205
remorse, *see* guilt
renewal, ix, 42
repentance, 27–8, 35–6
Resh Lakish, 134
respect, 114, 118, 160, 164
responsibility, xvii, 11, 23, 42, 137, 163–4,
    169, 196
revelation, 36, 53–4, 116, 163
revolution, 86–7, 121
righteous, 14, 56, 69, 82, 158, 165–6
Rishonim, 4
ritual impurity, 131, 134
Rorty, Richard, 109
Rosenzweig, Franz, xiii, xx, 62, 160,
    170–2, 182, 188, 196, 206
Russell, Bertrand, 136

S

Sabbath, 28n19, 71–2
Salanter, Rabbi Israel, 115
Sanhedrin, 6
Sartre, Jean-Paul, 79, 80, 81, 115, 122, 150, 203
Satan, 1, 5–14, 16, 18, 19
Shapira, Rabbi Kalonymus Kalman, 61
Shneur Zalman of Liadi, Rabbi, 30, 49,
    97, 112, 142, 178
Simha Bunim of Peshischa, Rabbi, 31
Sofer, Rabbi Moshe, 53, 155
Soloveitchik, Rabbi Joseph B., xiii, 2, 26,
    42, 44, 138–9, 145–6, 160, 197–200,
    206
Scholem, Gershom, 39
Schopenhauer, Arthur, 88
secularism, xii, xxii, 41–2, 44, 58–61, 67,
    120, 122, 129, 135, 140, 146, 155, 169, 175,
    178–9, 194, 196, 206
security, viii, ix, 95, 136, 147, 149, 160,
    185, 204
self-acceptance, 27, 33–4, 94–5, 98–102,
    162, 203, 207
self-actualization, 44n6, 133, 206
    and society, 153–172
self-annulment, 34, 167
self-deception, 52, 59, 98
self-denial, 143
self-sacrifice, xxi, 1, 114n16, 150–1
selfness, 79, 159
servitude to God, 69–70
Shekhina, God's presence, 38, 97, 154,
    161
Shimon b. Yoḥai, Rabbi, 8, 18
silence, 99–100, 112–115
sin, 10, 28, 69–71, 134, 176–7
    original, 34, 79, 81
    rectification of, 82
sincerity, 156, 171–2, 194
skepticism, xiv, xix, 197, 205

slavery, 69, 72, 82n26, 160
soul, 17, 27, 38, 46, 60, 63, 64n43, 76, 79,
 84, 93, 107, 114n16, 140, 145, 154, 157,
 160, 164, 166–7, 171–2
Spinoza, Baruch (Benedict de), 63, 73,
 76, 79, 203
spirituality, 29, 50, 100, 119
split personalities, 91
spontaneity, 57, 128n10, 137, 145
Steiner, George, 30
struggle, 7, 69, 72, 80, 82, 98–100, 109, 125,
 138, 194, 207, *see also* Battle
subjectivity, xix, 32–3, 35, 76, 79, 81, 87,
 117–8, 147, 159, 161–2, 169, 172, 194,
 201, 203
Sukkot, xii, 174
Syrians, viii

T
Talmud, ix, xi, xvi, xvii, 5–6, 9, 141, 173,
 193–4
Taoism, 120
Temple, 29, 54, 138, 174, 176–7
tolerance, xviii, 56, 167–70
Torah, xiii–xvi, xxii, xxiii, 8, 11, 15, 22, 26,
 37, 39, 52–56, 71–2, 112, 114, 137–138,
 154–6, 160–1, 166, 177–9, 184–5,
 187–8, 198
 im derekh eretz ("Torah with
  worldly involvement"), 42
Torat hasod, see esoterica
tradition, vii, ix, xii–xiii, xxi, 27, 29, 31, 42,
 58, 61, 63–5, 105, 116–7, 121, 202–7
 faith and, 38–9
 traditional rootedness, 45–7
trust, 28n19, 71n5, 93–5, 128, 160, 171,
 185
 distrust, 42, 44

truth, ix, xviii, xx, xxiii, 9, 13, 14, 24n8,
 27n17, 30, 33, 38, 48–55, 58–9, 64, 68,
 75, 77–9, 81–3, 87–9, 92, 95, 97, 99,
 101–3, 106, 109–18, 123–9, 146–8,
 156–8, 167, 197, 201–7
 absolute, xiv, 58–9, 77, 101–3, 196
 inner, 157
Twersky, Isadore, 37
Tzaddok HaCohen of Lublin, Rabbi, 54,
 64, 161, 162, 189

U
unanswerable questions, 30n25, 110–6
unity, xxii, 28, 57, 63, 70, 72, 79, 94, 98,
 147, 168, 171, 177, 179, 190–1
 of creation, 170
 of Israel, 188
 of God, 111, 115, 171, 188–9
 with God, 34, 83
universalism, 44, 118, 174, 182, 185–91, 197
university, xvi, 60
Urbach, Ephraim E., 49
Utopia, 12, 36–7, 44, 136, 162, 183

V
values, xiii–xiv, xviii, xix, 1–2, 25–26, 28,
 41–3, 51–2, 55, 59n35, 78, 80–1, 86, 99,
 106–18, 132, 136–7, 147, 171, 178, 196,
 204–6
Verne, Jules, 125
Vilna Gaon, 183
violence, 58, 106, 118
vision, 127, 136

W
wastefulness, 89, 204
Weber, Max, 87
Western culture, xxii

Wittgenstein, Ludwig, 25, 31, 50, 88–9, 100, 195, 197, 202

Y

Yehoshua b. Karha, Rabbi, 22
Yehoshua b. Levi, Rabbi, 154, 155
Yehuda b. Pedaya, Rabbi, 154
Yeshiva, vii–viii, ix, xiii, xvi, 120
  HaKotel, xv
  Kerem B'Yavneh, xv
  Merkaz HaRav, vii
Yisrael of Ruzhyn, Rabbi, 57
Yitzhak, Rabbi, 138
Yohanan, Rabbi, 3, 4, 6, 141, 173
yoke of the kingdom of heaven, 22n2, 27, 69–70, 96, 129

Yose b. Zimra, Rabbi, 6
Yom Kippur War, viii
youth, 9, 46, 60, 90, 146, 206

Z

Zedekiah, 5, 6
Zechariah, 174
Zeitlin, Hillel, 32
Zelazny, Roger, 124
Zizek, Slavoj, 32–3, 140, 188
Zionism, xiii, xv, 182, 206, *see also* hardal
  leaders, xiii
  religious, xiii, 22, 59, 146, 178, 195, 200
  secular, 178, 194
Zuriely, Odeya, xxiii, 105

The fonts used in this book are from the Arno family

Maggid Books
The best of contemporary Jewish thought from
Koren Publishers Jerusalem Ltd.